Philosophy of the Social Sciences

To Nicole

Philosophy of the Social Sciences: Towards Pragmatism

Patrick Baert

polity

The right of Patrick Baert to be identified as Author of this Work has been asserted in accordance with the UK Copyright, Designs and Patents Act 1988.

First published in 2005 by Polity Press

Polity Press
65 Bridge Street
Cambridge CB2 1UR, UK

Polity Press
350 Main Street
Malden, MA 02148, USA

ISBN: 0-7456-2246-1
ISBN: 0-7456-2247-X (pb)

A catalogue record for this book is available from the British Library.

Typeset in 10½ on 12pt Times
by SNP Best-set Typesetter Ltd, Hong Kong
Printed and bound in Great Britain by MPG Books Ltd, Bodmin, Cornwall

For further information on Polity, visit our website: www.polity.co.uk

Contents

Contents

Acknowledgements

I wish to thank the whole Polity team, especially Emma Longstaff and Caroline Richmond, for the professional work they managed to do with such poise and patience. I am particularly indebted to John Thompson for his ongoing support and encouragement. Over the years, I have benefited from conversations with colleagues. In particular, Sue Benson, Margareta Bertilsson, Alban Bouvier, Barbara Bodenhorn, Paul Connerton, Risto Heiskala, Claude Javeau, Martin Kusch, Alain Leplège, Hans-Peter Muller, William Outhwaite, William Pickering, Marie-Louise Stig Sorensen, Bryan Turner, Darin Weinberg and Alison Wylie spring to mind. I am grateful to Damien Catani, Julia Dover, Zahid Durrani, Simon Grimble, Iain Laing, Paul Lewis, William Outhwaite, Mark Roberts and Alan Shipman for reading through earlier drafts.

I presented papers related to chapters 5 and 6 of this book at the biannual conferences of the European Sociological Association held in Helsinki and Murcia, at the conference of the Association Internationale des Sociologues de Langue Française in Tours, and at the Westmarck Society in Jyväskylä. I gave talks at the universities of Copenhagen, West of England, Ghent, Leicester, Paris IV (Sorbonne), Sussex and Warwick, and I very much appreciated the comments I received. I also gained from long periods at the University of British Columbia, the Université Libre de Bruxelles, the Université de Paris I (Panthéon Sorbonne), the Université de Paris IV (Sorbonne) and the Humboldt Universität Berlin. All five were gracious hosts and provided the right intellectual climate. I also wish to express my appreciation towards the many students at Cambridge University, at both undergraduate and postgraduate level, who have unwittingly been sounding boards to and originators of some of the ideas expressed here.

Parts of chapters 5 and 6 draw on my articles 'Richard Rorty's Pragmatism and the Social Sciences', *History of the Human Sciences* 5 (2002), pp. 139–49; 'Pragmatism versus Sociological Hermeneutics', *Current Perspectives in Social Theory* 22 (2003), pp. 349–66; 'Pragmatism as a Philosophy of Social

Science', *European Journal of Social Theory* 7 (2004), pp. 355–70; and 'Towards a Pragmatist-Inspired Philosophy of Social Science', *Acta Sociologica* 48 (2005), pp. 191–203. I thank the publishers for allowing me to use some of this material.

Coffee breaks and late night drinks with Alex, Alison, Damien, David, Eleanor, Emile, Hugo, Mark, Simon, and Zahid kept me sane. So did Julia, who is a true companion in life.

This book is dedicated to Nicole, my wonderful sister.

Introduction

Philosophy of the social sciences is a meta-theoretical enterprise in so far as it reflects on the practices of social research. This reflection can take different forms. Most philosophers of the social sciences try to determine whether particular theories or methodological options are appropriate for *explaining* social phenomena. They may, for instance, investigate the coherence and explanatory power of evolutionary forms of explanation or of rational choice models, or they may wish, more broadly, to establish whether historical laws exist at all. My personal view is that the philosophy of the social sciences ought not to assume that the sole objective of social research is to explain an outer world. It should therefore also ponder alternative modes of knowledge acquisition. This perspective will become particularly apparent towards the latter part of the book, but it will also become clear in the earlier chapters that most philosophers of social science whom I discuss do not share my view. For many of them, social research is about explaining an external social realm; their task, then, is to reflect on this explanatory endeavour and the methodological strategies that accompany it.

This book has two objectives. The first aim is to advance a new approach to this discipline, one that is indebted to American pragmatism. The second aim is to present an advanced assessment of the main approaches in philosophy of the social sciences. The book is written so that it can be read in either way. Those interested in the latter should look at chapters 1 to 6; those interested in the former can read chapters 6 and 7, or, for those already familiar with pragmatism, chapter 7 only. This is not to say that chapters 1 to 6 are irrelevant to the concluding chapter. They are not, but it is possible to understand the last chapter without having read the preceding ones. The topics and authors covered in the first five chapters are chosen because their perspectives are central in the philosophy of the social sciences, not because they somehow fit into a narrative that ultimately leads towards my pragmatist view. The pragmatist stance developed in chapter 7 will develop a very different perspective to those advocated by the authors who appear in the preceding chapters. I will argue that philosophy of social science ought to take a new direction and ask different questions.

The assessment of the main approaches in philosophy of the social sciences is treated in chapters 1 to 6. The way I approach this task is different from that adopted by others, and this needs some elaboration. Firstly, rather than simply introducing ideas, I also focus on the authors and schools of thought behind them. The philosophy of the social sciences is often presented in a strictly analytical fashion, as a set of core topics or questions to which different answers can be given.[1] Alternatively, philosophy of the social sciences is conceived as a critical overview of the various theoretical frameworks that would serve within a naturalist or quasi-naturalist model of social science (that is, a model strongly or loosely based on the natural sciences).[2] *Who* gives the answers is relatively unimportant in this reconstruction. I concentrate instead on a limited number of thinkers and try to show, for each of them, how their views in different areas are linked to each other. For instance, Emile Durkheim held that the scientific study of the social enables us to reach decisions about ultimate values, believed in the virtue of a functional analysis, and was, by all accounts, a holistic thinker. In his case (though not necessarily for others) these three positions are interrelated: his functionalism *avant la lettre* was holistic, and he believed it would facilitate the inference of 'what ought to be' from 'what is'. Furthermore, these three positions tie in with broader visions Durkheim held about the discipline of sociology, its scope, and its relationship to social policy. Likewise, both Karl Popper's falsifiability criterion (as a line of demarcation between science and non-science) and his rejection of holism underscore his discomfort with various forms of historicism. These different stances form a coherent whole.

As well as focusing on its key authors, I prefer to sketch the philosophy of the social sciences in relation to other subjects, in particular (though not exclusively) in connection to disciplines that it is discussing, such as sociology or history. In the analytical tradition, to which I was referring in the above, philosophy of the social sciences tends to be treated as separate from other intellectual activities. I prefer to draw out the interconnectedness, for instance, by showing how the aspirations of some practitioners, such as Durkheim or Max Weber, spilled over into the domain of the philosophy of the social sciences. Once people come to the foreground, neat demarcations tend to fall apart. This is the case, not only for the 'sociological classics', but also for contemporary thinkers. For many critical realists, for example, taking one position or another is not simply an analytical game; it has serious consequences for the discipline in which they are working. Tony Lawson has shown that economics would be radically transformed if it were to take on a realist agenda. This book pays attention to the ramifications of philosophy of the social sciences for social research.

Organizing the book around questions or themes is a simpler task because there is more or less a consensus about the topics that are central to the discipline (holism versus individualism, naturalism versus anti-naturalism, etc.). To structure a manuscript around people or schools of thought is not a sinecure because it raises the question of whom to include and, more controversially, whom to exclude. I limit the analysis to six strands of thought, five among which are linked to an individual (Durkheim's 'scientific rationalism', Weber's attempt to transcend the opposition between hermeneutics and positivism, Popper's falsificationist agenda, critical realism, critical theory and Richard Rorty's neo-pragmatist proposal). This restriction has the advantage of offering an in-depth treatment and avoids bland discussions of various -isms. I will, for instance, demonstrate the extent to which the label of positivism is appropriate for Durkheim and where precisely he deviates from Comte's doctrine or from the later development of logical positivism. Given the small numbers involved, the criteria for selection are very important. Part of the rationale is linked to my own proposal in the final chapter, and indeed the chapters can be read as leading up to this. More importantly, however, I decided to select authors or strands of thought who have been decisive in the establishment of a social science or who have developed highly influential schools in the philosophy of the social sciences. Durkheim and Weber are examples of the former, Popper and critical realism of the latter. My decision to devote a chapter to pragmatism is based on the belief that, while it has hitherto been neglected, it is bound to become a decisive force in the philosophy of the social sciences, and, indeed, my own proposal will draw heavily on the intellectual tradition of pragmatism.

This brings me to the other objective of the book: I propose an outline of a pragmatically inspired philosophy of the social sciences. Not all histories of the philosophy of science assume that researchers might learn from the philosophical reflections that are being discussed, and some explicitly deny that researchers will benefit from reading about philosophy.[3] My historical overview is different from these views in that it is explicitly intended to help researchers think in a novel way about their research.[4] This proposal is partly based on a rejection of other strategies in the philosophy of the social sciences. One such strategy, known as naturalism, involves the search for *a single* scientific method appropriate for the study of both the social and the natural realms. Within this naturalist tradition, some believe they can find the key to scientific success by uncovering the logic of inquiry that is embedded in the history of the natural sciences and which can be emulated by the social sciences. Others prefer not to proceed historically and simply point out the logic of scientific inquiry, how it is superior to other forms of inquiry, and how it can be applied to the study of the social realm. Others again, such as Durkheim or Popper, argue along both lines by pointing out that the superior form of logic is also the one exhibited by natural scientists. Part of my argument is that this naturalist pursuit of the essence of science is misguided because there is no such thing that all scientific activities have in common.[5] But another strategy is to view the social researcher as a 'social cartographer' – someone who maps the social world as accurately and completely as possible – a view that underlies both critical realism and Anthony Giddens's structuration theory. As pragmatists have pointed out repeatedly, this view of knowledge as a mirroring or picturing device is deeply embedded in Western thought. I will show that this way of proceeding is also inconsistent and leads to an intellectual impasse. Both strategies – the naturalist and the cartography model – take for granted what knowledge is for. For naturalists, knowledge is about explaining and predicting an outer world; for cartographers, it is about depicting that realm. Neither reflects on the possibility of other forms of knowledge or, more accurately, on which other objectives of social research may be aimed at. One such objective is what I call self-knowledge, referring to the ability of individuals to question or redescribe themselves and their cultural presuppositions. I think this is a highly neglected component of social research, and one that I wish to promote in what follows.[6]

The first chapter tackles Durkheim's vision of the social sciences. Although Durkheim (1858–1917) was not a philosopher of the social sciences, he wanted to establish sociology as a scientific and autonomous discipline and spent a lot of his time writing about what a scientific social science should look like. Durkheim's methodology is the example par excellence of a naturalist outlook in that he was convinced that the examination of society ought to emulate the methods that have been employed in the natural sciences and have led to such remarkable results. The success of Newtonian physics enthralled French social philosophers such as Auguste Comte, and Durkheim was no exception, though his fascination for the developments in physics was matched by his ongoing interest in biological evolution. If only sociology would employ the same procedures with similar rigour and determination as in the natural sciences, it would not only become a scientific enterprise, but it would also be of practical use to policy-makers and politicians. The problem is that the discipline is still dominated by social philosophers and metaphysicians who consistently fall short of investigating empirical facts and who prefer to philosophize rather than embark on proper research. Durkheim was not the only one to call for a science of society and regard it as a base for the rational steering of the social, but he had a very distinct view of what science was about, what natural scientists have done and what sociologists ought to be doing. None of the usual labels that have been applied to him, such as positivism, deductivism, inductivism or empiricism, really fit. He presented a powerful and original view, one that has been as influential as it is contentious, even though ultimately proven incorrect. This view centred round the idea that sociology studies empirical regularities and can do so either through causal or functional analysis. This sociological research will help to decide upon the ultimate values appropriate for a given society. In this respect (and in this respect only) sociology will replace philosophy. Yet, the distinctiveness of Durkheim's sociology lay in his insistence that sociological regularities call for sociological explanations. As such, the myriad of psychological explanations is ultimately wrong.

Chapter 2 explores Weber's methodological reflections. Weber (1864–1920) did not share Durkheim's ambition to implement and institutionalize the emerging discipline of sociology. His systematic use of general concepts and comparative analysis, however, made his writings essential to the introduction of a historically sensitive and theoretically sophisticated form of sociological research. Contemplative by nature, Weber wrote extensively on the methodology of the social sciences, and did so in a more sophisticated (though more confusing) fashion than Durkheim. Whereas Durkheim situated himself unequivocally within the naturalist camp, Weber brought a more nuanced perspective and tried to steer clear of the pitfalls of both naturalism and anti-naturalism. For Weber, it is not sufficient simply to establish regularities of social life because social explanation demands more. To make sense of the observed regularities, it is necessary to bring in a hermeneutic component, to relive *why* people acted in the way they did. Contrary to several members of the hermeneutic school, Weber does not see this re-enactment as incompatible with causal analysis. Re-enactment is the start of a causal network because people's goals and desires made them do what they did, and these actions in turn led to various effects, some of which were intended, some unintended. The unintended or unanticipated outcomes of purposive action are especially central to Weber's analysis. Weber differed from Durkheim in other respects as well. Whereas Durkheim held that judgements regarding ultimate values might be inferred from empirical research, Weber strongly disagreed: 'what is' cannot inform 'what ought to be'. This is not to say that, for Weber, social research has no bearing on social policy – it does, but in a more modest way. Empirical investigations may help to establish which means are more effective for obtaining given goals or the unintended effects of pursuing a particular objective. As such, social research provides a kind of technical assistance to policy-makers but nothing more than that.

Chapter 3 moves on to Popper's philosophy of the social sciences. Popper (1902–1994) is a prime example of a philosopher searching for that which all proper scientific activities have in common and which therefore constitutes science. Popper started his career as a philosopher of the natural sciences and his knowledge of the social sciences was always limited. While he was acquainted with social and political philosophy, he knew little about sociology or political science. He gradually learned about economics but remained generally uninformed about the other social sciences. It is ironic that he exercised a massive influence on the philosophy of the social sciences, especially in the 1950s and 1960s, though his popularity has always been greater among natural scientists, partly because he portrayed their activities in an idyllic and heroic fashion. For Popper, scientists are imaginative and adventurous people who develop bold theories that are then put to the test. If a theory does not survive the test, then the search for a new theory is on. Theories, however, can be refuted only if they are refutable and, indeed, refutability (or what Popper famously coined 'falsifiability') is his chosen criterion to demarcate science from non-science. It is only because scientific theories are falsifiable that science can progress along the lines of trial and error. Most of the social sciences are not proper science since they construct and uphold theories that are immunized against empirical refutation. The main culprits are Karl Marx, Sigmund Freud and Alfred Adler – Popper admired all three as a young man and vilified them later on. The fact that their theories are non-falsifiable does not necessarily make them hopelessly redundant; they can still provide perceptive insights into the human psyche or society. Yet, as they stand, they are not scientific. For Popper the solution for the social sciences lies in methodological individualism: researchers must take individuals as the starting point of the analysis. They have to assume that people act purposefully and rationally though producing effects that they do not always intend. This does not mean that Popper believed people always acted rationally, but the assumption of rationality is a useful guide for social research, if only to find out where and when people deviated from it. The recent wave of rational choice theory in sociology and political sciences is perfectly in line with Popper's prescriptions.

Chapter 4 introduces critical realism, which first emerged in the 1970s and which has had a considerable impact in various social sciences, including sociology and economics. Like Popper's falsificationism, critical realism assumes a methodological unity between the social and the natural sciences. The starting point of this strand is that most social research functions according to positivist criteria and therefore does not move beyond the superficial realm of observed regularity conjunctions. To explain, however, must mean more than just pointing at regularities. It involves references to mechanisms, structures or powers that account for what has been recorded. Some of these mechanisms might not be immediately accessible to observation because their activities might be counteracted by the workings of other mechanisms. They exist nevertheless, and the task of science (including that of social science) is to gain reliable knowledge of them. This is possible with the help of a little imagination, for instance by drawing on analogies of and metaphors about what we already know. Scientists, indeed, learn about new phenomena by showing similarities with and differences from familiar phenomena. The task for social science is to remove the positivist straitjacket and delve for those underlying structures and powers which are not immediately visible but forever affecting the surface level. It is not surprising, therefore, that realists feel affinities with French structuralism, and indeed some of the 'first-wave' realists come from a Marxist structuralist tradition. Critical realists feel uneasy, however, about the structuralist neglect of agency in human affairs (to the point of denial), and they prefer to link some of the structuralist insights with actor-orientated models of social action. In this sense, their intellectual endeavour is close to Giddens's structuration theory or Bourdieu's genetic structuralism. More recently, they have exhibited a growing interest in evolutionary theory and, in that respect, are moving away from the Giddens–Bourdieu line of thought.

Critical realists emphasize that social research has an emancipatory dimension. This component becomes even more central in chapter 5, which deals with critical theory. For critical theorists, research is not just about describing or explaining; it also provides a platform for a critique of contemporary society. This critique will ultimately provide people with tools to remove societal restrictions and to make for a better society. Critical theorists are hostile to any philosophy of the social sciences that reduces social research to a descriptive enterprise. Positivism is a particular target. Critical theory was initially associated with the writings of the Frankfurt School, a group of left-wing intellectuals, among whom Theodor Adorno (1903–1969) and Max Horkheimer (1895–1973) were particularly prominent. They wrote at a time when logical positivism was influential, not just in philosophy but also in the social sciences. While sympathetic towards aspects of the transition towards modernity, they were concerned about its negative features, notably the spread of instrumental rationality and the loss of substantive rationality. People exhibit instrumental or means–end rationality if they reach given goals efficiently; they exhibit substantive rationality if they critically reflect on and evaluate the goals they pursue. For Adorno et al., positivist sociology is just another expression of the predominance of means–end rationality: it is technically sophisticated, possibly allowing for control, but lacking in critical judgement. Jürgen Habermas (b. 1929) followed in this intellectual tradition: he too felt strongly about the critical potential of sociology and was sceptical of the positivist orthodoxy in social sciences. However, his work differed substantially from that of the early Frankfurt School. Habermas was far more sympathetic to the Enlightenment tradition and tried to uncover its positive dimension: the transition towards modernity went hand in hand with the emergence of procedures of open discussion and criticism. He drew upon pragmatist philosophy to elaborate on the link between knowledge and cognitive interests. Later he would use speech act theory to develop a critical theory centred on language.

Richard Rorty's pragmatism is different again. It is the subject of the penultimate chapter and a prelude to my own exposition in the concluding chapter. Although Rorty's impact on the philosophy of the social sciences is limited, I regard Rorty (b. 1931) as important because he opens the path towards a different way of thinking about the philosophy of the social sciences, freed from the pointless search for an elusive essence of science. Rorty's original breakthrough in philosophy came with a sharp critique of epistemology (meaning any intellectual endeavour that aims to establish the atemporal base for superior forms of knowledge acquisition). Using Wittgenstein and recent developments in analytical philosophy, Rorty's point is that any attempt of philosophy to step outside language and find the master key to ethics or knowledge is ill-fated. In addition, the 'spectator view' of knowledge, which has impregnated contemporary philosophy and epistemology, is highly suspect. This view rests on a misguided representation of knowledge, as if it passively mirrors or reflects the essence of the outer world. Instead, Rorty suggests that we regard knowledge as active, as bringing something about. Later, Rorty finds allies among earlier generations of pragmatists, especially John Dewey. For him, Dewey came to radical conclusions regarding knowledge and truth that were remarkably similar to those of contemporary French deconstructionists such as Jacques Derrida and Michel Foucault. Although Rorty draws on the likes of Ludwig Wittgenstein and Martin Heidegger, his argument is truly pragmatist, not just in the way he rebuffs transcendental forms of inquiry and the spectator theory of knowledge, but also in the way he adjudicates theories on the basis of practical success rather than truth, and the way he shuns theoretical debates that do not make any substantial practical difference. Most of these pragmatist ideas have significant repercussions for the philosophy of the social sciences. Rorty goes further, however. For him, many methodological disputes in the social sciences are pseudo-debates. The *Methodenstreit*, for instance, is not really a quarrel about methods because this would require a consensus regarding which goals to achieve. Naturalists and anti-naturalists simply want different things. Research objectives are central to Rorty's philosophical reflections on the social sciences. They underlie his uneasiness with the way left-leaning social scientists in the United States have moved away from the liberal pragmatism of Dewey and have embraced doctrinaire Marxism or, worse, a sterile and emasculated version of French deconstructionism.

Chapter 6 ends with some critical notes on Rorty, forming a prologue to the concluding chapter. In chapter 7, I discuss a way forward for the social sciences. I suggest that we move beyond the spectre of naturalism that has been haunting the social sciences for a long time, not just because it erroneously assumes that there is something that all sciences have in common, but also because it reduces knowledge to just one type (adequately referred to by Habermas as an empirical-analytical form of knowledge). I elaborate on the possibility of a social science that aims at self-referential knowledge acquisition. This research explores and questions deep-seated presuppositions prevalent in contemporary culture and strives to become aware of other forms of life. This view of the social sciences, therefore, is perfectly in line with the pragmatist perspective that language and knowledge, rather than acts of representation, allow people to increase the scope of human possibilities. Various forms of social research, in a wide range of disciplines, have already explored this self-referential knowledge. Nietzsche's genealogical method is an obvious illustration, which has recently found applications in several academic subjects such as history and sociology. There are also less well-known or at least more discipline-bound examples, such as the emergence of post-processual archaeology and the critical turn in anthropology. These examples show that, rather than being a mere theoretical construct, the pursuit of self-referential knowledge acquisition can form highly successful research strategies in a multitude of fields.

1
Emile Durkheim's Naturalism

Introduction

One of the intellectual achievements of the French sociologist Emile Durkheim was to develop a coherent empirical method for the study of the social. He was not the first to make such an attempt. Others had preceded him in France and elsewhere, but they either lacked precision (as was the case for Auguste Comte) or they conceived of sociology as an aggregate of psychological mechanisms (like John Stuart Mill and Herbert Spencer). Durkheim managed to distinguish sociology from other sciences, not only in terms of its subject matter but also in terms of how it ought to be approached. He designed a distinctly sociological method – different from economics and psychology. Unlike many others, he did not merely theorize about the method he proposed; he also put it into practice. His methodological writings were informed by his sociological investigations and vice versa. This interplay is obvious in the case of *Rules of Sociological Method* (*Les Règles de la méthode sociologique*)[1] and *Suicide* (*Le Suicide*);[2] the former includes guidelines about how to conduct sociological research and the latter applies them to explain suicide patterns. His other research monographs also include many references to methodological problems. For instance, several sections of *The Division of Labour in Society* (*De la division du travail social*)[3] are devoted to methodological issues, ranging from arguments in favour of sociological explanations to assaults on *a priori* accounts of ethical problems. These reflections then feed back into his analysis of empirical phenomena.

Throughout his life, Durkheim was preoccupied with turning the emerging discipline of sociology into a science. Although he came from a religious Jewish background, he quickly substituted a secular, rationalist outlook for his original faith. This adherence to rationalism explains his dislike of the literary and speculative intellectual style that dominated Parisian intellectual life. He preferred conceptual and methodological rigour, and he felt uncomfortable with sociological analysis that indulged in conjectural or metaphysical reasoning. It is not surprising, then, that he explored systematically the possibility of a naturalist programme for the social sciences. The doctrine of naturalism assumes that the social and natural sciences have a great deal in common. Others had contemplated this naturalist perspective before him, but very few came near the boldness and clarity of Durkheim's approach. Durkheim promoted *methodological* naturalism: the philosophical position that the methodological rules that apply in the natural sciences could and should be employed in the social sciences. A number of presuppositions underscore this naturalist project. For instance, it assumes that most, if not all, natural sciences operate with roughly the same logic or according to similar procedures, and it presupposes that there is methodological unity *within* each discipline in the natural sciences. This naturalist approach has had a huge impact on the development of social sciences and in particular on sociology; it was particularly dominant in the first half of the twentieth century and is still prevalent today.

It is important to put Durkheim's naturalism within the intellectual context at the time. Nineteenth-century France was preoccupied with how to maintain or restore solidarity, consensus and cohesion within society. After the French Revolution and the repression that followed, intellectuals became very sensitive to the various issues surrounding social order. Order was no longer regarded as something that could be taken for granted: if it existed, it was not because of religious providence, but because people made it happen. If, however, social order can be achieved, it can also be undone. Recent historical events had shown the fragility of social order – the extent to which it can rapidly dissolve into chaos – so the question arose as to how to bring about a type of solidarity or cohesion that fits a modern society. Most philosophers realized that it made no sense to restore the mechanisms of solidarity that preceded the French Revolution. It was futile to seek a return to the *ancien régime*; a modern society needed modern ties. Rationalist philosophers such as Auguste Comte looked to science for a solution; a scientific account of the workings of society would allow for accurate prediction and effective control. Durkheim thought along similar lines: if we are able to study society like natural scientists study their objects, then we will be better placed to find the right solutions for our problems today. In *Division of Labour*, he applied this scientific approach to make proposals for the running of society. Whereas societies without division of labour are characterized by mechanical solidarity based on similarity of sentiments, contemporary societies have reached such levels of complexity that they can no longer rely on this form of solidarity. They require organic solidarity, predicated on complementary and interdependent roles.

Durkheim lived all his adult life through the Third Republic – a precarious period in French history fraught with social upheaval and political scandal. The socio-political context of the Third Republic helps to explain why

Durkheim was so preoccupied with the lack of sufficient integrative and regulative forces in contemporary society. This concern, which was shared by other French intellectuals at the time, was central to *Division of Labour* and *Suicide*. Durkheim believed that his scientific approach – a combination of causal and functional analysis – would enable us to steer society away from various calamities. It is telling that he employed a medical vocabulary to talk about contemporary society: society is described as 'unhealthy', some of its institutions as 'pathological'. The right scientific method would establish what is 'normal' versus what is 'pathological' – what ought to be kept and what should be eradicated. With the help of this method, he wanted to show that anomie (as the lack of normative regulations) was both widespread and destructive in modern France. In short, methodological considerations are not simply a matter of academic interest; they are crucial to the making of an ordered society. The future of French society (and of any contemporary society for that matter) depends on the right sociological method.

Like many social scientists in the nineteenth century, Durkheim was fascinated with the progress of the natural sciences. In awe of the achievements of Newtonian physics, he used the method of physics as a yardstick for sociology. He was aware that the differences between the social and the physical world were such that sociologists could not quite emulate the methods of physics, but he thought that they should try to come as close as possible. His admiration for Newtonian physics strengthened his belief in the virtues of methodological rigour and observable phenomena. It also fuelled his disdain towards anything remotely speculative or metaphysical. Besides physics, biology was an important source of inspiration for him. He accounted for societal evolution by drawing on analogies with biological evolution, with division of labour as an evolutionary 'solution' to rapid population growth and increasing moral density. Like organisms, societies become increasingly complex with time. Durkheim's use of biological metaphors also underscored his holistic approach to the social, according to which society needs to be understood in its entirety. Society cannot be seen as an aggregate of its components; there is more to society than simply the sum of its individuals. Durkheim regularly compared societies to biological organisms in which various components play a significant part in maintaining the whole. Societies are portrayed as having a need for integration or regulation, and sociological analysis ought to establish which parts of society are fulfilling these central functions.

Durkheim regarded himself as a social scientist who was interested in philosophy in so far as it helped him to establish the right methodological pathway. This is particularly obvious in his *The Rules of Sociological Method*. This book, which originally appeared in the *Revue philosophique*, is not Durkheim's most subtle work. Rather than developing the highly sophisticated arguments that can be found in *Division of Labour* or *The Elementary Forms of Religious Life*, he intended to state forcefully a case for the new science of sociology. Sociology was still associated with Auguste Comte, not quite as unacceptable as in the first half of the nineteenth century, but certainly in need of a proper defence, hence Durkheim's blunt and didactic style. Durkheim, however, had written on methodology long before *Rules*. His inaugural lecture in Bordeaux in 1887, entitled 'Course in Sociology' (*Cours de science sociale: leçon d'ouverture*), dealt with the methodology of the social sciences.[4] In this lecture, he set out the main principles of a new science of society and elaborated on its differences from previous philosophical perspectives on society. He also explained how Auguste Comte and Herbert Spencer were its founding fathers, and what role the new science could serve in contemporary French society. In 1892 he completed his dissertation on Montesquieu, which showed how the French philosopher already employed the methodology of the new science, though in a rudimentary and incomplete fashion.[5] After *The Rules of Sociological Method*, Durkheim published other articles about methodology. Among them, 'Sociology and the Social Sciences' (*Sociologie et sciences sociales*) explored the complex relationship between the new science and its neighbouring disciplines. This article put forward taxonomies of its various subdivisions. It also set out the key methodological rules that ought to accompany any sociological study and how it may differ from a historical study.[6]

An uneasy relationship with positivism

It is ironic that, while secondary sources have often labelled Durkheim's methodology as positivist,[7] Durkheim was anxious throughout his life to distance himself from that label. Instead Durkheim used 'rationalism', 'scientific rationalism' or 'rationalist empiricism' to describe his viewpoint, and by doing so distinguished it from what he called the 'positivist metaphysics' of Comte and Spencer.[8] Although he later expressed the need for some changes to 'traditional rationalism' he did so without abandoning its core ideas.[9] The fact that he chose 'rationalism' to refer to his view is partly indicative of his loathing for what he saw as the literary obscurantism that permeated the Parisian intelligentsia and with which he had become acquainted during his student days at the Ecole normale. Rationalism, as both conceptual clarity and scientific method, opposes the 'dilettantism' and 'mysticism' of contemporary intellectual life. Sometimes Durkheim opposed the scientific sociological method to what he called 'art', which is unmethodical and stirred by emotions.[10] A rationalist method consists of finding 'relationships of cause and effect' based on observations so as to steer society effectively. Durkheim pointed out that the principle of causality has been applied effectively in various domains of inquiry, ranging from the physical world to psychology.

It is therefore legitimate also to apply it to the social realm.[11] This is not to say that Durkheim believed that sociology would ever obtain certainties as there are in mathematics, logic, or even the natural sciences. He considered it unlikely that sociology will ever discover the indisputable truths that can be found, say, in geometry. Nevertheless, it would provide a type of knowledge that is preferable over philosophical speculation, metaphysics or religion, because it is grounded in empirical experience. As such, it is well placed to provide reliable guidance for effective future action.[12]

Durkheim was, of course, deeply influenced by the positivism of Auguste Comte, Hippolyte Taine and Ernest Renan.[13] He accepted Comte's view that, in the course of recent history, the positive method had been applied to increasingly complex domains of reality (respectively physics, chemistry, biology and psychology). As a consequence, it was probably only a matter of time before this method could be applied to society as well.[14] Durkheim agreed with the positivist school that sociology ought to emulate the methods of the natural sciences, hence his insistence that social facts should be treated like things. Sociology ought to adopt a similar objectivity to the natural sciences, and aim at law-like generalizations, using the comparative method. Like various positivists, he drew a distinction between science and metaphysics and emphasized that sociology is irrelevant with regard to metaphysical questions. It is wrong to assume, as some do, that the uncovering of societal laws undermines the notion of free will.[15] Like Comte, Durkheim held that in various spheres of life philosophical speculation has become superseded by science, as can be inferred from his view that, instead of *a priori* arguments about ethics, we should study empirically the extent to which various societies need different ethical systems. Like Comte's positivist school, he believed that the scientific study of society, rather than being contemplative, is a stepping stone towards the steering of the social, hence his interest, for instance, in distinguishing normal versus pathological forms. As society has become increasingly complex, its reliance on scientifically based steering has intensified.[16]

Durkheim felt strongly, however, that positivist knowledge was not sufficiently embedded in the empirical realm, and that it had become what it had tried to replace, a new orthodoxy and a new religion. It is probably indicative of Durkheim's stance *vis-à-vis* Comte that he initially used the term 'social science' ('*science sociale*') rather than Comte's neologism 'sociology' ('*sociologie*'). From the beginning, he was keen to distance himself from Comte's project, which he did not consider sufficiently scientific. For Durkheim, Comte did not carry out proper empirical research, and so failed to recognize the rich diversity among societies.[17] He recognized only one 'social species', and treated his law of three stages as a dogma rather than a scientific fact. Durkheim decided that there is no guarantee, as Comte believed, that societal evolution would continue evolving in the same direction as it has done so far.[18] Other positivist-inclined philosophers, such as Taine and Renan, were too literary for Durkheim's taste. While he had some sympathy for Taine's wish to reconcile rationalism and empiricism, he had none for Renan's elitist view that only a handful of people are able to embrace the new reason. French positivists were too much embedded in the very same literary-philosophical climate that they sought to replace. Identical reservations underlie the opening paragraphs of *Suicide*, in which Durkheim drew attention to the fact that, while the science of sociology has become remarkably fashionable, it has not accomplished much. He felt that too many unfounded generalizations and 'hasty intuitions' are made in the name of sociology. If sociology 'is to satisfy the hopes placed in it, it must try to become more than a new sort of philosophical literature. Instead of contenting himself with metaphysical reflection on social themes, the sociologist must take as the object of his research groups of facts clearly circumscribed, capable of ready definition, with definite limits, and adhere strictly to them.'[19]

There are other ways in which Durkheim's philosophical position contrasts with that of positivism, not just its nineteenth-century manifestation but also its more recent developments. Early twentieth-century positivism has often been associated with the doctrine of phenomenalism, according to which reality can only be attributed to phenomena that are immediately accessible or perceptible. In contrast, Durkheim assumed a two-level worldview, which downgrades the surface level of sensory observations and attributes epistemological priority to a structural level that is less accessible. While the former is illusory, the latter is real. Durkheim viewed science as capable of delving beneath the surface and uncovering the underlying mechanisms that account for the observed regularities. By doing so, science challenges people's preconceptions, showing that what is *prima facie* real is not reality. He regarded sociology as more iconoclastic than many other sciences because people, as part of society, have various preconceptions about its workings and they are likely to exhibit substantial emotional loyalty to their lay views. The act of questioning these ideas is not a sinecure, but it is central to the *métier* of the sociologist. Durkheim's two-level worldview meant that he preferred explanations that attribute causal power, not to the intentions or assessment of the people involved, but to unconscious or unacknowledged conditions. The reason for this is that people are often mistaken about the motivations behind their actions, and about what happens around them. Durkheim summarized his position clearly in a debate with the historian C. Seignobos: 'all those who engage in the study of the past know full well that the immediately perceptible motives and apparent causes are by far the least important. We must penetrate much more deeply into reality in order to understand it.'[20] History was a particular target for Durkheim. In his dissertation on Montesquieu, he had already deplored the tendency among historians to explain events in terms of individual decisions, as if history can be seen as an intended outcome of choices made by powerful kings, religious leaders and law-makers.[21] In a similar vein, Durkheim warned against explaining suicide patterns in terms of motives, for he regarded motives or reasons as merely 'apparent' causes. The real causes are social.[22] Likewise, reviewing one of Antonio Labriola's articles on historical materialism, Durkheim applauded Marxist historians for recognizing that social life must be explained not by the representations, motives or reasons of the individuals involved, but by underlying causes, which elude the consciousness of these individuals.[23] This is not to say that Durkheim totally embraced Marxism. For instance, he was unconvinced by the Marxist principle whereby these causes were embedded in the mode of production. He was even less persuaded by the dogmatic fashion in which this principle was upheld. However, he subscribed fully to the two-level worldview.[24]

Positivism has often been associated with an atomistic view.[25] According to atomism, the world is divided up into indivisible unconnected components. In the social sciences, these particles are often seen as individuals endowed with purposes and beliefs. In this case, we tend to talk about 'methodological individualism' – that is, the methodological orientation that regards social processes as the partly intended, partly unintended, outcome of people's purposive conduct. Methodological individualists are reluctant to attribute causal powers to extra-individual entities such as social structure. In contrast, Durkheim regarded society as an entity *sui generis* with its own internal mechanisms and complexity.[26] He adopted a holistic view, in which a social system is taken in its entirety, irreducible to its constituent parts. This explains why he saw Rousseau as one of the forerunners of sociology, because he too 'was keenly aware of the specificity of the social order. He conceived it clearly as an order of facts generically different from purely individual facts. It is a new world superimposed on the purely psychological world.'[27] Other French thinkers, such as Comte and Boutroux, would follow this holistic tradition, but Durkheim's holism differed from theirs as well as Rousseau's in that he drew more explicitly on analogies with biological organisms. Durkheim saw parts of a system as interrelated, each part contributing to the persistence of the very system in which it is embedded. Observed social patterns are causally affected by other social regularities, and their continuity is explainable by how they add to the maintenance and survival of a larger social body. Durkheim's commitment to an 'organicist' outlook also underscores his distinction between the 'normal' and the 'pathological' (about which more later), one of the differences being that the former is a functional fit whereas the latter is dysfunctional. The biological metaphor might be even more apparent in Durkheim's definition of organic solidarity as a moral bond based not on similarity between people, but on their mutual dependency. Long before functionalism and structuralism became fashionable schools, Durkheim had adopted the holistic perspective that became one of their hallmarks.

Twentieth-century positivism has often been identified with the so-called fact–value distinction. Here again Durkheim escapes a straightforward positivist label. By the fact–value distinction, philosophers may refer to two very different philosophical positions. First of all, they might refer to the methodological stance that, whereas values and norms affect the choice of the subject matter, these values and norms should not interfere with *how* the research is carried out. To postulate the desirability of value-free research is to assume that it is *possible* to conduct research that is not contaminated by value systems and normative regulations. Durkheim adhered to the fact–value distinction in this sense: he assumed value-free sociology is feasible and preferable. However, the fact–value distinction may also refer to an altogether different position, where science cannot help people to make judgements about ultimate values. Social science observes, describes and explains social phenomena, and it may enable people to establish the causes of given ends and the means for achieving them. It cannot, however, help to decide about the desirability of the ends themselves, nor can it help to choose ends. Durkheim rejected the fact–value distinction in this sense: if properly conceived, social science could tell people what is desirable and good. It is misleading to say that social science can establish only the means for achieving given goals because, from one viewpoint, every means is a goal. Why should science inform us about the fastest route to achieving our goal rather than the least costly one, or the most likely rather than the least complex one, and so on? If it cannot instruct people as to what ultimate aims to choose, then surely it will be equally inadequate in telling people which of the subordinate 'ends' are legitimate 'means'.[28] Building on this argument, Durkheim attempted to distinguish between normal and pathological forms: the former are desirable, the latter to be eradicated. He dissociated himself, though, from those who simply speculated about what ought to be, insisting that his distinction was founded on empirical investigations. Foreshadowing Popper, he was repelled by the Marxist view that philosophers and statesmen tried to accomplish their utopian vision. Idealists in general 'study reality in very cursory fashion. Often they merely content themselves with elevating some impulse of their sensibility, a rather sudden inspiration of the heart . . . into a kind of imperative before which their reason bows low, and they ask us to do likewise.'[29] Instead, sociologists and statesmen should become like doctors: they forestall illness by sustaining good hygiene, and if illness breaks out, they try to treat it.[30] 'Scientists of morality' are inevitably more cautious than idealists because they realize that social facts cannot easily be altered, and, as social facts are linked to other social facts, it is difficult to foresee the outcome of these 'series of repercussions'.[31]

It is worth elaborating on Durkheim's arguments against various speculative views of what society should be. As early as his inaugural lecture at Bordeaux, he warned against a dominant view among philosophers that treats society as a preconceived machine, as if at some point people simply decided to live together because they realized its usefulness. In this view, there is no particular affinity between the nature of what it is to be a human being and the nature of society; there is nothing intrinsic to human nature that propels people to form society in the way in which they have. It follows that a society can be undone or changed whenever people decide to do so. As long as they are clear about what kind of society they want to achieve, they can create it. They only have to exert their will, organize themselves and co-ordinate. There is nothing, however, in people's nature that could prevent them from achieving their utopian project.[32] Against this perspective, Durkheim proposed to view society as a 'natural product', an 'organism'. Like any organism, it grows and develops, and the various parts become interrelated. Just as the cells of an organism are interrelated in particular ways, the different parts of society have developed specific connections. When people decide to implement change without considering these connections (without taking notice of what is to be human), their efforts may be useless or even harmful.[33] Sociologists need to study society in order to find out about the functional relationships that hold the organism together. This can allow us to distinguish the normal from the pathological. Durkheim recognized that economists were the first to realize that there are social laws like physical laws. These laws really exist: they make certain interventions counter-productive and detrimental, others productive and beneficial. Political economists stopped halfway because they regarded the individual as the only discernible reality. Society and the nation were mere nominal entities, with laws based on aggregates of a psychological logic.[34]

One of the recurrent themes in Durkheim's writings is that sociology is distinct from other disciplines. Sociology's differences from philosophy were of particular importance to Durkheim. He insisted that sociology is an empirical discipline and therefore is not philosophy. Whereas the metaphysician studies the 'transcendental finality' of morality, sociology studies how it functions in society. Whereas philosophy pursues atemporal features applicable to different cultural settings, sociology is sensitive to the extent to which morality alters through time; it conceives of these changes in relationship to transformations within the social structure.[35] Durkheim saw philosophy as antithetical to sociology because philosophical doctrines had resisted the emergence of sociology for a long time. In particular, he thought that the predominance of metaphysical dualism made a science of society impossible. Metaphysical dualism postulated two different realms, one of nature and one of society. Whereas determinism reigned over the world of natural objects, what is manmade would mysteriously escape the principles of cause and effect. In order to make sociology possible, Durkheim wanted to expand the notion of scientific law to include human activities and artefacts. Given this intellectual context, he was not surprised that the arguments in favour of a science of society were first put forward in philosophy itself. For Durkheim, it took a philosopher such as Comte to rebut all the arguments in favour of meta-physical dualism while not succumbing to the materialist monism which was equally prevalent at the time. Both Comte's positivist philosophy and materialist monism recognized that people are subjected to laws, just as in nature. Whereas materialist monists regarded social and psychological phenomena as ultimately explainable in terms of their material foundations, Comte insisted that society had its own complexity and laws.[36] Durkheim rec-ognized that Comte's rebuttal of both metaphysical dualism and materialist monism was a considerable philosophical feat, but the price to pay for this intellectual liberation was that sociology became firmly fixed in philosophy. Being at once 'inventor' of sociology and high priest of positivist philosophy, Comte never managed to live up to his own positivist ideals, and ended up developing a highly abstract theory of society that failed to do justice to the vast array of human experiences. Trying to fit his data into a unilinear evolu-tionary narrative, he showed little empirical interest in different types of society.[37] Durkheim noted that most followers of Comte never practised proper science; instead they applied religiously his law of three stages. For Durkheim, science occurs only as people work on a wide variety of problems and are willing to reassess previous theoretical constructions in the light of new empirical evidence. Comte was not the last one to reduce the world to a single problem. This can be inferred from the search among various self-acclaimed sociologists for 'the cause which dominates all causes', be it the law of evolution, the law of imitation or the law of adaptation. Spencer is a good example. Although Spencer showed more interest than Comte in a detailed analysis of the workings of society, this energy was directed not towards the study of social facts for their own sake, but towards supporting his law of universal evolution.[38]

Durkheim's view of science prefigured aspects of realist philosophy of science. Firstly, although Durkheim thought that social science should ulti-mately have practical repercussions, he did not adhere to an instrumentalist view of science. Instead, he combined his Cartesian rationalism with a realist notion of science: he believed that definitions capture the inherent properties of social phenomena. Concepts of social phenomena ought to be a function of 'some integrating element in their nature and not according to whether they conform to some more or less ideal notion.'[39] Sociologists should then be able to shed their preconceptions and study the social realm as objectively as natural scientists relate to their domain of research. Secondly, Durkheim's two-level worldview precedes the realist distinction between the empirical and the deep. All through his life, Durkheim was conscious of the pitfalls of extreme empiricism, whether in the form of the mindless pursuit of empirical regularities or in the form of what Michel Foucault called the *histoire événe-mentielle* (the history of great figures or important dates that have shaped our past). A scientific explanation aims at uncovering underlying structures of reality that are not immediately accessible to observation. Thirdly, long before Mary Hesse and Rom Harré developed their realist perspective, Durkheim had already emphasized the part analogies and metaphors play in scientific analysis. He discussed their role in his inaugural lecture in Bordeaux. On the one hand, Durkheim repeated his well-known view that society cannot be reduced to biology because it contains something new that eludes biological research, just as biological phenomena could not be captured through chemistry and chemical elements could not be reduced to physics. On the other hand, he pointed out that the mind could only account for something new by relying on analogies with something with which it is already familiar. There is no creation *de novo*: a new idea is actually an established idea applied to a new object. As a realist *avant la lettre*, he argued that sociologists must rely on analogies with biological evolution in order to account for social processes. Of course, they need to do this with caution so that the social is not subordinate to the biological. But if sociology is to make any progress at all, these insights from other disciplines are crucial.[40] Durkheim realized that his analogies with biological evolution marked a sharp difference with Comte's unilinear evolutionism. He noted that Comte's view of science did not allow him to see society as a continuation of the biological. As such, he was incapable of seeing the former in terms of the latter.[41]

Durkheim's realist stance also appears in his treatment of pragmatism. Pragmatism was an American philosophical doctrine that rejected the view that science represents the world accurately. The value of science does not lie in accurate copying of the external world, but in a successful active engagement with that world. Durkheim disagreed, at least partly. Compared to Durkheim's views on positivism, his discussions of American pragmatism are not well known. Durkheim gave a number of lectures on pragmatism in the academic year 1913–14. At the time, pragmatism had some impact on French intellectuals, including Durkheim's teachers, Renouvier and Boutroux. Durkheim's lectures dealt not only with American pragmatism, but also with French philosophers whose views showed striking affinities with pragmatism (for instance, Henri Bergson). These lecture notes were published posthumously. They show Durkheim's in-depth knowledge of pragmatism, his admiration for John Dewey, but also his strong conviction that pragmatism posed a threat to the French rationalist tradition.[42] Interestingly, Durkheim failed to explore the implications of pragmatism for the methodology or philosophy of the social sciences. Instead, he noted remarkable similarities between his sociological project and pragmatism. In particular, each recognized that people's knowledge and truth are situated in real life, history and culture. Truth is no longer 'deified'; it is no longer 'above human life'.[43] Durkheim argued, however, that sociology was much better placed to account for knowledge and truth than pragmatism. Pragmatism tended to treat truth, reason and morality as psychological and arbitrary. Sociological explanations were more convincing. They pointed at the social processes that accompany and affect these categories. Durkheim insisted that truth is impersonal and necessary – not subjective and arbitrary. Against the pragmatist tendency towards 'local subjectivism', we need to find criteria to distinguish between opposing views. Pragmatism adopted a too fluid notion of truth as if devoid of any objectivity. The fact that things change does not imply that truth changes too. For Durkheim, truth is 'increased' and 'enlarged' through time, but its nature does not change. Truth cannot be defined solely as practical efficiency; truth corresponds to an external reality.[44] Truth is 'something that is independent of the facts of sensitivity and individual impulse. Such a universally held conception of truth must correspond to something real.'[45]

How to be a proper sociologist

By the end of the nineteenth century, numerous social sciences had already been established. Of these, historical research probably had the longest pedigree, but by Durkheim's time social statistics and economics had also gained prominence. Durkheim was forced to think about the relationship between sociology and the other social sciences. He decided that sociology was the system, the *corpus*, of the social sciences, and he regarded the latter as specific offshoots of the former. The other social sciences, however, had not developed within the same scientific spirit as sociology, and they must be reconfigured if they are to be integrated in sociology. The establishment of sociology should, therefore, go hand in hand not only with the reorganization of the social sciences, but also with a reassessment of their methods. This is not an easy task, as can easily be inferred from the hostile receptions that sociology received among the other disciplines.[46] Durkheim noted, however, that the task had recently been lightened by the fact that various disciplines, such as history and political economy, had been taking up methods that are quintessentially sociological. By focusing on institutions, history was no longer a narrative study. Whereas history traditionally reconstructed the flux of contingent events, the emerging history explored the more permanent features of social and political life and often used comparisons to search for similarities between different countries.[47] Political economy underwent similar transformations. It used to create a *Güterwelt*, an artificial model, in which individual actions are subordinated to iron economic laws, regardless of the society to which they belong. Instead the new political economy conceived of society as prior to individual action, and the notion of abstract economy became substituted by national economy or *Volkswirtschaft*.[48] In short, Durkheim recognized that the social sciences were already moving in the direction he wanted. The problem, as he saw it, was that scientists working in these different disciplines remained ignorant of what went on in aligned fields. Also, scholars still failed to acknowledge the distinct social nature of the phenomena that they study, preferring psychological types of explanation. This demonstrates again the importance for the sociological community of keeping a watchful eye on the academic developments in the different social sciences so as to coordinate and dictate their research agendas.[49]

Although Durkheim attributed a managerial role to the sociologist, he recognized that the other social sciences operated differently. While sociologists may draw on history, ethnography or statistics, he insisted that they study something different in a distinct way.[50] Of all the social sciences, however, he was particularly keen to draw a distinction from psychology, because he was convinced that many social philosophers had hitherto drawn upon pseudo-scientific psychological explanations.[51] There is no doubt that Comte and E. Boutroux were influential in this regard. They believed that there is a hierarchy of sciences based on the complexity of the domain of inquiry, and that, while the sciences higher up in the hierarchy rely to some extent on the mechanisms at the lower level, they cannot be reduced to them. In a similar vein, Durkheim extended Aristotle's dictum 'psychology by psychological principles, biology by biological ones' to the realm of sociology, which can no longer be seen an extension or aggregate of psychological factors.[52] Sociology has a different subject matter from psychology; its domain of inquiry necessitates a unique type of explanation. Sociology deals with collective representations, the collective conscience or behavioural patterns of groups of people – not individual representations, the mind or the personal act. During the nineteenth century, social scientists or philosophers tended to invoke two types of psychological explanations, and Durkheim was critical of both. Some referred to hereditary differences between individuals or groups of individuals to account for variations in observed tendencies. Sections in *Suicide* challenge those extra-social explanations on empirical grounds. Others alluded to innate psychological drives applicable to everybody, such as the proclivity to imitate others (Gabriel Tarde), the inclination towards progress (Comte) or the urge for happiness (Spencer).[53] Again, some of Durkheim's arguments against these explanations are empirical. From the observed variations between cultures (and between groups of people) he inferred that the notion of universal drives, if it exists at all, explains remarkably little. Foreshadowing the structuralist 'death of the subject', Durkheim saw society as pervading and moulding individual consciousness to the extent that any reference to 'human nature' or 'individual nature' becomes highly suspect.[54]

Durkheim did not simply believe that sociology employs different forms of explanations from those used in psychology. He also held that sociology has a distinct object of research. This point is important because, for Durkheim, a discipline is only a science if it has a clearly defined field of inquiry.[55] But if sociology has a distinct subject matter, as he claimed, he had to clarify what it consists of. He felt uneasy with those such as Comte who argued that sociology studies society because this only begs the question. What is it precisely about society that is being studied? Durkheim gave an unequivocal answer: social facts. The study of social facts is what distinguishes the mature science of society from the speculative pseudo-science of Comte. Social facts make sociology a focused discipline with an eye for empirical detail, far removed from the metaphysical lumber of social philosophy.[56] Durkheim's task was to define a social fact as distinct from other facts. He complained that many others use the term loosely, so loosely in practice that virtually everything would count as a social fact. For instance, there is little to be gained by defining social facts as facts that people have in common and that play a pivotal role in the reproduction of society. No one would, of course, doubt that all people drink, sleep and eat, and that these activities are central to the maintenance of the social, but to call these practices social facts would confuse the domain of sociology with biology and psychology.[57] Instead, Durkheim defined social facts as representations, feelings and actions that are not only general (in the sense of being shared by individuals) but also external to individuals, and which exercise coercive power over them.[58] Legal systems, moral frameworks, religious doctrines, monetary systems, languages and social currents are examples of social facts. Durkheim explained that 'externality' of social facts refers to their existence outside the consciousness of the individual, but he was ambiguous about what this meant precisely. In some passages 'externality' refers to how social facts exist before the individuals are born, or before they are faced with them. For instance, people's native language predates their birth or is temporally prior to people's usage. In other passages 'externality' seems to refer to the more contentious claim that the persistence of social facts is independent of the individual's action or beliefs. For instance, the survival or reproduction of a language is not contingent on the individual's compliance to the grammar and vocabulary that make up that language.[59] By the 'constraining' feature of social facts, Durkheim meant that they impose themselves onto the individual, partly because the individual has internalized the institutional matrix; as such he does not feel the urge to act differently. Even if the individual wishes to resist the social facts, however, they remain compelling because any resistance would immediately be accompanied by negative sanctions: for instance, any attempt to break the law may lead to a fine, a community service or a prison sentence.[60] Here, Durkheim took the opportunity to reiterate his point that social facts are not social simply because they are shared. It is precisely because social facts impose themselves onto each individual that they tend to be general – not the other way around.[61]

Durkheim's next task was to decide how social facts are to be observed. This may sound like a trivial issue, but it was not for Durkheim because he was very keen to distinguish science from ideology. People have various preconceptions (what Francis Bacon called *notiones vulgares* or *praenotiones*) about social life, and they tend to take these notions for reality. Observation is crucial to any science as it enables people to distinguish the real from the illusionary. There have been successful attempts to distinguish the true appearance of things from the *idola* in the natural sciences, but not in sociology. This is probably because in sociology people's definitions of things are constitutive of what is being studied.[62] There have, of course, been attempts to establish sociology on an empirical footing, but none has been successful. Just as Comte's 'progress of humanity' was ultimately not backed by facts, Spencer considered co-operation to be the essence of social life and mistook this preconception for a fact. He failed to check whether all forms of social life are indeed forms of co-operation as he assumed, and he used empirical research not to explain social phenomena, but to serve his preconceived notions.[63] The ideological nature of social research is particularly noticeable in some sub-fields of sociology such as ethics and political economy. For instance, while many scholars take the law of supply and demand as 'natural', there is no empirical research to support the claim that economic transactions operate according to this law.[64] In order to avoid the conflation between ideal and reality Durkheim suggested that social phenomena should be treated as things.[65] This dictum led to criticisms and misunderstandings, to which Durkheim replied in the prefaces of later editions of the book. He explained that a 'thing' is what is given; it forces itself upon the observation. To treat social facts as things is thus to approach them as data. This dictum is so interwoven with a Durkheimian outlook that he used 'social facts' and 'social things' interchangeably.[66] This modest prescription disguises a more radical agenda. He meant not only that the sociologist should eradicate his or her own preconceptions, but that he or she should also take distance from the preconceptions of the people involved. As such, the sociologist ought to study *actual* values exchanged in economic relations or *actual* moral rules that affect behaviour – not a moral ideal or some speculative notion of value – and, at least as importantly, he or she should do so independently of people's views of those relations or rules. In Durkheim's parlance, sociology should move from the 'subjective' to the 'objective' stage.[67] Likewise, the classification of facts ought to depend on the nature of things – not on their purported ideal or people's perception of them. So when the sociologist sets out to define a phenomenon, the definition ought to identify the 'common external characteristics' of the phenomenon. This often involves redefining commonly held concepts so as to ground them even more in the realm of 'sense-perceptions'.[68]

In one of his more contentious moves, Durkheim distinguished 'normal' from 'pathological' facts, the former referring to those phenomena that are 'appropriate' and the latter to those that should be different from what they are. The classification drew upon Saint-Simon and Comte's juxtaposition of 'organic' and 'critical' periods, the former harmonious, the latter times of crisis. For Durkheim the juxtaposition can also be traced back to Montesquieu's sociological approach to law.[69] The distinction is important for Durkheim because he wanted to show that his sociology would ultimately instruct people about what is desirable and what is not. Others had tried to make judgements about ultimate values, but Durkheim dismissed them as ideological because their suggestions were detached from reality.[70] He considered his approach to be scientific, using an 'objective criterion', 'inherent in the facts themselves'. The underlying principle is simple: a state of health is preferred over sickness. Durkheim was suspicious of any attempts to uncover the essence of the normal state; instead he decided to proceed empirically. Social facts are normal if firstly they are common in similar types of society at a corresponding phase of their evolution, and secondly if there is a convincing account for why they are so common. Those facts that do not fulfil these criteria are pathological or 'morbid'.[71] In practice, however, Durkheim tended to use the second criterion. The more societies go through massive transformations, he reasoned, the less empirical material is available about whether particular social facts under investigation occur in the average society at a corresponding level of evolution. As a result, he decided, in those circumstances, to establish which conditions in the past gave rise to the facts, and whether these conditions still exist. Social facts are deemed normal if they are related to the conditions of contemporary society. If not, they will be labelled as morbid.[72] Note that Durkheim's distinction between the normal and the pathological presupposes that what is normal for one type of society is not necessarily so for another, and this in turn assumes that there are different types of society or, as Durkheim put it, different 'social species'. Hence Durkheim's next task was to identify the different species and to justify the criteria used to identify them. He started with the observation that every society consists of various parts, and suggested that societies should be classified according to how the parts relate to each other. In Durkheim's 'social morphology', societies are classified depending on the degree of organization, ranging from single-segment societies to highly differentiated ones.[73] In *Division of Labour*, Durkheim drew upon both the distinction between the normal and the pathological and his taxonomy of societies. He tried to demonstrate that there is a lack of normative regulation within the contemporary economic system.[74] In the preface to the second edition, he argued that this pathological state would be rectified through the implementation of a professional ethic, and that this implies that professional organizations would be partly modelled on the way ancient corporations operate.[75]

How are social phenomena to be explained? For Durkheim there are two types of explanation: the efficient cause (which has led to the emergence of the social phenomenon) and the function that the phenomenon fulfils. In his essay on Montesquieu, Durkheim had already alluded to the importance of distinguishing efficient causes from final causes.[76] He pointed out that Montesquieu's statement that laws follow from the nature of societies is ambiguous. It could mean either that the particular characteristics of society *produce* certain laws, or that laws are *means* through which society is able to obtain its ends. It is precisely the same notion of efficient cause that reappears in his *Rules of Sociological Method*.[77] Sometimes he referred to it simply as 'cause'. Functions are very different from efficient causes. A social practice fulfils a function if it contributes to a particular need of the social system in which it is embedded; the effect is not necessarily intentional.[78] Both cause and effect are necessary, but they ought not to be conflated and should be studied separately.[79] For instance, the fact that organic solidarity reinforces social ties does not explain the fact that it emerged in the first place. Different religious systems emerge for different reasons, though, once in place, all strengthen social cohesion. The efficient cause of a social fact may help to establish the function it fulfils, so it is preferable to study the former before the latter.

Not any cause will do, however. Durkheim warned against those explanations that refer to psychological attributes or human nature. Sociology cannot be reduced to an aggregate of psychological phenomena because social facts constrain, intrude upon and shape individual consciousness. In *Suicide*, several chapters are devoted to the rejection of psychological explanations, such as those that attribute causal priority to mechanisms of imitation.[80] The explanation of social phenomena must be sought in society. To counter-argue that society in itself consists of individuals would be to ignore that society has its own 'psychical individuality'. The collective sentiments of an unorganized crowd, for instance, do not necessarily match the average sentiments of the people involved. The gulf is even greater in society because of the impact of previous generations and tradition on the collective consciousness.[81] The principal cause of any social phenomenon is to be found in the nature of the 'inner social environment' or 'general environment', in particular in the 'volume' of society and its 'dynamic density'. Whereas volume indicates the number of social units, dynamic density refers to the moral concentration of people. Montesquieu was one of the first philosophers to identify how social factors affect the type of society, but he focused mainly on the effect of how large society is, whereas for Durkheim dynamic density was more important.[82] Other causes are to be found in the characteristics of specific groups or 'special environments'. For example, the size of the family and the degree of its integration within the wider community will have an affect on domestic life. However, the general environment affects special environments, and so the impact of the former is more important than that of the latter.[83]

What evidence is needed to conclude that one fact has caused another? In the natural sciences, experiments provide sufficient evidence. In sociology, however, experiments cannot be conducted because the social facts concerned cannot be produced artificially.[84] Instead, the sociologist will use the comparative method to establish which cause corresponds to which effect. Durkheim realized that, for this method to be effective, it was crucial to hold that 'to the same effect there always corresponds the same cause.'[85] If the same fact has more than one cause, the comparative method would cease to supply reliable information. For Durkheim, then, there are as many crimes as there are causes of crime, and there are as many types of suicides as there are causes of suicide. Hence Durkheim described his classification of types of suicide as mainly aetiological – not morphological.[86] Durkheim's next task was to specify how precisely the comparative method is to be used to establish causality. The observation of regularities is central to the task of the sociologist. Take, for example, the correlation between social class and educational achievement, or between rates of suicide and education. The sociologist might be able to make sense of a given correlation by invoking a plausible theoretical framework. The theory would account for why one variable would have caused the other one. For instance, it is perfectly feasible to invoke a theory based on the idea that cultural capital, while being an instrument for educational success, is available to different degrees among different social classes. But often regularities are spurious and have to be explained by a third variable. For instance, it is unlikely that education as such has an effect on suicide rates. It is more likely that both are affected by the weakening of religious bonds, which reinforces the thirst for knowledge but also loosens social ties.[87] These examples might give the impression that, for Durkheim, the sociological method should be limited to the observation of regularities with a single society. Nothing is further from the truth. It is preferable to collect data from different countries, and it is also advisable to trace the development of social facts through time.

Application: the study of suicide

Durkheim did not see himself as a philosopher, but as a practising social scientist. His methodological prescriptions were not meant to be simply theoretical speculations; they were enshrined in actual empirical research. He insisted that sociology would only be taken seriously if, like any other established science, it was able to show empirical results. *The Division of Labour*, his doctoral dissertation, was an empirical study of the way in which societies have become increasingly complex and differentiated. The methodology of this study was very much in line with the guidelines set out in *The Rules of Sociological Method* two years later. Of all Durkheim's empirical works, however, *Suicide* counts as the archetypal example of his methodology concerning causal analysis. It was published in 1897, two years after *The Rules*, and it could be regarded as a straightforward application of *The Rules*. In *Suicide*, Durkheim was trying to show the power of his sociological research programme. One of the central tenets of that programme is the idea that, underneath the surface level of individual decisions and actions, there lies a deeper societal level, and that the latter affects the former. Pointedly, he restated this view in his preface to *Suicide*.[88] Durkheim saw suicide as a challenge to his sociology, because people regard suicide as among the most individual decisions one can make. Therefore, if he managed to show the impact of society in this instance, then he would have a strong case for his sociological project.[89] Durkheim was not arguing that his sociological perspective would be able to account for the origins of *individual* suicides. Every individual decision of that magnitude demands an in-depth psychological analysis. Durkheim insisted, however, that his sociological analysis would be able to tell us why certain *categories* of people seem more vulnerable than other categories; for instance, why Protestants are more likely to commit suicide than Catholics, and why individuals who are single have a higher probability than married people.[90]

Scientific analyses rest on 'comparable facts', which in turn rest on precise definitions; hence Durkheim's careful attention to what he meant by suicide. Given his methodological views, Durkheim was anxious to define suicide as independent of the subjective orientations of the people who committed it. For him, suicide should be limited neither to cases where people intentionally bring about their own death, nor to cases where there is an immediate link between the actions of the victims and the fatal outcome of those actions. Take, for example, the various individuals in history who have committed treason because they wanted to save certain ideals.[91] Although they did not commit treason to die, and although their act of treason did not immediately result in their death as a straightforward suicide attempt could have done, the traitors knew that their actions would most likely lead to capital punishment. There is, therefore, no reason to classify this act as anything other than suicide. Hence, Durkheim's broad definition of suicide as 'all cases of death resulting directly or indirectly from a positive or negative act of the victim himself, which he knows will produce this result.'[92] In other words, individuals commit suicide if their actions knowingly trigger a chain of events that eventually lead to their death. There is certainly something to be said for this definition, although, ironically, it could be used to question the validity of the official statistics, on which Durkheim himself relied. These official figures almost invariably used a stricter definition of suicide, excluding, for example, the case of the traitor.

In the first part of his book, Durkheim discussed alternative theories of suicide, eliminating them one by one. Durkheim often proceeded in this way. For each theory, he would be a fierce advocate and show its plausibility, before attacking it. Durkheim analysed four theories that provided extra-social explanations for suicide. The first theory explained suicide in terms of psychopathic traits, ranging from insanity to alcoholism.[93] With the help of statistics, Durkheim indicated that this theory lacked empirical support. Take, for example, the view that suicide can be explained by excessive alcohol consumption. Comparing various countries, he found hardly any correlation between suicide rates and rates of alcohol consumption. A comparative analysis of various states in Germany found no relationship between the two variables either. These results were not as fatal for the 'alcoholism thesis' as Durkheim suggested, because it is perfectly possible for a country or a state to have a low rate of average alcohol consumption and a high rate of alcoholism. More telling was Durkheim's comparison between various regions in France, where he found little correlation between suicide rates and cases of insanity as a result of alcoholism.[94]

The second alternative theory explained suicide rates by referring to race and heredity factors. With regard to race, within Europe Durkheim distinguished the Germanic, the Celto-Roman, the Slav and the Ural-Altaic type. This categorization was not atypical at the time. Durkheim argued that, if race played a significant role, then we would expect groups of the same race to display similar suicide patterns. The empirical evidence did not show this to be the case at all. Each type was characterized by internal diversity, with the Germanic type particularly heterogeneous, ranging from very low suicide rates for the Flemish to very high rates among the Danes. Figures from Austria showed little difference in suicide rates between the regions where the Germans tend to live and regions where the Slavs are in a majority. Results for Switzerland drew a similar picture, with the average suicide rate of French regions only slightly higher than that of German regions.[95] With regard to heredity, Durkheim's argument was puzzling. However convincing, it drew on the mechanism of imitation, which he rejected later in the book. For Durkheim, the evidence that supported suicide as hereditary was weak, not least because the observation that suicides run in some families can be explained more convincingly by the contagious nature of this ultimate self-destructive act. This alternative explanation, he continued, was supported by the fact that members of the same family often use the same method to kill themselves.[96]

The third alternative theory refers to 'cosmic' (*sic*) factors: climate and temperature. Within this framework, one hypothesis stood out, because it was apparently confirmed by most observations. This hypothesis was very simple: the higher the temperature, the higher the suicide rates. Those who advocated this hypothesis had seemingly strong evidence on their side: suicide rates are highest in summer and lowest in winter. Suicide rates increase every month from January until June, and they decrease from July until December.[97] Durkheim showed, however, that this *prima facie* evidence pointed at something else: the correlation between suicide rates and the length of the day. This alternative view was confirmed by the fact that people tend to commit suicide during the day, and during busy periods of the week and during busy hours. Once social life becomes more intense, certain categories of people become increasingly vulnerable.[98]

The fourth theory saw suicide in terms of imitation. Durkheim pointed out that many cases that seemed to support this theory did not involve imitation. Imitation is a very specific mechanism whereby individuals automatically repeat what others have done. Close scrutiny of most cases cited in support of this theory showed that they are indicative of something else. They referred either to the process by which a common feeling develops among a group, or to the mechanism by which people act through 'respect or fear of opinion'. But neither can be called imitation. Durkheim thought his view was supported by empirical findings that showed significantly low suicide rates for districts surrounding Paris.[99] If imitation were a factor at play, we would expect higher rates for those districts, exposed as they are to the Parisian 'centre of radiation'. Figures for other countries provided a similar picture: the image of a radiating nucleus, spreading out to neighbouring regions, is false.[100] Whether this observation in itself is evidence of the implausibility of the imitation theory might not be as obvious as Durkheim suggested (newspapers can affect people in faraway regions). For Durkheim, however, it was clear that the concentration of suicides in certain geographical areas does not result from mechanisms of contagion. It is indicative of the sociological fact that people with a similar social environment share various features, including the propensity to commit suicide.[101]

After eliminating these theories, Durkheim proceeded to propose his own view, according to which suicide patterns needed to be explained by social variables. He classified types of suicide by the type of cause that produces them. The causes have to do with the levels of social integration and the amount of regulation. He arrived at four types depending on whether people were subjected to too much or too little social integration and regulation. Whereas 'egoistic suicide' is owing to a lack of social integration and 'anomic suicide' caused by too little social regulation, too much integration is responsible for 'altruistic suicide' and excessive regulation for 'fatalistic suicide'. The egoistic and anomic types are more widespread in contemporary than in traditional societies.

Egoistic suicide is caused by a lack of social integration. Protestants are far less integrated than Catholics, and this explains their consistently higher rates of suicide in various countries. It also explains why England, a Protestant country, has relatively low suicide rates: compared to other Protestant countries, it still has many shared obligatory beliefs and practices, and it has a lot of clergy, which is a sign of an intense religious community. The importance of social integration also explains the very low suicide rates among Jewish people, who are part of a very cohesive religion and have a great sense of internal solidarity. The figures for Jewish people are remarkable, given that the latter tend to live in cities and occupy intellectual occupations (both factors increase the probability of suicide).[102] Religion was, however, not the only evidence cited by Durkheim to support his view of egoistic suicide. He also referred to figures concerning the marital status and family situation. He noted that married people are more immune to suicide than unmarried people and that, compared to individuals living in smaller family units, those in larger families are less vulnerable. For Durkheim, these observations showed that it is untrue that suicides occur as a result of 'life's burdens'. On the contrary, the rates increase with decreasing family burdens. The weakening of social ties and 'common sentiments' increases the propensity for suicide, and vice versa.[103] This also explains why suicide rates increase during periods of social and political upheaval. When societies are faced with internal strife (revolutions, election crises) or external conflict (national wars), suicide rates almost invariably go down. Most of these events 'excite the passions' and make life more intense. In contrast, dynastic wars, which do not affect ordinary people, have little effect on suicide rates.[104]

Whereas egoistic suicide occurs because of 'excessive individuation', altruistic suicide occurs in societies with 'too rudimentary individuation'. The two are opposed to each other. 'One is detached from life because, seeing no goal to which he may attach himself, he feels himself useless and purposeless; the other because he has a goal but one outside his life, which henceforth seems merely an obstacle to him.'[105] Durkheim distinguished between various subtypes of altruistic suicide, although the distinctions are not always so clearcut as to warrant separate categories. The most obvious examples of altruistic suicide are cases where the act of self-destruction is a duty. In those instances, Durkheim talked about 'obligatory altruistic suicide'. In some traditional societies, for instance, individuals sometimes commit suicide when they no longer feel they have a place in society, either because their partner or master died or because they are ill and a burden on the family.[106] Not every altruistic suicide is obligatory, though. In some societies, individuals who have lost honour may gain prestige by giving up life. Durkheim gave the example of Polynesia, where the smallest offence may lead to suicide. Durkheim coined the term 'optional altruistic suicide' to refer to these cases, because the suicides are not strictly obligatory. A third type is 'acute altruistic suicide', typical for Asian societies steeped in Hinduism and Buddhism, where people considered suicide as a secure route towards salvation or happiness.[107] All three types of suicide are typical for 'lower' societies, but a fourth type, 'military suicide', can be found in contemporary societies. In most societies, soldiers have higher suicide rates than civilians. The explanation for this is that military organizations undermine individualism and promote obedience and submission. Military suicide is one of the rare cases of altruistic suicide in modern society.[108]

Like egoistic suicide, anomic suicide is very much indicative of contemporary society. Both result from a lack of societal presence for the individual. But whereas egoistic suicide refers to the absence of intense social relationships, anomic suicide is attributable to the failure of society to control or regulate the individual. Durkheim had already explored the nature and consequences of anomie in contemporary society in his *Division of Labour*. Anomie means literally 'normlessness', but lack of normative regulation would be more appropriate. The upshot of this state of 'anomie' is that people's expectations and desires might be out of sync with the means to accomplish them. People might want various things that are unachievable for them. This explains increasing suicide rates during economic crises, when people's means are suddenly reduced. It also explains increasing suicide rates during economic booms, because people's expectations and desires increase dramatically during these periods.[109] Anomie is not restricted to such economic anomie. The lack of normative regulation might also manifest itself in non-economic areas. This explains why the weakening of marital regulations is often accompanied by higher suicide rates.[110]

For Durkheim, this analysis showed the overwhelming impact of the social environment on people's choices and actions, and it confirmed his view that social facts are to be explained and predicted by other social facts. This analysis was meant to explain 'social suicide patterns' – not individual suicides. Each individual case would have its own story. In-depth studies might teach us that one individual committed suicide because of the loss of a fortune, another because of an unhappy marriage, and yet another because of shame or guilt. A sociological analysis does not rule out the contribution of such negative experiences to people's decisions to commit suicide, but it insists that some social environments make individuals more vulnerable so that these experiences are more likely to tip them over the edge. Other environments are more benign, so that individuals, faced with severe problems, will be better equipped to deal with them.[111]

Evaluation

Those who wish to combine a normative project with an empirical agenda may find in Durkheim a powerful ally. For a long time philosophers have speculated about the good life or the just society, but these conjectures were devoid of empirical grounding. It is possible to think of sociology and the social sciences as irrelevant to debates of this kind by arguing that they deal with empirical material – with what is, not with what would be, good for us. In Durkheim we find a different view of sociology. For him, sociology, at least in its mature form, would not only prove helpful in tackling these philosophical issues, it would be paramount for answering these questions and vastly superior to the philosophical pathway. He hoped to base the central values and direction of society on a social scientific footing, and he believed that it would be possible to do this primarily with the help of a functional analysis.[112] But this is where the problem comes in. It is not obvious how we can establish the difference between what is functional and what is not, between the normal and the pathological, health and sickness. For Durkheim the distinction is unproblematic: something is functional if it is beneficial to the needs of the system. It is not clear, however, why systemic needs would count as an objective criterion, as opposed to, say, the needs of the individual. Durkheim's judgement regarding which 'needs' count among the societal needs seems equally arbitrary. For instance, Durkheim chose solidarity,[113] but it seems as plausible to argue that all societies need a certain amount of dissensus or conflict. Even leaving this aside, it is impossibly difficult to judge whether a specific set of practices or institutions would contribute to a particular societal need, and indeed we can use Durkheim's methodology and arrive at very different conclusions. For example, we could, with the same plausibility and forcefulness as Durkheim, argue that religion is still functional today. It is telling that Durkheim ended up using his functionalist logic to defend his own ideological and political convictions, such as his commitment to secular values in education, to social democracy in politics and to a non-utilitarian form of individualism in culture.[114] Virtually any institution or set of practices can be reconstructed as having functional consequences, and it is therefore not surprising that Durkheim concluded that the policies that follow from his own convictions were also the ones that were found to be functional for contemporary society.

Durkheim presented his methodology as one that is devoid of ideology or prejudice, and based on solid facts only. However, a closer look shows an inherent bias, which, for lack of a better word, I call conservative. There have already been a lot of accusations against Durkheim for his conservatism, not all them clear. Whether the label is appropriate for Durkheim depends on what is meant by conservatism and which aspects of his work we are talking about. It is important to make a distinction between the content of his sociopolitical views and the methodology he employed to arrive at or defend these views. The latter are particularly important in the context of this discussion. Durkheim's distinction between health and morbidity implies a conservative view, not in the sense that he was arguing that things ought to remain as they are or that the past used to be better than the present, but in that it is important that society is an organic, well-oiled, cohesive whole and that various other factors (that might be about justice or equality) should be subordinated to this. Therefore, it is intrinsic to his methodology that he conceived of change only within the contours of other things present, and that he did not suggest anything too radical or divisive. This distinctive form of conservatism is mirrored in his political and ethical writings, in which he advocated that we develop a new ethical system, but one in line with the requirements of a differentiated society and therefore based on interdependency and sound individualism.[115] His preoccupation with cohesion and solidarity made him prone to politically dubious conclusions, such as when he suggested that we should learn from and partly copy the practices of medieval corporatism.[116] The most important point here is that Durkheim's own work demonstrates that, even with the best intentions, a sociology that is free of ideology and prejudice seems to be an impossible enterprise. It seems more fruitful to acknowledge that these factors come into play, to be aware about how they are constitutive of our accounts and to be willing to reassess them in the light of new experiences.

Durkheim's ambition was to eradicate metaphysics from the study of society so that it can finally become a proper science, on a par with, say, physics or chemistry. Sociology ought to rest on hard facts, on empirical evidence – not on some speculative storyline. That is why ultimately he found Comte's project disappointing: while Comte heralded the age of positivism, he had failed to put the empirical method into practice. Durkheim felt that Comte remained entrenched in the very same metaphysical era which the latter had so repeatedly rejected.[117] In the same way, Durkheim was particularly critical of those explanations that refer to human nature. Ironically, a similar argument applies to Durkheim. Durkheim himself could not help relying on various untested presuppositions about the essence of what it is to be a human being or about the nature of society. They ranged from the statement that people need societal regulations to the assertion that society is an organic whole.[118] Relying on untested assumptions, as Durkheim did, is not a problem in itself; it is not possible to eradicate metaphysics completely anyway. What is problematic is his failure to acknowledge the non-empirical dimension of some of his claims, his intolerance towards the use of theoretical assertions by others, and especially the assumption that it is possible to eradicate metaphysics altogether. It is difficult to see how any substantial endeavour to explain the social would be possible without the reliance on at least some assumptions that are not immediately accessible to observation and that can be categorized as metaphysical. This phenomenon is not limited simply to the social sciences. Durkheim's belief that the natural sciences are devoid of metaphysical considerations is deeply problematic, especially in the light of more recent developments in physics and chemistry.

Durkheim insisted that a mature science studies facts that are objectively gathered. This, he assumed, is already the case in physics, and the identification of social facts ought to be established on similar solid grounds. Large sections of *Rules of Sociological Method* are devoted to this task. Here again, Durkheim hoped to remove any hint of subjectivism and eradicate the suggestion that the facts are just a matter of perspective.[119] If successful, his method implies that, however different people's background, they would agree with the criteria for identifying the facts, with what the facts really mean, and with where precisely the boundaries between the different categories ought to be drawn. Durkheim wanted to achieve what is now known in philosophy as the 'view from nowhere',[120] and he hoped to do so by establishing criteria that are independent of people's biography, interests and values. It is worth mentioning that, although Durkheim was acquainted with pragmatism, he did not properly engage with those aspects of pragmatism that question the pursuit of the 'view from nowhere'. He quickly denounced those features of pragmatism as leading the way towards subjectivism. The problem for Durkheim, however, is that no such neutral algorithm is available. People attribute meanings to their surroundings and are therefore likely to have different notions of what religion, language or education mean. There is not one concept of crime, nor one of class. Even suicide means different things to different people. It is difficult to see how these divergences in opinion can be settled in an objective fashion, how it would be possible for Durkheim, or anyone, to step outside history and resolve these discrepancies once and for all. Durkheim's identification and categorization of suicides is just one among many, probably an incisive and useful perspective, but certainly not the final one. As social researchers, we can debate which notion of suicide is more appropriate, but there is no set of rules prior to the conversation that would settle the controversy.

I have already indicated that Durkheim's methodology reflects a broader view, according to which it is possible and desirable for researchers to adopt a neutral algorithm, an objective standpoint, independent of their interests and presuppositions. In the face of recent philosophical developments, the view that it is possible to obtain such a neutral vantage point seems untenable, and, indeed, as will become clear later on, my own pragmatist alternative asserts that this position is implausible. I will discuss some of these philosophical changes in chapters 5 and 6, but it is worth mentioning at this stage that, during Durkheim's lifetime, various authors had already expressed serious reservations about the feasibility of objectivist accounts of social science such as the one suggested by Durkheim. This is certainly the case for Max Weber, one of the most insightful writers about methodology of the social sciences of his generation. This is not to say that Weber addressed Durkheim directly. He actually shunned mentioning him altogether, but he dealt with similar methodological problems. His position was more sophisticated than Durkheim's, albeit also less clear at times. Most importantly, however, Weber did not subscribe to the Durkheimian 'view from nowhere'; he underscored that presuppositions are *sine qua non* for any research, and he regarded interpretative understanding as central to historical and social explanation. He was aware of some of the limitations of the kind of naturalism that Durkheim was proposing. He anticipated some philosophical developments long before they became mainstream, and his view is much closer to what I will be proposing. His writings in the philosophy of the social sciences will be explored in the next chapter.

Further reading

Durkheim sums up his views on the philosophy of social science and methodology in *Rules of Sociological Method*. The 1982 English edition includes some other writings on methodology by Durkheim, plus a sharp introduction by Steven Lukes, in which he confronts Durkheim's perspective with recent developments in philosophy. Among the other articles by Durkheim in this volume are 'Marxism and Sociology: The Materialist Conception of History' and 'Sociology and the Social Sciences'. The former consists of a critical assessment of historical materialism, and the latter elaborates on the relationship between sociology and aligned social sciences such as history. Durkheim's methodological outlook is also clearly stated in his *Montesquieu and Rousseau: Forerunners of Sociology*, although it is not as detailed as in the *Rules*. Although Durkheim's *Pragmatism and Sociology* (posthumously published and based on student notes) does not deal with the philosophy of the social sciences, he used the comparison with American pragmatism to elaborate on his overall position with regard to a number of philosophical notions, such as method, truth and knowledge. Of all introductions to Durkheim (and there are many), Lukes's *Emile Durkheim, his Life and Work* is one of the best in terms of both analytical clarity and comprehension. With exceptions such as Hirst's *Durkheim, Bernard and Epistemology*, most interesting work on Durkheim's methodology appeared in French, of which little has been translated. François Chazel's *Durkheim: les règles de la méthode sociologique* is a lucid and critical account of Durkheim's methodological position. Around the one hundredth anniversary of the publication of Durkheim's *Rules of Sociological Method*, various books and articles were published, among which Jean-Michel Berthelot's *1895 Durkheim: l'avènement de la sociologie scientifique* stands out as a highly useful introduction. Cuin's edited volume, *Durkheim d'un siècle à l'autre*, contains various innovative readings of Durkheim's methodology. For those who are interested in locating Durkheim within the wider methodological debates of the late nineteenth century, I suggest two outstanding works: Turner's *The Search for a Methodology of Social Science* and Alexander's second volume of his *Theoretical Logic in Sociology*. Please note, for the sake of simplicity, that I did not discuss Durkheim's later structuralist and anthropological turn in *Primitive Classification* (*De quelques formes primitives de classification*) and *The Elementary Forms of Religious Life* (*Les Formes élémentaires de la vie religieuse*). There is a debate as to whether these works constitute a significant departure from his earlier methodological position. For a further exploration of positivist sociology, see Halfpenny's *Positivism and Sociology* and the first volume of Alexander's *Theoretical Logic in Sociology*.

2
Max Weber's Interpretative Method

Introduction

In 1918, Max Weber was asked to give a keynote speech at the University of Munich. The talk was about the current status of science; the title was 'Science as a Vocation' (*Wissenschaft als Beruf*). He talked about various issues, in particular the difference between German and American universities. But at some point he drew attention to the extent to which scientific activities had become increasingly specialized and compartmentalized.[1] Contemporary academics should be pleased to master only a fraction of the fields that their predecessors used to cover. This is not to say that researchers knew less than previously. There was simply more known in each field, and therefore more to be known in order to carry out research properly. Weber did not deplore this trend, nor did he applaud it. He simply recorded how things had changed and what they had become, and suggested to prospective academics that they bear all this in mind. 'A really definitive and good accomplishment is today always a specialised accomplishment. And whoever lacks the capacity to put on blinders, so to speak, and to come up to the idea that the fate of his soul depends upon whether or not he makes the correct conjecture at this passage of this manuscript may as well stay away from science.'[2] It is ironic that Weber, of all people, should point to this functional specialization of science and to the need for scholars to adapt, for he is remembered as a Renaissance figure whose encyclopedic knowledge entailed detailed acquaintance with such disparate subjects as theology, history and political economy. It is ironic because his interest in focused questions tended to be informed by empirical knowledge of related, but different, issues. His historical research was subordinated to broader existential and philosophical concerns. He was anything but a specialist.

Weber's point about specialization is an enticing one. It was not that specialization is preferable as such, but that, given the exponential growth of academic research, any contribution can now only be significant in *so far as* it relies on an in-depth scrutiny of the topic concerned. With the accumulation of knowledge, it has become even more untenable to make sweeping generalizations, and researchers now have to comply with scientific principles even more rigidly. So, for Weber, functional specialization and the institutionalization of scientific axioms are two sides of the same coin. It is therefore not surprising that throughout his life Weber was anxious to delineate scientific practice from other activities. He deplored the way in which contemporary academics, such as H. Treitschke, misused their position and treated it as an effective platform for political action, and he despaired at the way in which some of them misrepresented reality or selectively appropriated material simply to fit in with and confirm their beliefs. Above all, he was outraged by the cult of personality, which he perceived to have permeated German academia at the time. Too many wanted to be visionaries or prophets and scorned the meticulous work of the specialized scholar. They failed to recognize that there is a lot of dignity in the 'inner devotion' to this task.[3]

Weber personally did not lack breadth, vision or political commitment, nor was his work devoid of a distinctive *Weltanschauung*. He made, however, a concerted effort, in his own empirical research, to comply with rational scientific principles and to study the social in painstaking detail. While his sociopolitical views directed *what* he researched, he made sure that these views did not interfere with *how* the investigation took place. In this context, it is understandable that the methodology of the social sciences was at the centre of Weber's intellectual preoccupations. For him, rigorous methods were intrinsic to the vocation of modern researchers, who, more than ever before, had become experts in a specific field. Weber wrote extensively about the methods and philosophy of the social sciences. Unlike Durkheim he never produced a single monograph that summarized his position, but he wrote several long articles. These articles tend to start off with a discussion of one or two authors or a book but inevitably end up with a broader argument. Together these pieces present a remarkably coherent picture about what can and cannot be expected from social research, how it ought to be conducted, and what should not be done (at least, not under the banner of science).

Underlying these articles is an ongoing attempt to show the dangers of Marxist history, and this might explain why Weber's methodology has often been portrayed in contrast with Marx's. This is partly correct. His overt criticisms seemed to target a particular kind of Marxism – certainly not Marx. Weber was especially hostile to scholars who subscribed uncritically to the 'materialist conception of history' as a methodological device for explaining social phenomena. He did not, as is sometimes suggested, substitute a cultural determinist view for historical materialism, but he did point out the inadequacy of a Marxist framework whenever empirical events seem to contradict it. For example, in his 1895 inaugural lecture in Freiburg (*Der Nationalstaat und die Volkswirtschaftspolitik*) he gave empirical instances in which national and ethnic determinants overshadow economic ones. Prefiguring Popper's critical rationalism, Weber objected to the work of contemporary Marxists because they employed various illegitimate forms of ad hoc reasoning to protect their materialist view. When confronted with a historical event that seems to elude an explanation in economic terms, they either regarded the event as a scientifically unimportant 'accident', or they broadened the meaning of the term 'economic' so that it comprised the event. Historical materialists overlook the fact that these 'accidents' are also subjected to laws – non-economic laws but laws nevertheless – and that it would be equally convincing to treat the economic conditions as historically accidental.[4] Also, whereas historical materialists present history in terms of irreversible laws, as if corroborated by historical evidence, Weber insisted that Marx's 'stages' of historical development do not mirror reality; they are ideal types, which capture the essential features of a particular mode of production. Theoretical constructs should not be conflated with empirical descriptions.[5] On a related point, Weber felt uneasy about the way in which the political views and values of some Marxists tend to interfere with how they record and interpret social and political phenomena. As will be explained later, Weber was the first to acknowledge that the facts do not 'speak for themselves', and that, on the contrary, social researchers necessarily select according to what is significant to them. So Weber was, by no stretch of the imagination, a naïve 'objectivist' if by the latter is meant somebody who holds that values have no role to play in sociological investigations. But he did object to the way in which some commentators would forego the scientific principles of critical scrutiny and empirical demonstration so as to fit historical events with their political outlooks. It is the duty of the researcher to honour these principles. Several Marxists have failed to do so.

These objections to Marxism all come down to the fact that, generally speaking, it does not proceed scientifically, that it operates ideologically. But Weber also has another objection, quite different from the previous ones. He distrusted Marxism because, like Popper, he associated it with holistic forms of explanation, which account for social phenomena by situating them within, and subordinating them to, a larger system. While Weber's reconstruction of Marxist methodology is diametrically opposed to the analytical Marxism of Jon Elster, his own methodological position is remarkably close to that of Elster and other contemporary rational choice or rational action theorists. Weber, too, subscribed to methodological individualism, which conceives of social analysis as a complex interplay between purposive action and unintended effects, and his discomfort with Marxism was, indeed, partly based on what he considered to be its systematic disregard for individuals' abilities to reflect upon, transform and act upon their surroundings. Like the more sophisticated rational choice or action theorists, Weber not only ascribed a prominent role to models that assumed rational behaviour, but realized that people often operate differently. Like them, Weber was convinced that, even in those circumstances, the models would still be informative. Marxism was not Weber's only target in his crusade against holistic approaches. He regularly criticized the 'organic' school of sociology of Schäffe, and saw great dangers of reification in the functional explanations presented. He thought that functionalist frameworks ought to be seen as heuristic devices, as a 'practical illustration' and 'provisional orientation'. But if they are seen as anything more or as the end point of sociological analysis, then they risk attributing agency to systems. Systems do not exercise agency; individuals do.[6]

Weber's *Gesammelte Aufsätze zur Wissenschaftslehre* is a complete collection of his articles on methodological issues. It was published a couple of years after his death. I personally think that five works are important. To adhere to a chronological order, there were, first of all, three articles published ('Roscher und Knies und die logischen Probleme der historischen National-ökonomie') in *Schmoller's Jahrbuch für Gesetzgebung, Verwaltung und Volkswirtschaft* in 1903, 1905 and 1906. In 1902 he had been asked to contribute to a *Festschrift* for Knies, who was his predecessor at Heidelberg. He agreed to write a piece on Roscher, Knies and the methodology of 'historical economics' (hence the title) but did not manage to complete the project in time for the book and, instead, published his material in the journal. The translation (of all three articles) into English is available in book format as *Roscher and Knies: The Logical Problems of Historical Economics.*[7] Secondly, there is 'Die Objektivität sozialwissenschaftlicher und sozialpolitischer Erkennt-nis', which appeared in the *Archiv für Sozialwissenschaft und Sozialpolitik*. The article is an editorial for the journal, in which Weber, as a co-editor, tried to set out the latter's methodological orientation. This explains the distinctly normative tone of the article. Its translation, 'Objectivity in Social Science and Social Policy', can be found in Weber's *The Methodology of the Social Sciences.*[8] There followed, thirdly, 'Kritische Studien auf dem Gebiet der kulturwissenschaftlichen Logik', which came out in the *Archiv* in 1905. This article starts with a long critical commentary on the methodology of Eduard Meyer, which, as in the case of the Roscher and Knies articles, eventually leads to the elaboration of Weber's own ideas. The English version, entitled 'Critical Studies in the Logic of the Cultural Sciences', appears as chapter 2 in *The Methodology of the Social Sciences.*[9] Fourthly, Weber wrote 'Über einige Kategorien der verstehenden Soziologie', published in *Logos* in 1913, which sets out the basic concepts of his proposal for an interpretative sociology. It formed the basis for chapter 1 of the posthumous *Wirtschaft und Gesellschaft.* This chapter is available as 'The Fundamental Concepts in Sociology' in *The Theory of Social and Economic Organization.*[10] Fifthly, in 1917 he published 'Der Sinn der "Wertfreiheit" der soziologischen und ökono-mischen Wissenschaften' in *Logos.* Here Weber expressed his anger towards those German professors who thought that their political views could be inferred from detailed empirical research, and who also used their academic position to spread their political views. In English, it appears as 'The Meaning of "Ethical Neutrality" in Sociology and Economics' in *The Methodology of the Social* Sciences.[11]

Transcending the *Methodenstreit*

Some of Weber's most perspicacious observations on methodological issues are found in his commentaries on the *Methodenstreit* in his editorial for the *Archiv für Sozialwissenschaft und Sozialpolitik*. The term *Methodenstreit* refers to the academic debate about methodology of the social sciences held in Germany in the second half of the nineteenth century. Traditionally the debate is represented or remembered as involving two opposing camps. Some scholars deemed that, if properly conceived, history and the other social sciences should emulate the methodological strategy of the natural sciences, whereas others held that, partly because of their subject matter, the *Geisteswissenschaften* ought to adopt a different methodology from the one employed in the natural sciences. Analytically speaking, however, two separate issues can be distinguished in this debate. First, there was a dispute about the 'value-neutrality' of those disciplines studying social and historical phenomena. The question was whether, given the nature of the social world, it is possible to hold on to the distinction between what is (that is, the set of objectively valid findings) and what ought to be (the set of value-judgements). Second, there was a controversy about the applicability of 'nomological' knowledge to the social realm. The problem here was whether social and historical phenomena are subject to laws that are, in form, comparable to laws in physics.

The topic of value-neutrality in itself incorporates two separate questions. There was firstly the controversy surrounding the 'objectivity' of the social sciences, which centred round the question whether or not value-judgements necessarily interfere with the empirical study of the social world. Several adherents of the hermeneutic tradition deemed this to be the case, and inferred from this that the social sciences could never obtain the same level of objectivity as the natural sciences; others disagreed and regarded the social sciences as a perfectly objective enterprise. There was secondly the debate regarding the 'practical efficacy' of the social sciences. Its central problem was whether or not it is possible to glean judgements about ultimate values from empirical investigations into the social world. Some believed (explicitly or otherwise) that the task of social research was to inform people about the good life or about the ideal society; others thought this was impossible.

Weber took a middle ground position on the issue of objectivity, and he did so by distinguishing between the research question and the research process itself. He agreed with some hermeneutic authors that the values and norms held by the researchers affect their choice of topic or what is being put into focus. There is no 'objective' analysis of culture in the sense of an analysis independent of any viewpoint that may select or organize the phenomena. Underlying this position is the proposition that the social sciences face 'absolute infinitude', even when one single object (for example, a particular act of exchange) is being studied. 'Life with its irrational reality and its store of possible meanings is inexhaustible.'[12] Weber insisted that only a small part of the infinite world could be described as 'culture' to the people and the researcher involved, by which he meant that only this small section has relevance to their central values. Facing this infinite world, those who study the social are bound selectively to appropriate and represent the material dependent on their value-orientation to it, and only this small section will be explored. This selective process is also at work when researchers explore the causes of an individual phenomenon; an exhaustive causal investigation would be equally unfeasible and nonsensical.[13] In Weber's parlance, the researcher 'cannot discover . . . what is meaningful . . . by means of a "presupposition-less" investigation of empirical data',[14] and the study of socio-cultural phenomena 'involves "subjective" presuppositions insofar as it concerns itself only with those components of reality which have some relationship, however indirect, to events to which we attach cultural significance.'[15] Given that it is the theoretical interest (*Erkenntnisinteresse*) of the socio-cultural sciences to account for the social in relation to a limited, arbitrary set of values, none of the sociological accounts can ever be complete. They always remain partial accounts. While they are relevant to the concerns of some people, they continue to be incomplete.[16]

Weber also used a similar argument to assail the widespread conviction that social science will become 'objective' if it manages to uncover laws, the gist of his argument being that knowledge about a specific social reality is different from knowledge about its laws. The latter might be a means for obtaining the former, but knowledge of social phenomena is intertwined with the significance which events acquire in concrete situations, and no law can reveal how and in which situations such events acquire that significance. Searching for socio-cultural laws, similar to natural-scientific laws, would result in the creation of ridiculously abstract formulae, devoid of any empirical content.[17] Weber's views on the intricate relationship between presuppositions and historical research help to explain the importance he attached to ideal types. It is precisely because proving 'concrete relationships' is a meaningless endeavour that analytical constructs are needed to help select and categorize phenomena in the light of their cultural significance.[18] It could, of course, be retorted that one of the tasks of the historian is to ascertain the 'real' and 'true' meaning of the concepts introduced, but Weber's point is that this is impossible. Different researchers may define the same ideal type differently, and so will end up centring on different issues depending on their cognitive interest. While no ideal typological construct can ever grasp the 'infinite richness' of life, every ideal type makes for a welcome reduction of complexity, and this bringing 'order into the chaos' is a *sine qua non* for understanding.[19]

From the proposition that presuppositions guide research in the way spelled out above, some hermeneutic philosophers were eager to infer that, as far as the study of the social is concerned, the research process in itself is necessarily 'subjective'. Here Weber distanced himself from what he regarded as an unnecessarily defeatist attitude. The truth-value of an 'empirical fact' remains different from the validity of a 'practical evaluation'. While an empirical fact refers to an observation about social phenomena (which often covers the value-orientated actions of people), a practical evaluation is a verdict about whether or not these recorded phenomena are satisfactory or beneficial.[20] It is of course true that the accounting for social phenomena is often eased by the making sense of the individuals' evaluations (and, indeed, the latter is frequently a *sine qua non* for the former), but it does not follow that the researcher identifies with or approves those evaluations.[21] Weber insisted that, while conducting their research, gathering data and reporting, researchers will be tied to general normative regulations and procedures that are not only applicable and meaningful in their own context, but valid to everybody seeking truth.[22] For Weber, all empirical knowledge is, thus, 'objectively valid': although the 'subjective' ordering of reality is a precondition for empirical knowledge, the latter is directed towards and only makes sense to those cultures or individuals for whom scientific truth is a significant value.[23] Weber's commitment to the objectivity of science permeates various other aspects of his work; for instance his attempt to distinguish his own use of the ideal type, that is in its 'logical sense', from the ideal type in the 'practical sense'. Whereas Weber's notion of ideal type is a logical device to assist empirical research, the ideal type in the practical sense refers to a 'model type' that comprises features of a phenomenon that, from the viewpoint of the researcher, are perpetually worthy. Whereas the former is a *sine qua non* for comparative and historical research, the latter is introduced to make value-judgements of reality. Weber suggested that any scientific endeavour should seek the assistance of the ideal type in the logical sense, while avoiding the temptation of the ideal type in the practical sense. Moreover, it should ensure that the distinction between the two, so easily blurred, remains intact.[24] In the same vein, Weber repeatedly lashed out at those who regarded history as outside the realm of empirical science. A number of hermeneutic authors emphasized that historical insights relied on the genius of intuition – the ability to empathize with others – and that claims about causality are notoriously unreliable. For Weber these hermeneutic dogmas conflate the psychological mechanisms that accompany historical conjectures, on the one hand, with the logical structure of historical knowledge, on the other. Just as in the natural sciences, historians may rely on flashes of insight or imagination to develop hypotheses, but they still use logically valid procedures to validate the hypotheses.[25] Although historical research relies on counterfactuals (the imagining of what would have occurred if something had been different), this does not imply that it is subjective, arbitrary or whimsical.[26] Finally, the same insistence on scientific objectivity is consistent with those passages, in Weber's guidelines on history teaching, in which he asserted that lecturers ought to make a concerted effort to clarify to their audience which of their statements are 'statements of empirically observed facts' and which are 'practical evaluations'. It is unnecessary (and, furthermore, undesirable) to ask teachers to be dispassionate, but it is certainly their duty to make clear to their pupils when precisely fact turns to value.[27]

As for the practical efficacy of social research, Weber believed that 'existential knowledge' (that is, knowledge about what 'is') could never instruct people about 'normative knowledge' (that is, knowledge about what 'should be'). The fallacious belief that it is possible to infer normative from existential knowledge has often been predicated on the equally erroneous conviction that the study of the social consists of disclosing invariant laws or trends that indicate both the ideal and the inevitable.[28] For Weber, in so far as there are trends in history, they can never be irreversible cast-iron laws that transcend human agency, nor can they ever give a clear indication about that which is preferable or desirable. Weber was even more incensed by those historians who conflated what is and what ought to be by reconstructing and articulating historical development in terms of the nebulous term 'progress'. It is indeed nonsensical to claim that there is progress in the realm of 'ultimate evaluations'; the term only made sense in relation to an unambiguous end. There can, therefore, only be progress in a technical sense.[29] Weber fully acknowledged that existential knowledge entails 'technical criticism' – that is, information about which means are more likely to achieve given ends, the possible unintended consequences of various paths, and the incompatibility of some pursuits.[30] But Weber insisted that existential knowledge could not dictate those normative regulations or value-judgements from which guidelines about 'practical activity' can be inferred. Judgements about values are, after all, a matter of faith and can never be decided on the basis of empirical science, and, in the same way, any application of 'technical criticism' is, ultimately, the responsibility of the acting, willing individual.[31] In short, while 'evaluative ideas' help people to select from the infinitude of life and study empirically what is significant to them, no such study can ever be sufficient to justify or concur with these evaluative ideas.[32] Social science cannot even help alleviate the burden of responsibility when faced with elementary questions such as, for instance, whether various undesirable effects ought to be taken into account, or whether the ends justify the means, or which criteria to use to judge between incompatible aims. 'There is no (rational or empirical) scientific procedure of any kind whatsoever which can provide us with a decision here. The social sciences, which are strictly empirical sciences, are the least fitted to presume to save the individual the difficulty of making a choice, and they should therefore not create the impression that they can do so.'[33]

Weber also took a middle position on the issue of nomological knowledge (that is, knowledge about laws or law-like generalizations). He disagreed with members of the Historical School, in particular with their recommendation that the task of historians is to accumulate knowledge about empirical regularities so as, eventually, to develop an all-embracing deductive science.[34] Instead, Weber argued for a different methodology between the cultural and natural sciences. He could, as some anti-naturalists have done, have based his argument against the unified nature of scientific inquiry on ontological grounds, on the grounds that the intrinsic features of the social and the natural necessitate a different methodology. But he did not, and, as a matter fact, he repudiated any attempt to do so. His appeal for a difference in method was, instead, based on 'axiological' grounds: it was founded on the distinctiveness of people's theoretical *interest* in meaningful action, an interest that requires *Verstehen* or *Deutung*. Weber concurred with hermeneutics that the selection and organization of social reality from the angle of its cultural significance is distinct from and has no necessary logical connection to the study of social phenomena in terms of laws and general concepts. For example, researchers might be interested in money-exchange because it is so widespread in modern society. However imperative, studying the general features of exchange remains a preparatory endeavour because, in itself, it does not answer the question how exchange, in particular money-exchange, has become so important in modernity. The example is meant to show that, in so far as research is conducted from the point of view of its cultural significance, its objective will not be accomplished by exposing regularities or general concepts. Knowledge about causal laws might, of course, be a stepping stone towards establishing causes of individual phenomena, but it can never be sufficient in itself. Moreover, the more general or abstract laws are, the less valuable they are because the more they will be devoid of content and, therefore, the more removed they will be from the richness of reality.[35] By defending his anti-naturalist position on axiological grounds, Weber foreshadowed the pragmatist view that methodological questions can only be addressed if there is clarity on what the research in question wants to achieve. Unlike pragmatism, however, Weber did not further elaborate on the role of cognitive interests.

This is not to say that Weber concurred with the view that the study of the social depends on an unfathomable ability for intuition. It has already been mentioned that he was sceptical of this perspective, almost scathing. It fails 'to provide a verifiable standard for distinguishing the *causally* "essential" from the *causally* "inessential". A foreign city can produce in us a "feeling of totality" which is absolutely arbitrary – i.e. irrelevant to those elements which are essential to a *causal* explanation of the "life-style" of its inhabitants.'[36]

The insistence on empathetic understanding is incompatible with the requirements of demonstration and verification, which are so central to the logic of historical inquiry.[37] It would also be misleading to attribute to Weber the position that statistical regularities are altogether irrelevant to sociological analysis. He thought there was a place for them, but he insisted that both 'adequacy of meaning' and 'adequacy of causality' needed to be fulfilled. Observed regularities are only significant in so far as it is possible to make sense of them in terms of 'subjectively understandable action'. Conversely, any reconstruction in terms of understandable subjective meaning only holds in so far as it has been corroborated by empirical observations.[38] It would be equally erroneous to infer from Weber's critique of positivism that knowledge of the social realm is necessarily acausal. He very much rejected this position held by some of his contemporaries. Knowledge about social phenomena provides equally powerful insight into causal mechanisms as does knowledge of the natural sciences, and the introduction of synthetic concepts is likely to facilitate the disclosure of these causal networks.[39] Likewise, Weber's definition of sociology is testimony to his conviction that its subject matter is not an impediment for causal accounts. For Weber, sociology is a science that employs 'interpretative understanding' of social action precisely in order to establish a 'causal explanation' of its itinerary and effects.[40]

Ideal types and different types of action

The issue of general concepts brings the role of theory to the forefront. While Weber remained throughout his life deeply sceptical of the use of highly abstract propositions for the empirical study of social life, he realized the relevance of the employment of theoretical devices in historical research and discussed them at great length. He wrote about the 'ideal type' as a mental construct (*Gedankenbild*) that indicates the essential features of a phenomenon.[41] The term came from Jellinek, though Weber's use of the concept is probably indebted to Simmel's *Philosophy of Money*. Ideal types have regularly been employed in the natural sciences as, for instance, in the ideal type of a particular species or the notion of ideal gas within the kinetic theory of gases.[42] 'Ideal' should not be understood in the normative sense of the word but in its 'strictest logical sense'. As the ideal type attempts to articulate the kernel of a notion it should be conflated neither with its average manifestation in the empirical realm nor with its most common appearance.[43] For example, Weber's ideal type of bureaucracy was not meant to refer to an average of present or past bureaucratic institutions; nor was it intended to capture its most prevalent form. Instead, Weber set out to capture the essential characteristics of a bureaucracy, that which differentiates it from other types of organization. He was at pains to point out that, although ideal types can never be found in reality, they are nevertheless remarkably useful devices for historians and sociologists because they provide an indispensable service to both comparative and historical endeavours.[44] For example, did sixteenth-century Calvinists exhibit or presage the capitalist ethos more than their contemporaries? Or, has Western society become increasingly rationalized, and, if so, in which areas and how? Those pertinent questions are put with the help of ideal-typical constructions: the ideal types of Calvinism, the capitalist worldview, and instrumental rationality.

It could, of course, be counter-argued that Weber was preaching to the converted, and, moreover, that those converted had (and have) no choice but to do what they have always done. As Weber himself recognized, any historical research aiming to delve beyond the obvious observational level has to lean on *Gedankenbilder*, and indeed most research does so, as can be inferred from the regular employment of mental constructs such as 'individualism', 'imperialism' or 'feudalism'.[45] In this light the prescription that historians ought to employ ideal types seems very feeble indeed. However, Weber's point was more subtle. His point was not simply that historians ought to utilize theoretical concepts (which indeed, in isolation, would not have been a particularly illuminating proposition), but that they should be aware of doing so in order to avoid misusing these concepts.[46] Weber's recommendation for a self-conscious use of ideal types seemed to mean two things. Firstly, he advised historians to make a concerted effort to define clearly the ideal types that they use. He warned against those historians who take the meaning of these abstract notions to be unproblematic, an understandable assumption given that these concepts are commonly used (even outside academic discourse), but a false one nevertheless and one which leads to various misunderstandings. In order to obtain research with a high degree of adequacy of meaning, theoretical terms ought to be designed consciously and defined properly.[47] If not, there is likely to remain confusion as to the precise definition of theoretical terms, and a lack of clarity concerning the differences, if any, with the meanings attached to them by laypersons, other researchers and, most importantly, the people under investigation.[48] The need to define theoretical concepts properly is probably exacerbated by the fact that, with society perpetually changing, the meanings of theoretical constructs continually alter too.[49] Secondly, Weber recommended that historians should be fully aware of the difference between ideal types and empirical phenomena, and do not conflate the two while analysing and reporting. It is not surprising that Weber was adamant that, too frequently, theoretical constructs are mistaken for observable phenomena, rather than seen as means for ordering observation. He wrote against the backdrop of nineteenth-century social thought in which, according to him, it was not uncommon to confuse an ideal constructed of a developmental sequence with an empirical series. He repeatedly criticized Marxists for conveniently overlooking the fact that Marx's 'laws' or 'developmental constructs' are actually ideal types.[50]

Another counter-argument (and one refuted by Weber himself) maintains that the recurrent use of ideal types in historical research is symptomatic of the immaturity of the discipline. While this critique acknowledges that most historians and social scientists employ abstract constructs on a regular basis, it asserts that they would not feel the need to do so if their specialization was more advanced, if it resembled more, say, chemistry or physics. Weber agreed with this counter-claim, but only partly. Firstly, he conceded that a number of advanced areas of study, such as philology, indeed *prima facie* shun the employment of ideal-typical concepts. He maintained, however, that closer scrutiny demonstrates that these disciplines remain, if only implicitly, reliant on theoretical constructions. Incidentally, this assertion suggests that Runciman is not entirely correct when he attributes to Weber the view that ideal types are unique to the social sciences.[51] Rather, Weber would have agreed with those passages in Runciman that vehemently denied this view. Secondly, while Weber did not object to the rank ordering of disciplines according to degrees of maturity, he disagreed with those who urge historians to make a concerted effort to join the ranks of the mature sciences. Weber disagreed because he regarded history as one of the sciences 'to which an eternal youth is granted'. For him, history is unable to progress to a more advanced state because of the nature of its subject matter, which is 'perpetually in flux, ever subject to change'.[52] In contrast to, say, physical or chemical phenomena, the constant flux of historical processes always brings about new problems. 'The light which emanates from those highest evaluative ideas always falls on an ever changing finite segment of the vast chaotic stream of events, which flows away through time.'[53] While the constant supply of novel issues implies that any ideal type, however significant at some point, eventually ceases to be effective, it also means that, continuously, new abstract notions need to be created in order to tackle the emergent problems.[54] This means that the historian needs to strike the right balance between what T. Vischer called 'subject matter specialists' and 'interpretative specialists'. While the former remain remarkably loyal to the data collected, the latter are particularly keen to develop new interpretative frameworks. In the age of specialization, the subject matter specialist is dominant. But whenever significant cultural transformations take place, the interpretative specialist comes to the forefront.[55]

Weber would have agreed with the Marxist dictum that 'history is made by individuals but not under conditions of their own choice', though he would have put the emphasis on the first part of the quote. For him, people are indeed first and foremost purposive individuals, who have the ability to assess information, reflect on various possibilities and plan ahead. This view underscores his definition of social action as 'all human behaviour when and in so far as the acting individual attaches a subjective meaning to it'.[56] People are often faced with situations which are not the product of their own making, but this does not necessarily imply that they are passive recipients to external factors. On the contrary, they regularly judge the situations and use this information to choose between various avenues. Whether their action consists 'of positive intervention in a situation, or of deliberately refraining from such intervention',[57] they are thinking, evaluating individuals. The historian does something very similar when deciding what people did and why they acted in this way. He or she reconstructs the situation in which people happened to find themselves, and tries to make sense of people's actions in the light of this context. He or she will do so with the help of various ideal-typical models, one of which assumes 'optimal logical rationality' on the part of the individuals involved. For Weber, this particular model has methodological priority over others, hence his reference to his own methodological outlook as 'rationalistic'.[58] While he was fully aware that people do not necessarily or predominantly act in this perfectly rational way, his point was that, in those cases where they do not, the discrepancy between this model and reality will be informative. The researcher will learn which irrational factors, whether affects or errors, are responsible for the deviation from a rational course of conduct. Among these factors are, for instance, incomplete or wrong information, erroneous strategies, logical errors and personal character traits.[59] The function of the model 'is the comparison with empirical reality in order to establish its divergences or similarities, to describe them with the *most unambiguously intelligible concepts*, and to understand and explain them causally.'[60] Such a model is a stepping stone towards counterfactual reasoning, a counterfactual being an attempt at ascertaining what might have happened if a particular event had not occurred. For Weber, any significant historical work uses counterfactuals, and tries to imagine what would have happened if, for instance, the emergence of Protestant sects had not been successful, or how history would have developed if the Battle of Marathon had turned out differently. Counterfactual thinking occurs with the help of ontological and nomological knowledge, the former relating to conjectures about the situation individuals were facing at the time, and the latter to empirical rules regarding the ways people react under certain conditions.[61] Historians use this technique, for instance, when they make a judgement about the significance of the Battle of Marathon by assessing the Persian impact where they have been victorious (for instance, Jerusalem and Egypt). Likewise, historians may want to study the impact of Protestantism by contrasting Protestant areas in Western Europe with those that remained a stronghold for Catholicism.[62]

The subject matter of Weber's sociology is what he called 'social action'. He was, of course, aware of the fact that there are other views of sociology, some of which do not restrict the study of society in this way. But he seemed to be convinced that confining the research object to social action would be beneficial for, and possibly even necessary to, a *science* of society.[63] What, then, is social action? It differs from other forms of action in that it is orientated towards the behaviour of at least one other individual.[64] The individuals concerned can be co-present (as in an ordinary conversation) but do not have to be (as in an email exchange). The individuals might be known to each other (say, a relationship between mother and child) or not at all (for example, money as a medium of exchange, in which the individuals accept money because they expect others, with whom they are not necessarily acquainted, to accept it). But Weber insisted that, in his definition, an individual's action is social only in so far as the behaviour of others has been taken into account, and he gave some examples of actions that are not social. For instance, in contrast with a Catholic confession that is obviously social, a solitary prayer is non-social because it is not geared towards other individuals. Crowd behaviour, an emerging object of interest at the time, can be social but is not necessarily so. While people might be affected by their presence within a crowd, it does not follow that they are meaningfully orientated towards others. The imitation of others is not social if it is merely reactive. If, however, the individual imitates others because it lends distinction or because it is fashionable, then it is social.[65]

Once Weber had confined sociology to the study of social action, his next task was to distinguish different forms of social action. He classified four ideal types of social action based on their 'mode of orientation', while adding a cautious note that this is not meant to be an exhaustive list. The four types are: instrumental-rational (*zweckrational*), value-rational (*wertrational*), affectual and traditional action.[66] The first two are rational; the last two are not. In the case of instrumental rationality (*Zweckrationalität*) the individual is contemplating between several goals, and he or she is, by anticipating the behaviour of others, weighing up the costs and benefits of obtaining each goal. Instrumental rationality comes into play, for instance, when an individual chooses between various holiday options by taking into account the different prices, modes of transport, facilities, and so on.[67] Value-rationality (*Wertrationalität*) refers to a mode of orientation in which the individual has one absolute value, whether aesthetic, ethical or religious. The individual holds this value dearly and wants to achieve it at all costs. He or she might still exhibit instrumental rationality but only in relation to the means for obtaining the central value; the goal itself is never beyond doubt. For instance, any action based primarily on duty or honour is value-rational.[68] Affectual action is action that is caused primarily by particular 'affects' and feelings – as, for instance, expressing joy or sorrow. Like value-rational action, affectual action is done for its own sake, not because of considerations about its consequences. Traditional action originates from deeply embedded practices which stretch over a long period of time. Various religious rituals are traditional in that sense. Both affectual and traditional actions are borderline cases in that they are not always social in the Weberian sense of the word. They might, indeed, be reactive or unconscious.[69]

Weber's concept of 'social relationship' follows on from his notion of social action. He talks about a social relationship in so far as people, in their actions, take account of each other. It therefore indicates the existence of a probability that a course of social action will take place.[70] The content of the orientation of people towards each other might be one of love, friendship, conflict or economic exchange. This is not to say that, for Weber, people necessarily attribute the same meanings to each other. They sometimes do (as, for instance, in the relationship between two colleagues both of whom treat the relationship as a professional one), in which case Weber talked about symmetrical relations. But sometimes they do not (as, for example, in the case of two colleagues, one of whom sees the other as a friend, whereas the other one treats him or her as a rival, to be eliminated), in which case Weber called the relations asymmetrical.[71] Nor did Weber assume that people's orientations towards others are necessarily constant. Sometimes the mutual attitudes of individuals indeed remain stable (as, for instance, in a stable loving relationship), but in other cases people's orientations change drastically over time (as, say, in changing political alliances). Finally, Weber was also aware that people's orientations differ according to degree of discursive articulation. Some are articulated in a rational form (take, for instance a business contract); others are not and are unlikely to be (for example, a friendship).[72]

Application: the Protestant ethic

Acting consistently with his methodological views, Max Weber carried out historical research with painstaking detail, going out of his way to avoid speculative, sweeping accounts of history and carefully separating the actual process of empirical investigation from his own political and moral agenda. This is particularly clear in his most famous work, *The Protestant Ethic and the Spirit of Capitalism*, originally published as two articles in the *Archiv für Sozialwissenschaft und Sozialpolitik* in 1904–5.[73] Weber would have been the first to admit that his personal biography and values had something to do with his choice of subject matter: he was descended from a long line of Protestant bourgeois and had struggled all his life with the strict values with which he had been brought up. He would have insisted, however, that this personal involvement did not interfere with the actual research process itself, and that he had made every effort to let the facts speak – not his values. So when Weber mentioned in the book the inadequacy of Marx's materialist interpretation of history,[74] he did not intend, as popular wisdom has had it, to replace materialism with cultural or religious determinism. He meant to warn us of any dogmatic account of history, whether materialist or otherwise. He wished to indicate what role the Reformation had played in the development of rational capitalism, but based only on detailed empirical research – not on a set of ideological preconceptions. He recognized that he researched 'one side of the causal chain' and that other studies would complement his. As in his methodological writings, Weber noted that he could not study everything. He inevitably had to be selective, but, once the selection was made, he applied rigorous scientific methods.[75]

In this book, Weber acknowledged using ideal-typical constructions, for instance of capitalism and the capitalist entrepreneur.[76] His definitions of capitalism shifted somewhat throughout the text. After spelling out that the pursuit of gain is not limited to capitalism, he defined capitalism as 'the pursuit of profit, and forever *renewed* profit, by means of continuous, rational, capitalist enterprise.'[77] Later the reader learns that 'calculation' is central to capitalism: entrepreneurs calculate anticipated profit and act accordingly.[78] Weber emphasized that capitalism has been widespread for a long time. This form of economic exchange existed even before the sixteenth and seventeenth centuries, and not just in Western Europe. What made the modern Western economic system distinctive, however, was the 'rational capitalistic organization' of free labour. The emphasis here is on 'rational'. The meaning of Weber's concepts of rationality and rationalization were not unambiguous, but, in the context of capitalism, it is clear that they referred to the methodical use of organization, technology and labour to pursue profit and renewed profit.[79] Partly influenced by the work of Sombart, Weber contrasted this form of capitalism with 'traditionalism' because it tried out and managed to implement new, more efficient methods and conducted careful calculations. For Weber, rationalization sums up the transition towards modernity: rationalization can be observed in various domains, ranging from science and technology to legal and economic systems. As such, rational capitalism fits into a broader cultural process.[80]

Weber's analysis started with a number of observations. Firstly, until roughly the fifteenth century, Western Europe and parts of the East were more or less on a par with each other, technologically and scientifically. Within two centuries (the period during which the Reformation took place), Western Europe had moved ahead considerably. Secondly, compared to Catholics, the average Protestant obtained a higher educational degree, reached higher positions in administration and skilled labour, and was more likely to become a successful entrepreneur. Thirdly, a close look at the economic situation in Western Europe during and after the Reformation shows that most areas that had become Protestant were economically more prosperous than 'Catholic' areas.[81] Of course, none of these observations are conclusive evidence of a causal link between Protestantism and capitalism, let alone about the strength and direction of the causality. Nor do the observations in themselves present an explanation. To provide a persuasive account, Weber decided he ought to capture the worldview of sixteenth-century Protestants and re-enact their fears and hopes. Consistent with his methodological writings, he used this method of *Verstehen* as a starting point of a causal analysis.

By the time Weber was writing, the dominant explanation for the emergence of rational capitalism in Western Europe was straightforward: capitalism flourished because of a relaxation of the strict rules of the Church, especially with the transition towards Protestantism. This theory would also explain why Protestants were successful entrepreneurs. Weber rejected this explanation outright. If anything, the rules of the Church had become stricter. Calvinism, for instance, implied what 'would be for us the most absolutely unbearable form of ecclesiastical control of the individual which could possibly exist.'[82] Another explanation pointed the finger at a supposed sudden increase in greed and unscrupulousness. Again, Weber rejected this explanation on historical grounds. On the contrary, unscrupulous pursuit of gain was universally characteristic of pre-capitalist societies, and this form of unprincipled greed was virtually absent among early capitalists.[83] Instead, Weber argued that Protestantism and in particular Calvinism implied that individuals would adopt a very different relationship to God, to the world and, ultimately, to themselves. The method of interpretation would help Weber to establish the precise nature of this shift and explain the 'elective affinity' (*Wahlverwandtschaft*) between Protestantism and capitalism. Note Weber's use of 'elective affinity', a term originally from chemistry and popularized by Goethe. This concept was supposed to indicate that, while it is unclear whether Protestantism or capitalism came first, they reinforced each other. Once in place, Protestantism and capitalism were a natural fit and fed into each other. Weber's analysis showed why this was the case, but he made very clear that the elective affinity was time-bound. At some point, capitalism would gain its own momentum and no longer need the Protestant basis.

Weber studied the various forms of Protestantism, and argued that they were conducive to capitalism because of the immense value attached to work and material success and the extent to which idleness was condemned. He paid, however, particular attention to Calvinism, which, in his opinion, was decisive in the development of rational capitalism and rationalization as a whole. What were the main features of the Calvinist doctrine? Weber's analysis of Calvin's teachings suggested two central points. Firstly, the doctrine stipulated that people could not fully understand God because he is infinite and they are not. They cannot fully grasp what decisions he has made for us. They can get a sense of what he wants – they can make inferences and intelligent guesses – but they can never be sure. Secondly, Calvinism promoted the doctrine of predestination. For each individual, God has already decided whether he or she is elected or damned at the moment of his or her birth. He or she cannot do anything to change God's decision. Good works or a pious existence cannot make you one of the elect, nor can priests or sacraments bring about salvation. Note that the combination of these two principles led to huge 'salvation anxiety': only a few were elected, and nobody could know for certain that they were among the few. This 'inner loneliness' was increased by a significant reduction in the role of the priest.[84]

We would normally expect anyone to be paralysed in the face of this uncertainty. After all, in the Calvinist view, none of people's actions made any difference as to whether they were elected or not. So it is all the more remarkable that the early Calvinists were not in the least passive; they worked tremendously hard and were very successful. Why should this have been the case? Weber's answer was threefold. Firstly, the doctrine postulated that people have to work for the glory of God. Through work people honour and celebrate God, while idleness was regarded as essentially evil. Secondly, Calvinists considered it a duty to regard themselves as chosen, because they thought that any manifestation of insufficient self-confidence was a sign of a lack of faith and therefore a sign of 'imperfect grace'. Thirdly, Weber pointed out that, for Calvinists, someone's hard work and material success were signs of the fact that he or she was elected. Unbearable levels of salvation anxiety encouraged an unconscious drive to look for such signs, to find confirmation of the fact that one was among the very few, hence the drive for hard work and commercial and material success.[85] It would be wrong, therefore, to say that Protestants were enterprising *in spite* of the predestination doctrine. They were successful precisely *because* of it.

Calvinism was inner-worldly because it was concerned with the here and now – this life. It was also ascetic because it did not want its members to indulge in any sensuous pleasures.[86] Very few religions are both inner-worldly and ascetic. Many Eastern religions are ascetic but outer-worldly – that is, concerned with the spiritual or the afterlife. Medieval asceticism was equally outer-worldly. According to Weber, the combination of inner-worldliness and asceticism made for a remarkably dynamic approach to life, which would change the face of Western Europe for ever. The concept of unintended consequences was central in Weber's analysis. In his depiction, none of the Protestants meant to bring about rational capitalism and rationalization of culture. They were concerned about very different things – their own relationship to God and their afterlife – and they unintentionally brought about these broader societal changes. In the long run, further unintended effects would occur: the rationalization process ultimately led to the erosion of religion itself. Capitalism would be able to survive without Protestantism.

Whereas Durkheim published *Suicide* in part to promote his methodological position, there is little evidence that Weber had such a purpose in mind

when he wrote *The Protestant Ethic and the Spirit of Capitalism*. His methodological agenda is, nevertheless, clearly exemplified in this book. The key
notions of his methodology are visibly present. Once the ideal types of the
Calvinists and capitalist entrepreneurs were established, Weber employed
the method of interpretative understanding to grasp the Protestant mindset
and preoccupations that turned devout Christians into methodical, calculating
entrepreneurs and unintentionally brought about rational capitalism. The question is, of course, whether ordinary Calvinists wholeheartedly believed in their
Protestant doctrine to the extent to which Weber assumed they did. Weber portrayed them as entirely at one with their religion, and his theory (with reference to the predestination doctrine and the Calvinists' need to reduce salvation
anxiety) depended on it, but the evidence presented was not always convincing. Most of this was based on extracts from Calvin's teaching, and it goes
without saying that it was perfectly possible for Calvinists to have taken more
critical distance towards these ideas than Weber suggested, or at least to have
been more selective in appropriating them.

Evaluation

Like Nietzsche, Weber was right to point out that, however sophisticated,
people cannot resort to social science, or any other science, in order to judge
between competing values. This is precisely where Durkheim went astray. No
study about social inequality could help to ascertain whether equality is worth
striving for, and no piece of criminological research could settle whether
justice is worth pursuing. Weber was right to argue that no reference to what
is the case (*das Seiende*) could help clear up what ought to be (*das Seinsol-
lende*), although it is possible to defend this position more convincingly than
Weber did. My main problem with any attempt to infer values from facts is
that this endeavour itself draws on a set of ultimate goals. It therefore involves
a circular argument in which the formation of a system of values takes place
with the help of a set of values. This in turn would need a justification. This
is very obvious in the case of Durkheim, who tried to establish which ethical
system was appropriate or desirable for a given society. He did this by studying which of the sets of values might provide a functional contribution to
society, how it may prove to have beneficial effects for societal harmony and
survival.[87] He thereby implicitly drew on the assumption that cohesion and
stability are worthwhile goals, that there is something desirable about consensus and something unappealing about strife and discord. The point is not
that Durkheim was wrong in promoting cohesiveness and societal accord
(both this and the opposing view are perfectly defendable). Rather, it proved
impossible for him, as it would be for anyone, to infer values from facts,

because his attempt at doing so, like any attempt, draws on a collection of value patterns. Although Weber arrived at similar conclusions, he would have felt uncomfortable with this argument against Durkheim, for Weber did not quite want to acknowledge the extent to which values interfere with research. He still somehow adhered to the view that, in the actual process of empirical investigation, social researchers should (and therefore can) shed their values and interests. This explains why his stance against inferring values from facts is inadequately developed and poorly defended.

So Weber is vindicated on this score. But he also assumed that, if properly conducted, social science would be able to assist social policy in a more modest fashion, by providing information about which means are more likely to lead to the accomplishment of central values or about the possible unintended effects or incompatibility of various pathways.[88] Weber was vague as to what he meant by this. Social research might certainly assist in determining how certain values can be accomplished in a given setting, at a particular point in time and space. Sometimes Weber seemed to say precisely that, but at other times he seemed to mean that social science would be able to make those recommendations, independent of the setting in which the research took place. This is a far more problematic statement to make. It is unlikely that the advice, derived from a particular setting, would be as informative in other contexts, because so many correlations and intervening variables would play out differently. It is, for instance, perfectly reasonable to assume that certain research into the relationship between education and social stratification in a particular country might be helpful in bringing about some equality in that country, but it is less obvious how these research results would support policies in other parts of the world. Likewise, research might show how, in a particular environment, certain societal transformations produce unintended effects which eventually undermine the intentions that motivated the changes in the first place, and knowing that would indeed be helpful; however, it is not at all certain that similar transformations would be equally self-defeating in a very different context. So Weber was right to point out the usefulness of social research, but there are important limitations to it.

There are two ways in which values can interfere with social research. One such interference was acknowledged by Weber, as can be inferred from his critique of Marxism.[89] This refers to cases in which the investigator uses research with the *intention* not to establish existential knowledge (knowledge about what is), but to promote a particular vision or critique of society. Although the finding of societal facts and regularities might be part of this intellectual enterprise, it is subordinated to an ideological or political mission, because data are being used selectively to support a particular cause and argument. This is the kind of value-laden research that Weber very much deplored and condemned. But there is also another way in which values come into play in research. They come into play even if researchers are not pursuing normative knowledge, even if they self-consciously embark on value-free research and wish to eradicate their normative and political views. The point is that they *always* come into play, even if researchers do not want them to, and even if they monitor themselves on this score. The way in which social researchers use various conceptual tools (such as metaphors, models and analogies) to interpret findings and put them into a particular narrative necessarily draws on a number of assumptions that exhibit normative components. Whether in the process of accounting they refer to rational actors, fierce class struggles or dwindling social cohesion, implicit value-judgements are always being made. What these judgements are precisely may not be obvious and they might indeed be open to conflicting interpretations, but the point remains that the idea of a value-free social science (*Wertfreiheit*) is a chimerical construction. The fact that value-free science is non-existent does, of course, not necessarily imply that researchers should abandon all academic standards and subordinate knowledge to a normative project (although, under certain circumstances, this might be a defensible route to take). It does not mean either that it is necessarily worthless for social scientists to respect criteria of objectivity. But it does suggest that they ought to be aware that, however much they try, they cannot operate in a moral vacuum, and that therefore it might be particularly important to exhibit reflexivity and be aware of the various moral assumptions that underscore the research. So to argue, as Weber did, for value-neutrality as a regulative idea is a perfectly laudable proposal to make, particularly if it is meant to make researchers vigilant about which normative presuppositions they take on board, but not if it is simply meant to advise them to shed their values and interests.

Weber subscribed to what is now known as methodological individualism. He assumed that, for a proper explanation of the social, the sociologist or historian needs to accept that the people studied are purposive actors who know more or less why they are doing what they are doing, but whose actions produce effects that may go far beyond what was intended by any of them. Implicit in his argument is Donald Davidson's position that people's reasons for doing something are also the causes for doing it.[90] Not all philosophers share this treatment of reasons as causes, and indeed some strongly deny this, but it is certainly essential for defending the viability of methodological individualism. Once reasons are treated as causes, the grasping of people's reasons or motives can be a starting point for a causal analysis, in which reasons are conceived as bringing about actions. These actions in turn lead to effects, some of which are intended and some not. If, as I have argued, the assertion that reasons are causes is central to his research outline, it is all the more surprising that Weber did not present a clear argument to this effect, let alone defend it aptly, and his methodological programme is therefore incomplete. Some passages in his work might be interpreted as saying that reasons are causes, but he certainly did not elaborate on it. Even if he had made a proper case for this position, there would be other problems that need addressing. Although he recognized that the unconscious plays a role in history, it occupies an auxiliary position in his methodological writings. Because of the methodological priority on rational and in particular instrumental-rational action, there is a tendency in Weber's methodological programme to ignore the full extent to which people's unconscious motives and hidden desires impinge on their actions, the ways in which they might be driven by forces which are not always under their control or of which they are not necessarily aware. This problem becomes particularly obvious when Weber studied real scenarios, such as the emergence of Calvinism in early modern Europe, because he could not help deviating from his methodological prescriptions and regularly drew on an unconscious logic. His explanation for why there might be an empirical link between this form of Protestantism and capitalism rests partly on the conjecture that, in the face of salvation anxiety and inner loneliness, the Protestants at the time were looking for signs of the fact that they were elected. Given that hard work and material success were among those signs, Protestants were particularly prone to the kind of nervous energy and work ethic that would eventually lead to the spread of Western capitalism. Contrary to how various rational choice theorists[91] and others[92] have tried to interpret *The Protestant Ethic and the Spirit of Capitalism*, Weber's story does not quite gel with their model of a rational, self-determining agent, and the persuasiveness of his argument lies precisely in the fact that it does not.

I already mentioned towards the end of the previous chapter that, in some respects, Weber was very much ahead of his time, in particular in the way he broke with the positivist assumption that it is possible to reach a neutral vantage point. Weber recognized that researchers cannot 'step outside history' and always draw on a number of culturally embedded presuppositions in order to make sense of what they are studying. Equally interesting is Weber's defence of the interpretative method on axiological grounds. He did not argue that the ontology of the social necessitates a distinctive method; rather, a different cognitive interest was at stake. But in the course of our discussion it has also become clear that Weber did not go far enough. His concept of value-neutrality was problematic, and he did not fully explore the relationship between types of cognitive interests and methodology. As will become obvious from the latter parts of this book, a pragmatist philosophy of the social sciences will do away with the notion of value-neutrality and will put the notion of cognitive interest at the centre. My pragmatist view will also question Weber's implicit assumption that the natural sciences use a single method. At this stage, it is important to move on to Popper's philosophy of social science because it is, in crucial respects, compatible with Weber's position and can be read as a more advanced articulation of it. Like Weber, Popper insisted that observations are always theory-laden. Like Weber, Popper was sceptical of the way in which Marxist historians were proceeding: they were pretending to do science but were not really remaining faithful to scientific ideals. Like Weber, Popper opted for methodological individualism and took seriously the role of ideal types of action (although he did not use that term). But, in addition to Weber, Popper had clearly articulated notions of what science is about, what the difference is between science and, say, ideology or religion. Unlike Weber, Popper was a philosopher of science and his reflections on sociology or psychology were guided by his philosophy. Popper presented a coherent philosophical project.

Further reading

One of the first of Weber's pieces on the philosophy of social science is a text on Roscher and Knies which appeared between 1903 and 1906 in three parts in *Schmoller's Jahrbuch für Gesetzgebung, Verwaltung und Volkswirtschaft*. The text is now available in English as a little book entitled *Roscher and Knies: The Logical Problems of Historical Economics*. Weber elucidates his position vis-à-vis the *Methodenstreit* in 'Objectivity in Social Science and Social Policy', which was initially published in 1904 in the *Archiv für Sozialwissenschaft und Sozialpolitik* when Edgar Jaffé, Werner Sombart and Max Weber took over the editorship of the journal. The article was meant to communicate the underlying philosophy of the journal to readers and possible contributors but actually goes far beyond an editorial or set of editorial guidelines. It is particularly significant because it explores systematically the use of ideal types to study historical phenomena. 'Critical Studies in the Logic of the Cultural Sciences' dates from 1905 and was originally published in the *Archiv*. It has a similar polemical tone to 'Objectivity in Social Science' but is different in that it explores in detail the use of counterfactuals. Weber's 'The Meaning of "Ethical Neutrality" in Sociology and Economics' was published in *Logos* in 1917 as a reworked version of an earlier communication to the *Verein für Sozialpolitik*. It is in part a polemical piece directed against those German professors who used their academic status to give weight to and propound their political positions. Echoing Nietzsche and heralding the existentialist movement, Weber insisted that individuals were condemned to make choices and that no science can help them escape this. Finally, there is 'The Fundamental Concepts in Sociology', originally published in 1913 and reprinted in *Gesammelte Aufsätze zur Wissenschaftslehre* in 1922. The first sections are devoted to the methodology of the social sciences; the later sections explore some central sociological concepts such as 'social action'. There are a few books that deal exclusively with Weber's methodology. There is Gary Runciman's *A Critique of Max Weber's Philosophy of Social Science* and, more recently, Fritz Ringer's *Max Weber's Methodology*. Ringer's book puts Weber's philosophy of the social sciences in its intellectual context, and it is a lucid introduction to a notoriously difficult topic. Runciman offers a sympathetic critique of Weber's methodological writings, but, in spite of his overall positive disposition, he subjects Weber's arguments to relentless analytical scrutiny. For those interested in understanding Weber's significance within the methodological debates of his time, I suggest the third volume of Alexander's *Theoretical Logic in Sociology* and Turner's *The Search for a Methodology of Social Science*. For an overview of Weber's influence on sociology and sociological theory, I suggest Collins's *Weberian Sociological Theory*.

3
Karl Popper's Falsificationism

Introduction

Few philosophical doctrines in the modern era are associated with only one person. Almost every significant philosophical school consisted of a number of people who helped elaborate and refine the doctrine, as if the contribution of each was not enough to keep the strand afloat. It took, for instance, the intellectual weight of Schlick, Rudolf Carnap, the early Wittgenstein and many others to build the fortress of logical positivist philosophy. Likewise, it took the collaborative effort of Adorno, Horkheimer and others to develop the critical theory of the Frankfurt School. In contrast, falsificationism has always been a one-man act. It was Karl Popper's brainchild and, although it has over the years accumulated a coterie of followers, most significant contributions to the school have been by Popper himself. There are, of course, a number of philosophers who have followed Popper's lead, such as Ian Jarvie, Imre Lakatos, David Miller and John Watkins, but none of them has substantially altered the Popperian framework. Whether this is testimony to Popper's intellectual brilliance, to the idiosyncrasies of his philosophy or to his notorious lack of tolerance for others' views would be an interesting question, but not one that I will pursue here. What I want to suggest, instead, is that it is perfectly legitimate to treat, as I will do in the remainder of the chapter, Popper and falsificationism as virtually interchangeable. This becomes an even more persuasive strategy given that other significant contributors to falsificationism, such as Lakatos, had remarkably little to say about the social sciences.

Earlier I wrote about 'methodological naturalism'. Methodological naturalists assume that similar methodological guidelines are applicable to the social and the natural sciences. They do not necessarily commit themselves to ontological naturalism, which is the doctrine that the various domains of inquiry ultimately consist of the same material. But they assume that the social and the natural sciences proceed alike. Methodological naturalists can defend their position in two ways. They may, firstly, refer to the essence of science, its superior logic, from which they infer methodological guidelines for the social sciences. Or they may argue that it is sufficient to look at the history of the natural sciences – a tale of progress, to be emulated in the social realm. It will become clear that Popper used both arguments: he referred to some essence of science, the logic of falsification, which is somehow embodied in the practice of natural scientists.[1] For Popper, this explains why the natural sciences have made such progress, and he urged social scientists to follow the codes of practice of natural scientists. One such code is to construct refutable theories that are then put to the test. Refutable theories are lucid, specific and informative. The social sciences are misguided by shrewd conmen such as Marx, Freud and Adler, who pretend to be able to explain everything, but who, by doing so, fail to say anything significant. The problem with the likes of Marx is not that what they say is wrong, but that they are not clear enough to be wrong.

It is difficult to overestimate Popper's towering presence after World War II. Testament to his influence is the series of honours that came his way, uniquely among British-based philosophers, receiving a knighthood in 1962, being elected a Fellow of the Royal Society in 1975, and becoming a Companion of Honour in 1982. Across the world, foundations and universities have been set up around Popperian principles, from a private university, called LUISS, in Rome to George Soros's Open Society Foundation in Eastern Europe. Popper inspired otherwise diverse intellectual projects such as Peter Medawar's medical science, Ernst Gombrich's philosophy of art, Hayek's economics, and Ernest Gellner's social and political theory.[2] For a long time, natural scientists habitually brought up his falsificationist philosophy of science to describe, guide or justify their actions, and a lot of them still do so today. His political theory has often been employed to defend or promote the principles of liberal democracy and to condemn various totalitarian regimes, whether left or right of the political spectrum, all around the world. It is difficult to think of any intellectual, in the twentieth century, with such a vast impact on so many different spheres of life.

Popper's popularity can partly be ascribed to the various ways in which his philosophy fitted in with and legitimized the political and intellectual priorities of the day. He presented a remarkably flattering portrayal of the natural sciences, portraying scientists as adventurous, risk-taking individuals who develop bold conjectures while being prepared, if necessary, to face their destruction, and so ready to take the responsibility of forming new conjectures. This portrayal of the natural sciences, which was particularly lucidly explained in his *Conjectures and Refutations*,[3] was infinitely more attractive than, for instance, the one presented by the doctrine of inductivism, according to which the activities of natural scientists are hardly more than laborious, fact-finding ones, interrupted by the occasional generalization.

Popper's notion of the open society presents an equally idealistic depiction of liberal democracy. That portrait, together with his critique of historicism, developed and provided the necessary motivational energy for and justification of the Western political system, especially during the Cold War. Like other advocates of the liberal cause, such as Friedrich Hayek, Isaiah Berlin and John Plamenatz, Popper provided in his writings a sense that the West was on the right track. He argued (in *The Poverty of Historicism* and *The Open Society and its Enemies*) that Marxist history rests on shaky philosophical foundations, and that, like other utopias, socialism is irreconcilable with liberty.[4] It is not unimportant that, while fascism had been destroyed and the Soviet bloc became a major opponent, Popper focused on the similarities between Marxism and fascism and so created a feeling of continuity in liberalism's enemies. Popper's critique of Marxism complemented Hayek's: whereas the economist Hayek argued that centralized planning is not economically viable, Popper asserted that utopian social engineering was incompatible with liberty.[5]

Popper was first and foremost a philosopher of the natural sciences. His initial training was mainly in that area, and his knowledge of the natural sciences was more sophisticated than his knowledge of the social sciences. The social sciences hardly played any role in his earlier writings. His first book, *Logic of Scientific Discovery* (*Logik der Forschung*), was entirely devoted to the natural sciences.[6] However, soon afterwards he started to write about the philosophy of the social sciences, and he did so for a variety of reasons. We should first of all mention that Popper's autobiography identified Marxism and psychoanalysis, together with the theory of relativity, as the most popular doctrines among the Viennese intelligentsia during his formative years, and, indeed, Popper's initial acquaintance with both doctrines goes back to that period.[7] For a short while, the young Popper was even a committed Marxist, although there is no evidence that he ever developed a similar liking of, let alone enthusiasm for, psychoanalysis. The honeymoon with Marx's theorizing was soon to be followed by Popper's concerns with its intellectual flaws, which, for Popper, also extend to Freud's framework but not to Einstein's. A not insignificant part of Popper's writings was, indeed, concerned with why various theories in the natural sciences, such as the theory of relativity, are superior to the theories of Marx and Freud. While the former allow for predictions, the latter are immunized against refutation.[8]

The second point is that Popper's *The Open Society and its Enemies* and *The Poverty of Historicism* were initiated by, and a response to, the extreme political circumstances of the 1930s and 1940s in Europe. Popper's main concern here was to warn us against utopian blueprints of society, such as Marx's, which, although superficially enticing, are ultimately very dangerous. These blueprints are often accompanied by a 'historicist' view, according to which the study of the past will allow us to foresee the future, which, incidentally, happens to coincide with the desired utopia. Popper was appalled by the widespread appeal of Marxist historicism, even among fellow ratio- nalists and eminent scientists; he viewed them as terribly misguided in regard- ing historicism as a scientific endeavour.[9] Whereas *The Open Society* presents both a political theory and a critical history of philosophy, *The Poverty of His- toricism* is the closest to a treatise in the philosophy of the social sciences. It is a carefully argued assault on the widespread doctrine of historicism and its attendant holism in the social sciences. Popper's criticisms of historicism and holism are certainly not limited to *The Poverty of Historicism* – they are scat- tered across his numerous publications – but they do find in that book their most systematic articulation. Some sections of *The Poverty of Historicism* also incorporate positive rules about how to conduct social research, which brings me to my next point.

A third observation to be made is that Popper's long-term professional asso- ciation with the London School of Economics and Political Science after the war led him to develop a further interest in the philosophy of economics. This was in line with his long-running respect for economics, which predated his arrival at the LSE. Popper was already acquainted with the Austrian School of economics, and his further contact with his LSE sponsor F. A. Hayek served to strengthen his respect for the work of Ludwig von Mises and his follow- ers.[10] Of all social sciences, Popper tended to regard economics as the most rational, providing refutable (rather than immunized) forms of knowledge, and therefore an example to be followed by the other social disciplines. Like several contemporary rational choice theorists, Popper believed that the formal structure of reasoning in economics should be extended to the other social sciences, and that this 'economic approach' rests upon atomistic forms of explanation, in which individuals' purposive action and these actions' unin- tended or unanticipated effects play a central role. Note that Popper's earlier writings in the philosophy of the social sciences – his comparison between Marx and Einstein or the critique of historicism – were mainly, though not exclusively, negative endeavours, warning as they did of the dangers of succumbing to non-refutable doctrines. In contrast, Popper's writings on rationality and rational action mark a decisively positive turn in his work: he intended to give us clear guidelines for carrying out proper social research. Interestingly, compared to the vast impact of his criticisms of Marx and others, Popper's proposals for a methodological individualist research programme met, at the time, largely with indifference, at least in sociological circles. At the time Popper wrote about these methodological guidelines, a lot of sociol- ogy was still very much steeped in functionalist and structuralist reasoning. It was only later, especially from the 1980s onwards, that methodological indi- vidualism started to occupy a more prominent position.

Fourthly, although Popper gradually showed more interest in the philoso- phy of the social sciences, his knowledge of contemporary sociology and aligned disciplines always remained rudimentary. Whereas his knowledge of the natural sciences was remarkably sophisticated, his knowledge of the social sciences was limited basically to economics. He was, of course, familiar with the rough outlines of the *history* of social philosophy, but he was out of touch with recent developments in the social sciences. Take, for instance, his reflections on the sociology of knowledge, which can be summarized in two propositions.[11] First, the sociology of knowledge rightly opposes the naïve view that scientific objectivity is secured if the individual scientist has the right psychological attitude and necessary detachment – that view does, indeed, neglect the various institutional structures that are essential for the possibility of objective knowledge. Secondly, the sociology of knowledge is deficient when it asserts that scientists can never be objective, and that scientific results are always 'relative'. The sociology of knowledge neglects what should be one of its main insights, namely that science is a social and public endeavour and that therefore objectivity too can be achieved given the right conditions. However, Popper's expertise concerning the sociology of knowledge seems limited mainly to Karl Mannheim's writings on this topic. The sociology of knowledge was, of course, not the wide-ranging sub-discipline that it later became, but Popper's ignorance or neglect of other approaches is nevertheless striking. In a chapter in *The Open Society and its Enemies* devoted to the sociology of knowledge, there is no mention of Emile Durkheim's work on the social origins and conditions of systems of classification.[12] Nor is there any substantial discussion of Max Scheler's attempt to reconcile the cultural specificity of knowledge and the Platonic notion of atemporal essences.[13] These lacunae are not unimportant because Durkheim's legacy in the sociology of knowledge is at least as important as Mannheim's. Furthermore, Popper's treatment of Mannheim focuses on his *Ideology and Utopia*, and Popper's critique of that book is remarkably superficial; he dismisses it as yet another Hegelian narrative (something which is blatantly incorrect) and then spends most of the time reiterating why Hegel was wrong.

What science is about

Popper's views about the philosophy of science need to be set against the background of the Vienna Circle. He agreed with Rudolph Carnap and others that philosophy ought to learn from how the natural sciences operate. Scientists tend to adopt a critical attitude, which means that they are continually willing to confront their views and predictions with empirical evidence. Unfortunately few philosophers think like that. Instead, Popper claimed, they spout their 'pretentious wisdom, and their arrogation of knowledge which they present to us with a minimum of rational, or critical argument.'[14] The Vienna Circle had rightly promoted procedures of 'rational discussion', the necessity of stating our problems clearly and examining them critically.[15] In this sense, Carnap and his Viennese colleagues embodied the Enlightenment principles which Popper felt so strongly about. This is the route that philosophy should follow, which eventually should bring about a better society. But Popper also credited himself with destroying logical positivism, for pointing out its major flaws, in particular its adherence to 'inductivism' and 'verificationism'. Both doctrines rely on a mistaken view of what science is about.

Popper differed from some members of the Vienna Circle in that he was highly sceptical of the doctrine of inductivism. This assumes that via inductive methods we are able to gain secure scientific knowledge. An inference is inductive if it obtains universal statements (such as hypotheses or theories) from singular statements (such as statements about our observations). Inductivists argue that the inference is perfectly legitimate if a sufficient number of singular or observational statements are gathered under a wide variety of circumstances. Because they record immediate observations or perceptions, 'protocol sentences' are thought to provide the solid bedrock from which we can induce our laws.[16] But some critics, such as Hume, point out that we cannot obtain certainty about the validity of a universal statement on the basis of any set of singular statements, because it is always possible that we will face future observations that contradict the universal statement. However large the number of singular statements might be and however wide the variety of circumstances in which they are gathered, the problem of induction still remains. Popper agreed. He was of the opinion that the difficulties of inductive logic are not solvable, and that induction can never be justified on rational grounds. Some counter-argued that, even if that is the case, it is also true that scientists have always used the inductive method and have been successful in doing so, and that this in itself should be sufficient for us to be persuaded by the value of the inductive method. But Popper rightly pointed out the circularity of this argument, the fact that it attempts to defend the method of induction by relying on the very same method.[17]

So far Popper's views are close to Hume's. But Hume was resigned to the idea that knowledge, being an inductive procedure, could not be rationally justified. Hume's 'psychological' solution was that our belief in inductively inferred laws is merely on account of habit or custom, and it follows that even scientific knowledge is irrational. Popper disagreed, and promoted a deductive view of knowledge: it is true that induction cannot be justified, but deduction can, and it is precisely deduction that rules the scientific world.[18] To develop this idea, he pointed out that, whereas we have already established that we can never obtain certainty about the validity of a theory even when confronted with numerous empirical confirmations, it takes only one empirical refutation to know with certainty that a theory is false. Popper called this 'the asymmetry between verifiability and falsifiability': while we can never infer universal statements from singular statements, the latter can contradict the former.[19] This asymmetry is at the heart of Popper's philosophy of science, and, according to him, ties in with the practice of scientists who are indeed ready to abandon their theories in the face of counter-evidence. The solution to the problem of inductivism lies, therefore, in abandoning the method of induction and embracing the deductive method.[20] According to this view, scientists start with a problem, and come up with a theoretical system to tackle the problem. From this theoretical system, which consists of universal statements and initial conditions, they deduce hypotheses that are subsequently tested. If corroborated, the theory survives; if falsified, it is abandoned. This view of science in terms of trial and error depends, of course, on theories being constructed so that they *can* be refuted. Popper therefore suggested falsifiability as the criterion of demarcation between the 'empirical sciences' and the rest. Logic, mathematics and metaphysical systems are non-falsifiable. Falsifiability is not a criterion of meaning; both falsifiable and non-falsifiable statements are meaningful.[21] Instead it is meant to distinguish science from non-science. 'It must be possible for an empirical scientific system to be refuted by experience.'[22] We could also say that a theory is falsifiable if the class of its potential falsifiers (the set of all basic statements with which it is inconsistent) is not empty. Note that, while a theory makes claims that its potential falsifiers are false, it does not assert that any of the basic statements that it permits are true. It actually permits mutually exclusive statements.[23]

There are degrees of falsifiability. Compare, for instance, 'T1: all orbits of heavenly bodies are circles', 'T2: all orbits of planets are circles' and 'T3: all orbits of planets are ellipses'. Theory T1 is 'falsifiable in a higher degree' than T2 because it has more potential falsifiers and T2 is more falsifiable than T3 for the same reason. It follows, Popper argued, that T1 provides more information about the world than T2 because it excludes a larger class of observational statements, and for the same reason T2 is more informative than T3. It could be counter-argued that the class of permitted statements of T1 is smaller than that of T2, which in turn is smaller than that of T3. But this does not undermine Popper's argument that T1 is more informative than T2 and that T2 is more informative than T3. The reason for this is that, as we mentioned before, theories do not assert anything about the class of permitted statements; they only make assertions about the class of potential falsifiers. This is not just a logical point, because degrees of falsifiability do matter to science. Scientists should not only aim at formulating falsifiable theories; they should prefer highly refutable theories instead of modestly falsifiable ones, because the former theories are more informative and bolder than the latter.[24] Popper explained convincingly that, the higher the degree of universality and of precision of a theory, the more falsifiable the theory is. In our example, T1 is more universal than T2, and T2 is more precise than T3. In a similar vein, Popper was able to justify why simplicity is so important in science. Simple propositions are desirable because they are more refutable; their empirical content (that is, the class of their potential falsifiers) is greater.[25] More contentious was Popper's critique of the view of Carnap and other logical positivists, according to whom the aim of science is to obtain theories with high probability. Contra Carnap, the bolder a theory is the better, because bold theories have a high empirical content. We should be pursuing theories with low probability.[26]

Science proceeds by making bold conjectures, testing them and, if falsified, replacing them by even bolder conjectures. But we only replace a theory by another one if the former has been empirically refuted, and if the latter explains what the former managed to explain, leads to new predictions, and successfully passes new empirical tests.[27] Leaving aside for a moment the problem in establishing whether the old theory is false, would it make sense to say that the new theory is true? After all, the new theory manages to explain what the previous one explained, and has led to several new predictions that have been corroborated. Popper's answer was categorically negative. We can never conclusively establish the validity of a theory, because future tests may cast doubt over what was previously held to be true. The irony is that, however stringent the testing, the 'method of elimination' still leaves us at any moment in time with an infinite number of possibly true theories.[28] There is an element of progress, however, for the new theory is *closer* to the truth than the previous one. Here, Popper drew on Tarski's notion of truth,[29] and introduced the 'notion of degree of verisimilitude' or 'truthlikeness': that is, the extent to which a theory approximates the truth. Assuming that the truth-content of a theory is the class of its true consequences and falsity-content is the class of its false consequences, there are two ways in which the verisimilitude of a theory T2 exceeds that of T1. T2 might have a higher truth-content (and not a higher falsity-content) than T1; alternatively, the falsity-content of T1 (and not the truth-content) is higher than that of T2.[30] Leaving the technical sophistication of Popper's argument, it suffices to point out that the scientific logic of trial and error is such that with every new theory the degree of verisimilitude has increased. This means that we are continually getting closer to the truth, although we can never say that we have reached it.

The controversy with Kuhn

In 1962 Thomas Kuhn published *The Structure of Scientific Revolutions*.[31] His book created a huge controversy with Popper. At first sight, Kuhn's work did not seem to have any repercussions for Popper because the two men were focusing on different issues. Contrary to Popper, Kuhn's main objective was not to develop a normative philosophy of science. His aim was not to present guidelines to scientists about how to proceed. Instead, his book was mainly a *historical* view of the development of science: it was not so much about what scientists ought to do, but about what they have actually done. Secondly, Kuhn tried to *explain* why scientists operated in this way. His explanations were sociological. Whereas Popper conceived of scientists as individuals, Kuhn emphasized that they do not operate in a sociological vacuum. Scientists belong to a scientific community with rules and expectations. These sociological factors explain why scientists are not always willing to change their theories even when confronted with a wealth of counter-evidence.

In spite of these differences in focus, it quickly became apparent that *The Structure of Scientific Revolutions* was problematic for Popper's philosophy. Kuhn's history showed that, most of the time, scientists did not operate in the way that Popper prescribed. Kuhn used the phrase 'normal science' to refer to the way in which scientists usually work. Normal science is characterized by a dominant paradigm. In Kuhn's terminology, a paradigm is a set of practical guidelines, skills and tacit knowledge about how to work. They are 'universally recognized scientific achievements that for a time provide model problems and solutions to a community of practitioners.'[32] During a period of normal science, scientists share a paradigm, which is transmitted from one generation to another. Contrary to Popper, Kuhn's historical evidence seemed to suggest that, during periods of normal science, researchers do not try to undermine the paradigm in which they are working. They are trying to articulate the paradigm, for instance, by finding new applications or through various 'puzzle-solving' activities. Solving scientific puzzles is different from what Popper had in mind: researchers do not search for unexpected findings or theories. They actually know what the outcome of their research will be, but they do not know from the outset how to achieve the expected outcome. The challenge is to accomplish these expected results by using various mathematical, experimental and conceptual tools.[33] Kuhn also noticed, again contra Popper, that scientists do not blame the paradigm when confronted with anomalous results. They might question their own calculations or they might blame the instruments they use. However, the confrontation with anomalous results does not seem to encourage researchers to question the broader framework in which they have hitherto been working. Scientists will start questioning the paradigm only when confronted with an enormous amount of counter-evidence.[34] This period of 'crisis' is followed by a discussion of which alternative paradigms might be more suitable. This leads to a period of 'scientific revolution' in which eventually one paradigm becomes victorious.[35]

Kuhn argued that his historical research showed that Popper had overstated the importance of 'occasional revolutionary episodes' at the expense of 'everyday research'. Most of the time, researchers do not work in ways Popper described and promoted. When they do, a crisis has preceded their activities.[36] Popper's reply to Kuhn was remarkably weak. For instance, he argued that

Kuhn's historical reconstruction was incorrect, but he failed to provide any proper historical evidence to back up this view.[37] Popper simply asserted that Kuhn's 'picture of science clashes with the facts as I see them. For there was, ever since antiquity, constant and fruitful discussion between the competing dominant theories of matter.'[38] Given the historical craft and accuracy underlying Kuhn's arguments, it was absurd to brush them aside like that. Other arguments by Popper were slightly stronger. For instance, he maintained that he had focused on what scientists ought to do, not on what some of them have done: he developed guidelines about how to proceed, regardless of whether or not most scientists actually worked in this way. Normal scientists had been taught badly; they were 'applied' rather than 'pure' scientists.[39] Closer scrutiny, however, shows that this counter-argument is also problematic. Firstly, it becomes increasingly difficult to sustain the view that scientists need to follow Popper's guidelines once we acknowledge that very few actually followed these rules, especially if, like Popper, we maintain that scientific progress has nevertheless been made. To prescribe, like Popper did, we need the history of science to be on our side, and Popper himself had used the history of the natural sciences to support his normative argument. It now turned out that his historical reconstruction was highly selective. He had focused on a few innovative theorists and had disregarded large chunks of 'normal science'. Secondly, Kuhn's argument was not merely descriptive or explanatory. There was also a prescriptive component to it. There are various passages in which he pointed out the benefits of normal science. During periods of normal science scientists are able to carry out their research without having to question too much. They are able to continue with their experiments and they may find some interesting results. 'We have . . . noted that once the reception of a common paradigm has freed the scientific community from the need to re-examine its first principles, the members of that community can concentrate exclusively upon the subtlest and most esoteric of the phenomena that concern it. Inevitably, that does increase both the effectiveness and the efficiency with which the group as a whole solves new problems.'[40] This would not have been possible if scientists continually followed Popper's guidelines. Popper's world would not have provided the stability that is necessary.

Popper also criticized Kuhn for paving the way for irrationalism and relativism. The reason for this accusation lay in two statements made by Kuhn. Firstly, Kuhn argued that, with every new paradigm, the world seemed to change. He talked about a 'gestalt switch' or religious conversion: people suddenly see things differently.[41] Kuhn held these views because he believed in a holistic theory of meaning and a discontinuity thesis. According to a holistic theory of meaning, the meaning of a term is dependent on the structure or paradigm in which it is embedded. For instance, the meaning of velocity depends on the paradigm we are using. The discontinuity thesis assumes that there is a rupture or epistemological break between paradigms. From the holistic perspective and the discontinuity thesis, it follows that, with every new paradigm, the meaning of a term shifts and a radically different world emerges. It becomes very difficult to compare scientific theories. Secondly, Kuhn argued that it does not make sense to say that, with time, scientific theories represent the world more accurately or are gradually approaching the truth. We are not representing the world any better, nor are we getting closer to the truth. This does not mean, however, that we cannot speak of progress in science. We can, but it is a different type of progress. Through time, we become more astute in manipulating our world and in solving scientific puzzles. With every new paradigm, our ability to solve intellectual puzzles increases.[42]

In this context, Popper accused Kuhn of adhering to the 'myth of the framework'. The myth of the framework assumes that rationality depends on a common language and a common set of assumptions. It presupposes that we can only have a rational discussion and criticism if we agree on fundamentals. If we do not share the fundamentals, then rational debate is not possible.[43] Popper strongly disagreed with this view. He acknowledged that a common framework makes a rational debate more plausible, and he also agreed that we always operate within a framework. He disagreed, however, with the view that the existence of different frameworks makes for the impossibility of communication between them. It might make it more difficult but not impossible. People are always able to break away from their framework. They will then enter a new framework but it will be a broader one. It is not the case that people are for ever stuck in their framework. It is also not true that different frameworks are so different that translation becomes impossible. Different frameworks always have enough in common so that people can compare and judge them regardless of which framework they belong to.[44]

How to make social science scientific

However limited Popper's knowledge about the state of the social sciences, he held strong views about how social scientists ought to operate. One of his recurrent statements is that the same method underlies the social and the natural sciences. Anti-naturalists tend to point out that the experimental method does not apply to the social sciences because we cannot reproduce identical experimental conditions; some go further in arguing that natural scientists restrict themselves largely to the study of 'closed' systems, whose conditions can be reproduced with change only in the causal variable under study, whereas social scientists confront a system which is inherently 'open' because of the innumerable simultaneous, imprecisely interdependent changes always occurring within it. They also argue that the differences in social environment are so vast that generalizations are confined to particular settings or periods. But Popper's riposte is that the variability of conditions also applies to the natural sciences, and that this variability is perfectly compatible with the method of trial and error.[45] Commenting on Hayek's views, Popper emphasized that other *prima facie* differences between the social and the natural sciences can also be disregarded. It has often been asserted that 'sympathetic imagination' or intuition plays a more significant role in the social sciences, that it is more difficult to predict concrete social situations than concrete cases in the natural world, or that the social is more complex than the natural world. Even if it is true that intuition comes into play in the creation of hypotheses in the social sciences, empirical hypotheses are still arrived at via deduction from general laws and initial conditions, the hypotheses are still testable empirically, and they are abandoned if such tests fail.

Likewise, although it is true that we are not able to predict accurately *concrete* social situations, it would be a gross error to assume that we are regularly able to do so in the natural sciences. With the exception of the solar system, we can only predict physical events placed under artificial experimental isolation. We are not able to predict the precise result of *concrete* phenomena, such as, for instance, weather conditions. Finally, it is not true in Popper's opinion that social situations are more complex than physical ones. This error is based partly on a misguided comparison between concrete social situations and experimental physical situations. Popper regards the two as incommensurable. It is also based on the erroneous assumption that the description of a social situation should incorporate descriptions of all mental and physical states of everybody involved. In fact, social science is less complicated than physics or chemistry, and social situations are less complex than physical ones. They are less complicated because people tend to act rationally. They hardly ever act completely rationally, but they do act more or less rationally, and this allows for the application of relatively simple models that approximate real life.[46] Ironically, Popper's assumption that the consequences of rational action are easier to model and predict than those of non-rational or habitual action has been challenged mainly within the economic literature.[47]

The unity of scientific method even extends to history, but this does not mean that we have to give up the distinction between the theoretical and historical sciences. The interest of history is in actual or specific events, whereas the interest of the theoretical sciences is in laws or generalizations. The theoretical sciences attempt to discover and test universal laws, whereas the historical sciences take various universal laws for granted while attempting to find and test singular statements. Many of those laws are so trivial that we do not feel the need to articulate them. Take, for example, a historian who writes that the immediate cause of the death of Anne Frank was that she was gassed in a concentration camp. The historian then assumes the universal law that all human beings die when they are exposed to such intense levels of gas, but this law is so obvious that he or she does not feel the need to state it explicitly. Not every tacit law needs to be so trivial. Some might be quite sophisticated sociological or social-psychological laws, such as de Tocqueville's statement that progress (rather than deterioration) in material conditions might lead to revolutionary movements. Nevertheless the historian tends to employ these laws implicitly, similar to the way in which practical science operates. A chemist, for instance, employs routine techniques to analyse a particular compound, and in so doing draws upon universal laws, which, as in the case of history, are not normally articulated. History is thus not unique in using universal laws implicitly to tackle a specific problem; it is intrinsic to any applied scientific activity.[48]

Popper insisted that, while historians cannot help introducing a selective point of view, this does not undermine the scientific status of their activities. Historical observation shaped by inappropriate preferences or prejudices on the part of the social scientist – like natural-world observation shaped by inappropriate theoretical presuppositions of the natural scientist – will be detected and rejected, because of the subjection of the hypotheses they generate to empirical test. Historians are selective in that they always write the kind of history that interests them – a history from a particular angle and with certain concerns in mind. They interpret history as a history of class struggle, or a history of religious clashes, or a history of nations and nationalism. It would be wrong, however, to assert that history is different from the natural sciences in this respect. After all, Popper rebuked what he called the 'bucket theory of mind', according to which science is a mere accumulation of raw data, and he suggested instead the 'searchlight theory of science', according to which what is made visible depends to some extent on the viewpoint of the scientist.[49] Some historians, however, pretend that they do not succumb to any preconceived view; they see themselves aiming at objectivity and simply holding on to the facts. Popper's point is that these historians are misguided in believing that their history is objective in that sense. Whether they intend to or not, historians will always present a history from a particular angle, but this in itself is not in opposition to the spirit of scientific inquiry.

As long as the theories are constructed so that they can be subjected to empirical scrutiny, the progress of scientific discovery is secured. Rather than denying their viewpoint, historians ought to acknowledge their angle and ought to be willing to shed their presuppositions if and when confronted with counter-evidence.[50] Whereas 'objective' history fails to recognize that history is always a narrative from a particular angle, 'historicism' makes the opposite mistake; it erroneously takes historical interpretations for theories. Historicism is defined as 'an approach to the social sciences which assumes that *historical prediction* is their principal aim, and which assumes that this aim is attainable by discovering the "rhythms" or the "patterns", the "laws" or the "trends" that underlie the evolution of society.'[51] Historicists take their particular angles, their particular views, as coherent theoretical constructions about the world, and when they find out that many events can be interpreted in that way, they see this as evidence of the truth-validity of the theory. For instance, Marxist historicists would *not* say that they interpret the past as a history of class struggle; they would say that *all* history *is* the history of class struggle, and the fact that their viewpoint can be applied to various situations is evidence, for them, that it is true. But nothing is further from the truth. The history of class struggle is simply a perspective, a fruitful one, but a viewpoint nevertheless. It is not a theory, and it is neither true nor false.[52]

We have seen so far that Popper criticized those who believe that the nature of the domain of historical inquiry is an impediment to adopting a scientific approach. But Popper was also appalled by the multitude of pseudo-scientific approaches to the social realm. There are various culprits, ranging from Sigmund Freud's psychoanalysis and Alfred Adler's 'individual psychology' to Marx's historical materialism. Like many others, the young Popper was seduced by the *prima facie* strength of these theories. The theories were regarded as having an extraordinary 'explanatory power': they were able to account for virtually everything, and verifications were found everywhere. But Popper soon realized that these strengths might reveal a serious weakness: the fact that they cannot be refuted. He took the example of a man who pushes a child into the water intending to drown it, and a man who goes out of his way to save a child from drowning.[53] Popper showed that both cases could be explained by using a Freudian and an Adlerian explanation. For Freudians, the first man suffered from such severe repression that it led to this disastrous act, whereas the second had sublimated his desires. For Adlerians, the first man suffered from a warped and destructive inferiority complex that manifested itself in this awful way, whereas the second man had the overwhelming desire to overcome the inferiority complex and so 'proved' himself to be worthwhile. The Marxist theory of history had similar failings. Some of Marx's predictions were falsified, but the followers then made ad hoc adjustments to the theory so as to make it irrefutable.[54]

The problem with historicism and utopianism

Marx's problem goes deeper than that; it lies with the way in which Marx employed history. Like Hegel, Marx was what Popper called a 'historicist', and there are two components to the Popperian notion of historicism. Firstly, it postulates the existence of laws of social evolution and our ability, given the right methods, to detect them; and, secondly, it presupposes that these laws of social evolution will allow us to foretell the future. It also assumes, of course, that it is desirable to know the future because we can then adjust our political actions accordingly. 'Utopianists' exhibit historicist tendencies: they try to imagine different social institutions from the ones under which they live, and, for them, thinking about new forms of action ought to be done within the contours set by the iron laws of history. Note that, because of its alleged predictive value, historicism is often portrayed as scientific; it certainly presents itself that way, as in 'scientific socialism' or 'scientific Marxism'. Marx's dialectical theory of history is indeed an example par excellence, though historicism is not limited to Marxism. G. W. F. Hegel, Auguste Comte and J. S. Mill also exhibited historicist tendencies, as before them did Heraclitus, Hesiod and Plato, and even the Jewish notion of the chosen people is rooted in historicist thinking.[55]

It is no coincidence that historicism has so many followers, and from different sides of the political spectrum, religious people and atheists alike. It is appealing to people because it allows them to avoid taking responsibility for their purpose in life: they do not have to face making choices because history has already made these for them.[56] Popper strongly objected to these attempts at uncovering universal statements regarding historical development. For him the evolution of human society is a unique phenomenon, which therefore allows for a singular historical statement, and singular statements are not universal laws. Some historicists would counter-argue that these historical descriptive statements allow for the inference of hypotheses regarding trends, directions or tendencies, and that these hypotheses can then be tested at some point in the future. For Popper this is an erroneous argument because trends are not laws: while trends refer to existential statements, laws are universal statements. Any trend so far may alter in the future. In *The Open Universe* and other publications Popper develops this argument further. The course of history is dependent on knowledge, but it is not possible to predict the fruits of the growth of knowledge, because to predict what we will know tomorrow would mean to acquire that knowledge now, and that acquisition would raise new problems and more knowledge for tomorrow. A variation of this argument is the paradox of self-prediction. Assuming that we have perfect knowledge of present and past initial conditions, we will not be able to infer our own future predictions, because to predict our own predictions is already to affect what will be predicted.[57]

Historicists are of the opinion that the identification of trends informs them about the future, but Popper disagreed. He suggested that we draw a distinction between prophecies and predictions, a distinction ignored by historicists. Whereas prophecies are unconditional statements ('X will occur'), predictions are conditional ('X will occur if Y occurs'). Historicists inform us about the future in that they make prophecies – not predictions – and prophecies are non-falsifiable, as opposed to predictions, which can be refuted. So historicist claims are so vague that they are indeed able to account for anything, but remember that statements that do not exclude events fail to explain anything.[58] Our task is to identify the conditions under which particular trends occur rather than to present the trends as unconditional regularities that will inevitably stretch into the future. Take, for example, the Marxist statement that there is a trend towards an accumulation of means of production. There is no reason why this trend ought necessarily to continue in the future because it depends on various conditions: for instance, the trend might be reversed in a rapidly decreasing population.[59] We could, of course, counter-argue that it is perfectly legitimate to infer prophecies from predictions as long as we are operating in well-isolated, stationary and recurrent systems. Popper agrees, and mentions the solar system as a case in point: it is a stable and repetitive system, and it therefore allows for accurate eclipse prophecies. But there are very few other systems that exhibit those features, and modern society certainly does not. Social conditions are constantly changing, and this makes for the impossibility of accurate prophecies.[60]

Popper agreed with Immanuel Kant that science should not simply be a matter of 'idle curiosity', and that the need and desire to tackle practical problems has led to most significant scientific advances. We should, of course, not yield to the opposite (and equally preposterous) view that science is worthwhile only if it proves to be a good investment. But most major scientific advances start with problems – often *practical* problems – and Popper gleaned from Hayek's work that this principle applies as much to the social as to the natural sciences.[61] Not any form of social engineering will do, however. Popper recommended 'piecemeal social engineering' as opposed to 'holistic or utopian social engineering'. Piecemeal technologists acknowledge that few social institutions are consciously designed; most are unintended outcomes of various forms of action. Even if consciously designed, they may turn out very differently from what was intended. Piecemeal engineers realize that their intervention, like any action, may lead to significant unforeseen effects, and some of these might even contradict the intentions behind the intervention. They also realize, though, that it is possible and desirable for us to learn from our mistakes. Faced with the effects encountered, piecemeal strategists are more than willing to reassess the theories that guided their intervention. Rather than pretending to know all the answers to our political problems, piecemeal engineers recognize the fallibility of their views and the need to learn from our errors. But they are willing not simply to adjust their theories when confronted with practical difficulties; they will also try out their theories in small-scale experiments before applying them on a wider scale. One of the pivotal functions of social science is to assist social policy by testing theories and related policies before implementing them.[62]

Contrast this with utopian engineers, who have a blueprint of society, and who want to implement that project *in toto*. They do not see the point in carrying out small-scale experiments because they cannot be generalized; social experiments only have value if they are carried out in their entirety. Contrary to the piecemeal approach, utopian engineers will not take into account that their project might turn out to be somehow flawed – that it might lead to undesirable effects. They fail to acknowledge that any intervention leads to unintended effects and that the greater the intervention the more striking the effects. Utopian engineers are not satisfied with small changes; they want to change society as a whole, and, by creating a social *tabula rasa*, end up destroying the institutions that would prevent or at least limit the extent of bad rule.[63] Furthermore, for their centralized policies to be effective, they ought to be able to centralize the knowledge that is distributed across society, but Hayek and others had demonstrated that this is an impossible feat. So the future will always have surprises in store for utopian planners, and they will, ironically, be forced to implement the piecemeal method to tackle the various problems. Popper used derogatory terms such as 'piecemeal improvisation' and 'unplanned planning' to refer to the various ways in which utopian social engineers are continually forced to repair things but are unprepared to do so.[64]

We might be inclined to infer from the multitude of ad hoc repairs that the utopian engineers are questioning and amending their own blueprint just like their piecemeal counterparts, but nothing is further from the truth. First, utopian engineering involves such grand-scale change that it becomes virtually impossible to trace back the causes of certain problems. The utopian engineer therefore cannot learn from his errors. We might therefore say that both are involved in experiments, but very different types of experiments. We can indeed use the word experiments to refer either to the way in which we test our hypotheses by comparing the results obtained with those expected, or to an activity whose outcome is unclear to those involved in it. Whereas piecemeal engineering draws on the former type of experiments, utopian projects use the latter. Second, utopian engineers are so persuaded by their blueprint that they will defend it against criticisms or evidence to the contrary; they will often do so by using force. Unable to centralize the knowledge that is dispersed in society, they will use propaganda to eliminate the multitude of individual differences and, by so doing, reduce rational criticism. It is therefore not surprising that utopian thinking and authoritarianism tend to go hand in hand. The inability of utopianism to recognize its own fallibility has indeed disastrous political consequences.[65]

Methodological individualism

Popper's methodological prescriptions are opposed to 'naïve collectivism' and the 'conspiracy theory of society'. Naïve collectivism assumes that the social sciences study social wholes such as social classes or nations. Naïve collectivism goes hand in hand with 'sociological determinism' or 'sociologism', which reduces human action to social influences. For Popper, these social wholes are not to be treated as empirical objects – they are ideal objects whose existence depends on theoretical presuppositions – and not every act is to be explained by social forces.[66] The conspiracy theory of society makes the opposite error in that it assumes that all significant social phenomena are the product of direct design by powerful individuals. Conspiracy theories have been around for a very long time – for instance, the ancient myth about the Homeric gods who were responsible for the Trojan War. Once in power, those who believe in the conspiracy theory sometimes use their force to combat alleged 'conspiracies' and, by doing so, unintentionally bring about the validity of their theory. But there are, in reality, very few of those conspiracies, and, more importantly, even fewer of them turn out to be successful.[67] This brings us to Popper's view, possibly influenced by Carl Menger, that the main task of the social sciences is to trace the unintended effects of purposive actions. So Popper is a 'methodological individualist' in that, firstly, he takes most social phenomena to be explained by referring to individual actions rather than any supra-individual entity, and that, secondly, he recognizes that most of these phenomena end up differently from what any of the individuals intended. Whereas we would have expected him, in this context, to find an ally in the likes of Alexis de Tocqueville or Max Weber, he chose Marx of all people as an exponent of the search for unanticipated effects. This is, of course, even more surprising given that he spent so much time rebuking Marx's holism, utopianism and historicism. But Popper's point is that *some* aspects of Marx are fine, and that Marxism has substituted for them the problematic ones.[68]

Let us distinguish the various components of Popper's methodological individualism. His starting point was that people act purposively. Few would disagree with that statement, but Popper then made two further claims. The first one is that, on the whole, people act rationally; they do not always act rationally, but they do so most of the time. The second claim is that people do not act in a vacuum; they operate in a particular context or situation. This brings us to Popper's notion of 'situational logic', a notion that initially acquired prominence in marginal utility economics. By 'logic of the situation', Popper meant that social action is to a large extent to be explained in terms of the situation in which it emerges. People will act differently in different situations because every situation sets its own constraints and possibilities. This in turn brings us to what Popper in *The Poverty of Historicism* called the 'zero method'. Similar to what J. Marschak called the 'null hypothesis' and Hayek the 'compositive method', the zero method works in two steps. It first creates a model that assumes complete rationality (and also possibly complete information) by all individuals involved, and subsequently compares the actual behaviour of people with the behaviour predicted by the model. For Popper, the possibility of using the zero method is probably the most crucial, if not the single, difference between the social and the natural sciences, although there are a few instances in the natural sciences in which a similar method is adopted.[69]

In an article, 'The Rationality Principle', originally published in French, Popper further developed these ideas. He argued that, in social research, we ought to construct models that assume that people act appropriately to the situation as they see it. Note that he writes about situations as seen from the viewpoint of the individuals involved, not as conceived by some external observer. To emphasize this point he took Winston's Churchill's war recollections. Churchill showed that a lot of decisions by generals during World War II were inadequate or even irrational.[70] Popper's point was that these decisions might well have been inadequate given what we now know, but they were probably perfectly rational given what the generals perceived to be the situation at the time. Popper defended himself against those critics who argued that he regards the rationality principle as *a priori* valid. Popper insisted that he certainly does not regard the principle as *a priori* valid; it would be absurd to claim that individuals always act in a manner appropriate to the situation in which they find themselves. But if the principle is false, why use it? Popper's answer is that, although untrue, the rationality principle remains a good approximation of the truth and, when our model is refuted, we should try to avoid blaming the rationality principle. The reason why we should not attribute responsibility for the refutation to the rationality principle is that we know it is false anyway, so we would not gain much by blaming it. We are bound to gain more from blaming the situational model.[71]

The attention to the unintended consequences of purposive action ties in neatly with Popper's naturalism. What is typical of scientific laws is that they state what cannot be done, and this is most obvious in the natural sciences. For instance, one of the consequences of the second law of thermodynamics is that we cannot build a machine that is entirely efficient. But the same applies to scientific laws about the social realm. Falsifiable laws have practical value in that they postulate what cannot be accomplished in the social world: for instance, 'you cannot accomplish full employment without inflation', or 'you cannot introduce agricultural tariffs and at the same time reduce the cost of living'.[72] It is possible to rephrase the laws in terms of unintended consequences. For instance, the first law suggests that pursuing full employment may unintentionally cause inflation, and the second law indicates that the introduction of agricultural tariffs unintentionally increases the cost of living. Note also that these laws are refutable. It takes one empirical instance where full employment goes together with zero inflation to refute the first law. It takes one case where agricultural tariffs are accompanied by a reduced cost of living for the second law to be refuted. To give an example outside economics: 'you cannot introduce a political reform without strengthening the opposing forces, to a degree roughly in ratio to the scope of the reform.' Other examples include Plato's dictum that 'you cannot make a successful revolution if the ruling class is not weakened by internal dissension or defeat in war', or Lord Acton's 'law of corruption' which says that 'the temptation to misuse one's power increases with the amount of power wielded.'[73]

Contemporary rational choice theory (or rational action theory, as some prefer to call it) can be seen as the logical extension of Popper's outlook on the social sciences.[74] Many rational choice theorists explicitly refer to Popper or falsificationism as a philosophical basis for their views. Rational choice theory explains social life as the intended and unintended outcome of rational, purposive action. The starting point is that, in general, people act not only intentionally, but also rationally. People act rationally if they have a clear preference ordering and if they have rational beliefs about how to pursue those preferences and about the sacrifices and benefits this pursuit would entail. Rational beliefs are not necessarily true beliefs. A belief is rational if, given various constraints (for instance, time constraint), people have made an effort to gather the appropriate information. Take, for instance, undergraduate students who have to decide whether they want to work or continue studying after their degree. The students will obtain information, by going to open days, checking the web, looking through brochures and talking to relevant people. They will try to ascertain the costs and benefits of different courses of action. This does not mean that the information acquired is correct, but they have come by rational beliefs about what to expect. Rational choice theorists are particularly interested in the interplay between purposive, rational action and unintended effects. For instance, faced with overwhelming evidence of the shortage of corporate lawyers, many students might decide to go to law school, expecting a lot of work and high salaries. Because so many students think along these lines, they unintentionally produce an excess of lawyers, resulting in a shortage of positions and lower salaries. For each individual, the decision to go to law school was perfectly rational, but the aggregate outcome contradicts the reasons why they wanted to become lawyers.

Evaluation

It is not difficult to see the attraction of Popper's writings for those who believe passionately in the legacy of the *Aufklärung*. Like Habermas, Popper sketched the importance of critical debate in the project of Enlightenment philosophy and in science in particular. In spite of their differences, both describe the transition towards modernity in terms of the implementation of procedures of open discussion, criticism and defence (what Habermas called 'communicative rationality'), and both identify the idea of an unconstrained debate among equals as the pillar and hope of contemporary civilization.[75] The notion of communicative rationality is, indeed, central to Popper's political writings, in particular to his distinction between 'open' and 'closed' societies. What distinguishes the former from the latter is not simply that it tolerates dissent, but also that it engenders that lack of consensus through rules of open debate and criticism. It seems to me that the open society is therefore 'open' in two ways. It is open in the sense that it tends not to exclude or sanction any particular views except for the ones that might undermine the open debate itself. It is also open as in 'open-ended': although the procedures, through which decisions are reached, might be more or less fixed so as to allow for open debate, the actual decisions are never 'given'. This contrasts with the closed society in which alternative views are prohibited and the future is a relatively closed one: its future path is to a large extent set and non-negotiable.

The very same notion of communicative rationality also underscores Popper's philosophy of science. First, this already becomes apparent in what Popper had to say about the cognitive structure that underlies closed societies. For Popper, closed societies are a corollary of closed systems of thought. Remember that utopian thinkers produce closed systems of thought in that they portray a perfect world and are unable to envisage the possibility of imperfections. So closed societies, based on these blueprints, often employ authoritarian means so as to protect their ideal vision against obvious real-life falsifications, and it is precisely the inability to recognize the incurable openness of the future that makes utopian thinking the handmaiden of a closed society. In Habermasian parlance, utopian thinking embodies the antithesis of undistorted communication and is, for that reason, likely to lead to those forms of government that stifle or repress the very same ideal of a 'discursive will-formation'. Second, for Popper, a falsifiable theory is formulated so that it *can* be scrutinized and criticized by the members of the scientific community with regard to its empirical validity. A non-falsifiable theory is immune to such examination, and is therefore likely to survive the most thorough procedures of open debate and criticism. The progress of science depends on successful scrutiny by the scientific community, on the successful implementation of procedures of open discussion and criticism, and ultimately on whether or not the theories can be the subject of this debate. Falsifiability is the cognitive counterpart of communicative rationality: only if theories are refutable does the power of communicative rationality take full force.

Note that, for someone who promoted open debate and criticism, Popper was remarkably restrictive about what that forum in the scientific realm may entail, confining the debate to one primarily about the empirical validity of hypotheses. This warrants two questions, the first of which is whether, as Popper assumed, empirical testing is the firm footing on which matters of cognitive validity are decided. We now know that the answer is no. A substantial part of Popper's critique of inductivism was that observational statements are fallible because they depend on theoretical assumptions that may be mistaken, but he refused to admit that this sheds serious doubt on his own methodological prescriptions. It is a blatant contradiction to opt, as Popper did, for a falsificationist methodology and to recognize the fallibility of observations that form the base of falsifications. It is therefore not surprising that, most of the time, scientists do not attempt to falsify their theoretical frameworks, and, when confronted with 'falsifications', decide to ignore the results.[76] It is wrong for Popper to dismiss these activities as simply unfortunate bouts of irrationality.[77] The anomalous experimental findings may well be due to the fallibility of the auxiliary theoretical assumptions that accompanied the observations. Also, the refusal on the part of scientists to question the theoretical structure in which they operate allows them simply 'to get on' with mundane research, which is not unimportant altogether.[78] It has also been shown, in some cases, that, if scientists had operated according to Popperian principles, they would not have made the progress that they did make: if they had toed Popper's party line, they would have abandoned research programmes that later turned out to be fruitful.[79]

The second question is whether researchers use criteria other than empirical testing to decide upon the validity of a theory or to judge between theories. The answer is an equivocally positive one. It matters, for instance, whether a theory has breadth or depth, whether it allows for counter-intuitive insights or, simply, whether it opens up new imaginary worlds.[80] This is especially relevant in the social sciences. For instance, when Popper criticizes Freud for producing theories that are immunized against falsification, he does not appreciate fully the obvious value or strengths of Freud's theory, nor does he take into account its place within the intellectual context of his time. Freud's psychoanalytic theory not only provided powerful insights into the human psyche and proved relevant to various aspects of human life, it also allowed people at the time to see things in a very different light, challenging, among other things, the widespread assumption of a Cartesian self-sufficient subject. Conversely, there are numerous contributions in the social sciences that are perfectly refutable, that have actually been corroborated *ad nauseam*, but which are, in the light of our cultural understanding today, ridiculously trifling or superficial. It would be preposterous to regard them as 'superior' to psychoanalysis or Marxism, which have after all helped to revolutionize our thinking about ourselves and about society.

There is also a striking contradiction between Popper's appeal for scientific indeterminism, on the one hand, and his falsificationist agenda, on the other. While pointing out the incurable openness of the universe,[81] he somehow failed to realize the extent to which similar arguments may undercut the validity of empirical testing for deciding upon the falsehood of empirical statements. This problem is particularly acute in the case of the social sciences, because social systems are open, probably more so, or at least more visibly so, than natural systems. Popper realized one consequence of the relative openness of social processes, namely that it becomes extremely difficult to predict the future, however much information one may have about the past. But he failed to take seriously another consequence; namely that we cannot infer straightforward conclusions from falsifications or corroborations, for the simple reason that we cannot anticipate (and therefore we cannot control for) the various generative mechanisms that may interfere with the observations. This is, for instance, a problem when we deal with a scientific law that stipulates some causal mechanism between variables. It would be rash to infer from the absence of the expected correlation between the variables that the law does not hold; the observed 'falsification' might well result from the interference of other mechanisms.

Equally contradictory is Popper's distrust of prophecies, on the one hand, and his strong appeal for scientific predictions, on the other. Remember that one of his pivotal arguments against historicist prophecies was that they are not falsifiable, that they are constructed so that they cannot be challenged on the basis of empirical evidence. No observation can refute these unconditional statements, Popper reminded the reader, because, if they have not been 'confirmed' yet, they can always be so in the future. But, however convincing this objection to prophecies, Popper failed to realize that, at least in the social realm, his argument can also be extended to predictions. Even if we stipulate the conditions under which a phenomenon will occur, we have not committed ourselves to any statement regarding *when* it will occur, save, of course, for the fact that it will occur *after* the conditions have been met. In the social world, faced with the right conditions, it remains unclear how much time needs to pass before the absence of any sign that the prediction will come about can be safely interpreted as an empirical refutation of the conditional statement. Needless to say, the inability to 'read' empirical data becomes even more acute in the case of probabilistic laws. Take, for instance, de Tocqueville's conditional statement that revolutions are more likely to emerge when people's material conditions have improved. Assuming we are confronted with rising material conditions and no sign of a revolution, it remains unclear how long an absence of revolution should finally lead us to decide that de Tocqueville's statement has been refuted.

There is an inconsistency between Popper's recognition that theoretical presuppositions necessarily guide historical research, on the one hand, and his suggestion that the social sciences emulate the methods of the natural sciences, on the other. Remember that Popper objected to the myth of theory-independent historical research, and his insistence that any research is theory-driven. But while Popper was right to recognize that the theory-laden nature of observation applies to both the social and the natural sciences, he did not seem to be willing to acknowledge the differences in degree between the two and how these differences might jeopardize his project. Anyone remotely familiar with social research is aware of how researchers not only attribute different meanings to the same concepts, but also use different techniques to measure the same thing. Popper's favourite example is the economic law that you cannot accomplish full employment without inflation, but he discarded the fact that economists disagree about what full employment is and how to measure it – for instance, whether we should we include part-time employment in the figures of employment. Likewise, Plato's law of revolutions depends on what we mean by 'revolution' and 'successful' revolution, how much 'internal dissension' and what kind of 'war' we are talking about, and finally how we are to measure all this. There are so many steps between Plato's dictum and the empirical research, so many decisions to be made on the way, that it is hard to see whether any empirical research can ever establish the authority to act as a clear-cut empirical refutation of the statement as presented.

Now that we have briefly discussed Popper's own examples of scientific laws or hypotheses in the social sciences, it might be appropriate to subject them to further scrutiny. It is remarkable that, for someone with such gusto for clarity and precision and who accused others relentlessly of being too obscure or imprecise, some of his own examples are vague or tautologous, and would not begin to match his own strict criteria of falsifiability. It is ironic that, after viciously attacking the nebulous language of Hegel and Marx and their deceitful scientific pretence, Popper found no better than to suggest developing hypotheses such as 'you cannot make a revolution without causing a reaction'.[82] It is difficult to imagine that it did not occur to him that this statement is so ridiculously general that it can never be refuted, that it is not clear what kind of reaction he is talking about, and that virtually any social phenomenon may be treated as a reaction. Likewise, the hypothesis that 'you cannot introduce a political reform without causing some repercussions that are undesirable from the point of view of the ends aimed at'[83] is, given the absence of a time specification, probably true in virtue of its logical structure. Again, it is difficult to see what the potential falsifiers might be. Other examples, such as the one about the incompatibility of full employment and zero inflation, exclude so little that their empirical content is too low.

There is a contradiction between the precise nature of Popper's commitment to the rationality principle, on the one hand, and his appeal for a falsificationist philosophy of social science, on the other. As we mentioned before, while Popper was aware that the rationality principle, as a universal claim, is incorrect, he advised researchers not to blame the rationality principle when confronted with empirical counter-evidence. Popper's argumentation for this position was hardly convincing, suggesting that we are bound to gain more from blaming the situational model than from impugning the rationality principle, which we already know not to be true. This rationale reveals two problems. First, it shows a general problem with critical rationalism: if a hypothesis has empirically been refuted, and assuming that we know that the auxiliary assumptions are not to be blamed, it still remains unclear which aspect of the theory ought to be adjusted. Second, it is from the viewpoint of falsificationism blatantly absurd to protect a principle that we know is incorrect. It is contradictory to say that we are certain to 'learn' more from adjusting the situational model, while admitting that it is perfectly plausible that the model might not be responsible for the empirical refutation. It also shows that Popper was not practising what he preached: in this instance at least, his recommendations seemed much closer to Lakatos's views of science, treating the rationality principle as a 'hard core', to be protected as long as the research programme proves to be fruitful.[84]

In chapters 5 and 6, I will argue more broadly against methodological naturalism. Before doing so, however, I will draw attention in the next chapter to critical realism, an approach that also adheres to methodological naturalism. Like Popper, critical realists are preoccupied with what characterizes science and distinguishes it from pseudo-science. Like Popper, critical realists assume that the social sciences can learn a lot from the natural sciences. Like Popper, they take the role of social science to be mainly about explaining, but they have a different notion of what explanation and causality are. They are less interested in falsifiability, and indeed less critical of the likes of Marx and Freud, whom they regard as very productive contributors to social and psychological research. They also differ from Popper in that they are far more preoccupied with ontological issues – with the nature of reality – and one of their main points is that ontological positions should not be derived from epistemological ones.

Further reading

Popper's views on the philosophy of science can be found in his *The Logic of Scientific Discovery* and his *Conjectures and Refutations,* of which chapters 15 to 20 are devoted to social and political issues. *The Poverty of Historicism* and some sections of both volumes of *The Open Society and its Enemies* deal with the philosophy of the social sciences. For his views about rational forms of explanation and the zero principle, Popper's 'The Rationality Principle' in *A Pocket Popper,* edited by D. Miller, is a must. There are various introductory works on Popper, of which Anthony O'Hear's *Karl Popper* is one of the most impressive. O'Hear is on the whole sympathetic but without ever losing his critical touch, and chapter 8 discusses partly Popper's philosophy of the social sciences. Popper's autobiographical work *Unended Quest* can also serve as an introduction, although his self-congratulatory style can be irritating at times. For those who wish to read about the intellectual influences on the early Popper, I recommend Hacohen's *Karl Popper: The Formative Years, 1902–1945.* He is able to show that Popper's early work is steeped in a tradition of progressive politics. There are not many books that deal substantially with Popper's views on the social sciences. Colin Simkin's

Popper's Views on Natural and Social Science is one of the exceptions; the second part of the book is a summary of Popper's philosophy of social science and gives a comprehensive overview of how others criticized, adopted or adjusted his views. Simkin's strength lies in elaborating the link between Popper's views and that of some leading economists, but the drawback of his approach is that, as a one-time colleague of Popper and a life-long friend, he remains uncritical of Popper's views. In contrast, Gregory Currie and Alan Musgrave's edited collection, *Popper and the Human Sciences*, contains some critical contributions. The large bulk of the articles in that book focus on Popper's political theory, but Alan Chalmers's and Peter Urbach's articles tackle issues in the philosophy of the social sciences. The link between Popper and economics is further developed in Neil de Marchi's edited collection *The Popperian Legacy in Economics*. Popper's criticisms of Marxism provoked a long-drawn-out controversy, and Maurice Cornforth's *The Open Philosophy and the Open Society* is a cogent defence of Marx's theory of society against Popper's fierce criticisms.

4
Critical Realism

Introduction

With the demise of logical positivism and critical rationalism in the second half of the twentieth century, both the natural and the social sciences faced a philosophical vacuum. There were, schematically speaking, two responses to this void. Some philosophers accentuated what they saw as the relativist implications of Kuhn's work. They maintained that the pursuit of *the* successful scientific method is a wild-goose chase, something that can never be achieved successfully. Their point was not that positivism and falsificationism were misguided about the nature of this method; rather it is simply a Sisyphean task to try to establish this universal algorithm in the first place. This view was introduced by Paul Feyerabend in his provocative *Against Method* and, subsequently, articulated more subtly by Richard Rorty.[1] Others dismissed this position as unnecessarily defeatist and dangerously irrational. While they agreed that logical atomism and falsificationism were flawed, they maintained that it is still worthwhile to attempt to make explicit the method which most successful scientific activities, in the social or natural sciences, have in common. Previous philosophies of science asked the right question; they answered it wrongly. They were right to pursue the issue of demarcation between science and non-science, but they were mistaken about how to go about finding those boundaries.

Taking the latter position was braver than might appear at first glance. Faced with both the recurrent failures of subsequent forms of naturalism and the early signs of a postmodernist bandwagon, it was quite audacious to postulate that there is a single method of inquiry after all, one that it is applicable to both social and natural sciences. So when, from the 1970s onwards, some academics, presenting themselves as realists or critical realists, tried to salvage the naturalist project while taking on board that knowledge is a social construct, it was, indeed, a bold step to make, and one worthy of careful consideration. Not that it has received a lot of coverage since its arrival. Or, more precisely, it did, but not in mainstream philosophical circles. Although critical realism is by any account a philosophical doctrine, most strait-laced philosophers have been remarkably indifferent to it. With its attention to social theory and its penchant for holistic reasoning, critical realism was regarded as well outside the contours of mainstream analytical philosophy. It did catch the attention of sociologists, and also, more unexpectedly, of a group of historians, social psychologists and economists. Sociologists felt that realism, in contrast to logical positivism or critical rationalism, represented more veraciously the methods which they employed. Also, the realist attention to social theory struck a chord with the sociological community, especially because some of the realist views on social theory, such as the transformational model of social action, were remarkably close to significant theoretical developments within sociology.[2] In particular, critical realism provided a philosophical base for those sociologists who had been schooled in Marxist structuralism or in evolutionary theory. The impact of realism in the other disciplines has been more moderate. Influenced by the Annales School, some historians saw realism as a foundation for their non-positivist approach that breaks with the *histoire événementielle* (the history of events or of great personalities who shaped the past). Several psychologists regarded realism as a base for a new methodology that treats people as self-steering and rule-employing individuals; others used it to defend psychoanalysis. Finally, heterodox economists see realism as a philosophical support for their disenchantment with mainstream economics and its preoccupation with quantification, deductivism and econometrics.

Critical realism has not been around for very long. Among the intellectual ancestors of the movement are Mary Hesse and Rom Harré. By the early 1960s, they had drawn attention away from Hempel's logical deductive view of scientific theories and pointed instead at the role of models and analogies.[3] Harré has since moved away from his early commitment to realism, is increasingly showing affinity with a social constructivist and discursivist agenda for the social sciences, and has of late distanced himself from what he calls the 'critical realist crowd'.[4] Roy Bhaskar, initially Harré's pupil, wrote two texts that are now considered to be cornerstones of the critical realist doctrine. They are *A Realist Theory of Science*, first published in 1975, and *The Possibility of Naturalism*, which came out four years later.[5] The former develops a transcendental argument to promote a realist approach to science; the latter uses this philosophy to discuss the nature of social science. Around the same time Russell Keat and John Urry wrote *Social Theory as Science* with similar ideas to Bhaskar's.[6] Since the 1980s a number of social scientists have further developed these ideas, among whom are Margaret Archer and Ted Benton in social theory, Derek Layder, Peter Manicas, Andrew Sayer and William Outhwaite in the philosophy of the social sciences, Tony Lawson in the methodology of economics and Christopher Lloyd in history.[7] Gradually, aligned contributions to the philosophy of science, such as those of Nancy Cartwright, were integrated within a critical realist framework. In psychology early work by Harré and Paul Secord attempted to merge realist philosophical insights with a Wittgensteinian social psychology; later D. Will would use critical realism to defend psychoanalysis against positivist criticisms.[8] From the mid-1980s onwards, critical realists such as Roy Bhaskar and Andrew Collier explained how their doctrine is a philosophical platform for a Marxist view of society; others followed on from this and argued that critical realism is a plausible base for a feminist critique.[9] Around the same time, a group of scholars around Harré started to explore the link between his realist agenda and a selectionist theory of social change.[10] A similar evolutionary research programme also underscores Geoff Hodgson's contributions to economics and David Harvey's to sociology; both tried to merge insights from chaos and complexity theory with critical realism.[11] In the course of the last decade Bhaskar extended his project by elaborating on the relationship between realism, dialectics and, more controversially, Eastern philosophy.[12] This latest journey has to some extent split the critical realist camp: some disciples regard his *From East to West* as a deviation from the original creed, while others are more sympathetic.[13] But this does not mean that critical realism is facing a crisis. Since the early 1990s a Centre for Critical Realism has been founded, and an annual conference is being held. The realist position is well represented in academic journals, especially (though certainly not exclusively) the *Journal of Social Behaviour* and the *Cambridge Journal of Economics*. If anything, critical realism seems very much in the ascendant.

In spite of Bhaskar's esoteric language, it is not difficult to see the appeal critical realism has had for social researchers. The new creed purports to establish social research as a *scientific* endeavour, in many respects on a par with the natural sciences, and it manages to do so without relying on a heavily discredited deductive-nomological outlook.[14] As a matter of fact, it does so while providing a long overdue cogent critique of positivist epistemology, and, significantly, one that avoids the looming spectre of relativism. In contrast with poststructuralism, which conceives of knowledge as forever entangled in (and unable to transcend) intricate power relations, critical realism reaffirms the emancipatory status of the social sciences. If properly conceived (i.e., carried out according to realist principles), the social sciences not only provide superior explanatory devices, but also help free people from previous constraints.[15] They may not be a sufficient condition for emancipation but they are necessary for it. So critical realism asserts both the scientific and the critical potential of social research, and therefore provides a welcome boost for the morale of social researchers, especially at a time when their activities have come under criticism. In addition, critical realism seems to confirm what a lot of social scientists are already doing. With the exception of highly descriptive forms of research and possibly mainstream economics, there are remarkably few pieces of empirical social research that are not somehow endorsed by the realist perspective. Structural Marxism is rehabilitated; so is psychoanalysis.[16] After being treated as a poor second to the natural sciences, now the social sciences are told that many of their practitioners have been getting it right anyway.

Realism, reality and causality

The first question that needs to be addressed is in what sense, if at all, is critical realism 'realist'. It is realist in both a strong and a weak sense of the word. It is realist in a weak sense in that it assumes that there is an external reality that exists independently of people's descriptions, and, in particular, of the conditions under which people gain access to it. It is realist in a strong sense in that it assumes that scientists are, in principle, able to gain access to this reality, though critical realists acknowledge that scientists can be mistaken in their assertions on this score. So, for critical realists, it is blatantly erroneous to say that there is no such thing as reality, or to argue that we cannot possibly gain access to it. It is equally misleading to regard theories as merely instrumental devices or acts of rhetoric. Those statements are, for critical realists, unfortunate shades of the spectre of postmodernism, a doctrine which most of them despise vehemently.[17] The realism advocated by critical realists is a metaphysical or transcendental one in that it tries to assess what the nature of reality must be for successful scientific, experimental practices to be possible. In this respect realists are indebted to Immanuel Kant's treatment of David Hume's empirical stance. Kant agreed with Hume that all scientific knowledge ought to be based on sense experience, but he continued with a transcendental argument by asking what *a priori* categories must exist for a coherent explanation of sense experience to be possible. Note that critical realists turn Kant's reasoning upside down: the realist question 'what must reality be like for science to be possible?' is substituted for the idealist 'what must the categories be like for science to be possible?' While there are a few critical realists who take a more overtly Kantian position,[18] most of them would indeed side with Bhaskar when he describes his transcendental argument as distinct from Kant's idealism. They would point out that they avoid what they describe as the 'epistemic fallacy' – that is, the assumption that ontological issues can be reduced to epistemological ones.[19] Rather than arguing that what we can know to exist depends on what we can know, realists advise that we infer what the world must be like from the existence of scientific knowledge. In short, critical realists pride themselves on avoiding the pitfalls of both radical empiricism, according to which reality can only be attributed to entities that are immediately accessible to observation, and transcendental idealism, according to which reality is only accessible to people as an individual or social construction.[20]

To validate their realist credentials critical realists draw a distinction between 'transitive' and 'intransitive' objects of knowledge.[21] Transitive objects of knowledge are like Aristotle's 'material causes', tools available to the researcher, such as previously established facts, or antecedent methods and theories. Intransitive objects refer to the 'real' events, structures and mechanisms that make up the world. Examples are planet rotations, molecular structures, fertility rates and suicide patterns. They all exist independent of people's knowledge of them.[22] Bhaskar then points out an interesting asymmetry. While it is possible to conceive of the existence of intransitive objects without people's knowledge of them, it is infeasible to envisage the production of knowledge about intransitive objects without the use of transitive objects. Scientists indeed rely on formerly established cognitive tools in that they regularly employ analogies with and models of familiar phenomena to account for novel ones. For instance, blood circulation has been articulated in terms of a hydraulic model or society in evolutionary terms. It is now possible to rephrase the differences between critical realism on the one hand and transcendental idealism and empiricism on the other. Critical realism is at variance with transcendental idealism in taking the objects of knowledge to be intransitive as opposed to transitive, and it opposes empiricism in treating the intransitive realm as layered, not simply limited to the instantly observable. In other words, while transcendental idealism erroneously downplays the fact that there is a reality unmediated by cognitive or discursive practices, empiricism fails to attribute reality to those layers that are not immediately observable.

Realists react against what they describe as a 'Humean conception of causality'.[23] I will not discuss the extent to which the realist depiction of a 'Humean concept of causality' corresponds to Hume's concept of causality. Suffice it to say that this is a point of contention, and that even some self-proclaimed realists doubt whether Bhaskar's depiction of Hume as an anti-realist is correct.[24] Let us for the sake of argument follow Bhaskar's reconstruction. According to Bhaskar's depiction, the Humean view assumes that the empirical content of a statement concerning a causal relation is merely a statement about the regular succession of events or states of affairs of one type (the cause) by events or states of affairs of another type (the effect).[25] Concretely, the observation of regular conjunctions between two discrete events is both sufficient and necessary to claim that there is a causal relationship between the two. People might invoke mechanisms to account for how the regularities are brought about, but this is only because of people's psychological disposition, not a move that can rationally be defended. This explains why the Humean notion of causality is sometimes referred to as the 'regularity theory' of causality or the 'successionist view'.[26] It stipulates that whenever event (or states of affairs) x occurs then event (or states of affairs) y occurs, or, in a probabilistic form, y is likely to occur. From a realist point of view, the Humean notion of causality is flawed for various reasons. First and foremost, regularities of this kind are extremely rare in nature. They tend to occur only in closed systems, such as the solar system. Closed systems are characterized by internal and external closure, the former referring to the absence of any changes to the internal workings of the system, the latter to stability in the relationship between the system and factors that may interfere with its workings. While these conditions can be created artificially, they are rarely met in reality. This would impel Humean philosophers to take the outlandish position that there are hardly any laws (besides those of astronomy) or, worse, that there are no laws, outside closed systems. To take the former position is to question the value of science. To take the latter implies a contradiction in terms because laws are, by definition, universal.[27]

Furthermore, this Humean view of causality conflates description and explanation: a causal explanation ought to go beyond the mere observational level and account for *how* the observed regularities were produced. Another way of expressing this is to say that the Humean notion of causality makes it difficult to distinguish between accidental and necessary regularities or, in W. E. Johnson's terminology, between 'universals of law' and 'universals of fact'. Accounting for *how* the regularities have been produced necessitates hinting at mechanisms, structures or powers that generate the regularities; and, crucially, these mechanisms do not have to be immediately observable. This generative theory relies on a notion of 'natural necessity', which explains change or stability of phenomena in terms of their intrinsic features.[28] Take, for instance, the case of a rock breaking glass. It is possible to argue that the rock caused the glass to break, and indeed whenever a rock hits glass it tends to break. But realists insist that the glass broke because of its internal structure. From a realist point of view, to account for the impact of the rock is to point out the molecular make-up of the glass, and the rock merely triggered off the mechanism. Of course, powers or mechanisms are potentialities that are not necessarily exercised, and it is not the case that exercised powers are always manifest in any outcome. That is why laws are interpreted 'normically' and scientific statements as 'transfactual' – not counterfactual.[29] That is, the laws indicate not what *would* happen, but what actually *is* happening although possibly not immediately observable. They are actualized in the laboratory or other closed systems, but may *not* be reflected in a regular sequence.[30] For critical realists, therefore, constant conjunctions are neither necessary nor sufficient to talk about a scientific law.

Based on their transcendental argument, realists subscribe to what they coin a stratified notion of reality. This notion attributes reality to three distinct levels or domains.[31] The domain of the actual refers to the patterns of events that take place, whereas the realm of the empirical refers to people's perceptions or observations of these events. For instance, unemployment, productivity, suicide or mortality rates are to be found at the level of the actual, but their measurements by social scientists belong to the empirical realm. It is the third level, however, that acquires importance in the critical realist creed, for it ties in with the latter's view of the scientific objects as not only intransitive but also structured. While the intransitive nature of reality means that scientific objects exist independently of people (infra), realists also talk about the 'structured' nature of reality, meaning that the scientific laws designate, not events, but underlying mechanisms that exercise powers. The domain of the real refers precisely to the underlying structures or mechanisms that generate events. Mechanisms operate in various scientific areas. Take a psychologist who refers to the death instinct, a linguist to a linguistic structure and a sociologist to society's tendency to equilibrium. These are underlying mechanisms; none of them is immediately observable, but each is alleged to be real and to affect the surface level. Two qualifications ought to be made. First, to postulate this philosophical ontology is not to make any commitment to a scientific ontology. That is, while this philosophical ontology stipulates the existence of mechanisms and structures beneath the observable surface, it does not specify further the precise nature of these entities. To speculate about them is the task of the various sciences – not philosophy. Second, from the realist conviction that there is an intransitive dimension to science (that is, that mechanisms exist independent of people's knowledge of them) it does not follow that every scientific attempt to uncover the real necessarily leads to valid assertions regarding the nature of the underlying mechanisms or structures. Nor does it necessarily follow that theories are becoming increasingly isomorphic with reality. Realists are fallibilists in that they acknowledge that, however persuasive the evidence provided, a scientist or a community of scientists can hold erroneous beliefs about their research object.[32]

The stratified notion of reality postulates the possibility of a lack of synchrony between the three levels. So the realm of the actual might be out of sync with the empirical in the case that people's perceptions or observations do not match the events. Or, alternatively, the actual and the deep might be out of sync, for instance when other structures counteract the effect of a particular structure, which is therefore not manifest in any outcome. This tends to happen in open systems, where various generative mechanisms interfere with one another.[33] Most systems found in nature are open, and therefore the actual and the deep are frequently out of sync with each other. Scientists often artificially create relatively closed systems in order to identify a particular underlying mechanism. They use experiments to control for the other mechanisms that otherwise would have intervened, and by doing so they are able to test hypotheses regarding the nature and effect of the mechanisms under investigation. But outside these artificial settings, systems tend to be open, other mechanisms are interfering, and it follows that a perfectly adequate explanation does not necessarily imply the ability to predict. The postulate of symmetry between explanation and prediction (the belief that to explain is to predict and vice versa) is therefore to be abandoned.[34] For instance, take a falling leaf, which obeys the law of gravity. According to the law of gravity, the leaf would fall to earth in a straight line according to the parameters set out in the law. In reality, the leaf is unlikely to fall in this way because other mechanisms, such as aerodynamic forces, are counteracting the gravitational pull.[35] This example shows that there is a lack of synchrony between the underlying mechanism (gravitational pull) and the observable manifestations at the surface level. It also shows that, because of the openness of the system (the existence of other mechanisms that interfere with the effect of the law of gravity), knowledge about the existence of the law of gravity does not allow for accurate predictions. While this may not apply to a closed system such as the solar system, it does apply to *most* systems, the social system certainly being one of them. Because people have genuine choice, social systems are open systems. It is therefore not surprising that economists have been remarkably unsuccessful in discovering event regularities. Because choice is real, knowledge of the workings of the social realm does not guarantee predictive power. Again, testimony of this is the recurrent failure of economics to establish itself as a predictive science.[36]

Creative scientists at work

Few philosophies of science systematically explore creativity, the process by which scientists proceed to develop novel theories or theories about previously unexplored phenomena. Realists are a welcome exception in this regard. It has already been mentioned that they pay attention to the *social* structure of science and, in particular, to the fact that scientists employ previously established facts and theories in order to explain new phenomena. This brings the realist notion of 'retroduction' to the foreground. Retroduction sums up the way in which knowledge depends on 'knowledge-like antecedents'.[37] Distinct from both induction and deduction, it indicates the process by which researchers account for new phenomena through analogies with phenomena with which they are already familiar. By doing so, the scientist endeavours to uncover mechanisms, structures and powers underneath the instantly observable surface level. For instance, Darwin's evolutionary theory was based on his knowledge of domestic breeding and Malthus's theory of population, while these insights into biological evolution, in turn, allowed Durkheim, in *The Division of Labour*, to develop his theory of societal change. Or, drawing upon the work of Jakobson, Claude Lévi-Strauss employed analogies with linguistic structures to account for non-linguistic, social phenomena such as myths or kinship. More recently, Niklas Luhmann employed insights from Maturana and Varela's autopoesis, initially a theory from biology, to account for the self-referential nature of society. Through retroduction theoretical entities are invoked, the reality of which can be inferred from the observation of their effects. For instance, although it is not possible to observe electricity as such, it can be detected through an electroscope. Likewise, radioactive materials can be identified through a Geiger counter.[38]

The prescriptive dimension of critical realism is now coming to the foreground. Scientific theories ought to indicate deeper mechanisms that go well beyond the Humean surface level. Theories ought not to be seen as simply logico-deductive devices; they are the outcome of a creative process in which the unfamiliar is apprehended through analogies with the familiar. Scientists ought subsequently to use empirical research to test the existence and causal power of the alleged mechanisms. Besides empirical validity, however, Bhaskar and Lawson suggest another criterion to decide between theories: that of explanatory power. Scientists ought to prefer theories with high explanatory power instead of those with less. There is some dispute among critical realists as to what explanatory power means, but most would agree that it indicates how wide a range of significant empirical phenomena has been 'accounted for', 'illuminated' or 'covered'.[39] The wider the range, the greater is the explanatory power, and the greater the explanatory power, the more desirable is the theory. So, a theory T_b is preferable over T_a if and only if T_b manages to explain most phenomena explained by T_a plus some other significant phenomena that T_a does not manage to explain. There is some ambiguity as to what 'most' and 'significant' mean in the previous sentence,[40] but the gist of the argument is clear: theories with a broader scope are preferable. As far as the social sciences are concerned, this prescription is not inconsequential. Whereas Popper regarded the all-encompassing nature of the theories of Marx and Freud with great suspicion, Bhaskar et al. consider the very same feature as a plus. This is not to say that critical realists necessarily wish to abandon the falsifiability criterion. Empirical testing remains a central methodological theme, and from this most critical realists would infer that theories ought to be empirically refutable. In practice, however, they seem less concerned about falsifiability (or, indeed, degrees of falsifiability) than about explanatory power.

As mentioned before, many critical realists are practising social scientists. Among self-declared critical realists are various economists, geographers, psychologists, historians and sociologists. This is maybe not surprising because initially critical realist philosophy had paid a lot of attention to social science and social theory, and in turn social scientists contributed to the realist doctrine. In contrast with several philosophers of science, such as Popper or Lakatos, whose knowledge of the social sciences is minimal and, if existent, limited to economics, Bhaskar and fellow realists have a sophisticated understanding of both the practice of social science and the theoretical and methodological considerations that accompany it. Their philosophy is meant to be a guide for the social rather than the natural sciences. Like Popper, however, critical realists defend a naturalist position. They want to demonstrate that, at some level, the social and the natural sciences employ the same method, and that therefore the idea of social *science* is not a fiction. Their point is that most anti-naturalists, such as Peter Winch, have made the crucial mistake of adopting a positivist view of science. Realists acknowledge that social researchers do not operate in a positivist fashion, but insist that natural scientists do not either. So Winch is right to point out that the regularity notion of causality is alien to social research but wrong in taking it as intrinsic to the practice of natural science. Once a realist notion of science is substituted for the positivist one, a qualified naturalism becomes a distinct possibility. Like the natural sciences, the social sciences attempt to uncover underlying social structures or mechanisms to account for observed 'demi-regularities'. Demi-regularities or 'partial regularities' are imperfect patterns, but patterns nevertheless. 'Women tend to be paid less than men for the same kind of work' or 'Protestants commit suicide more than Catholics' are examples of demi-regularities. They are typical of open systems, in which various mechanisms interfere with each other and in which perfect regularities are scarce. Demi-regularities allude to the existence of a mechanism or, indeed, of several mechanisms.[41] I mentioned a *qualified* naturalism because Bhaskar acknowledges three differences between the social and the natural sciences. As opposed to natural structures, social structures do not exist independently of the activities they affect, nor do they exist independently of people's conceptions. They are also subject to change to a far greater extent than natural structures.[42] It would also be an error to interpret Bhaskar's naturalist outlook as a carte blanche for reductionism, as if the social realm can be interpreted in natural science terms. Like Durkheim and Boutroux, critical realists tend to assume that, while laws applicable to more simple domains of reality also affect more complex ones, the latter cannot be reduced to aggregates of the former. Every domain has a complexity of its own that cannot be captured simply by laws of a lesser order. As much as it would be a gross error to reduce the biological world to the workings of chemicals, or the chemical to physical mechanisms, there are emergent properties to the social that cannot be addressed by any combination of the other sciences. Bhaskar's holistic outlook also excludes individualistic explanations because they too fail to pay sufficient justice to the exclusivity of the social.

Contributions to social theory

Critical realists such as Bhaskar also contribute to social theory. They try to avoid both societal determinism and voluntarism. The former downplays the role of human agency; the latter makes the opposite error. Both have in common that they erroneously oppose society and agency as if social structures preclude agency. For Bhaskar society is a precondition, not an impediment, for agency. In turn people's agency makes for the reproduction and transformation of society. Bhaskar calls this 'the transformational model of social action' according to which social structure is both the medium and the output of people's agency.[43] There is thus no creation *de novo*: like sculptors, only able to create something out of the materials available to them, individuals can only exercise agency by relying on structure. In Aristotelian terms, the individual acts as efficient cause and structure is material cause. Think of the sculptor again: the artist, not the clay, is able to initiate activity but the kind of clay that is being used affects the shape of what is being produced.[44] To what extent this contribution is innovative is a different matter, especially given that some realists acknowledge that other theorists expressed remarkably similar views earlier.[45] Those who are familiar with Giddens's structuration theory may have noticed that the transformational model resembles his 'duality of structure', according to which structure is both medium and unintended outcome of people's actions.[46] Like Giddens, critical realists tend to portray people as continuously monitoring themselves and able to do so because of tacit, practical knowledge about the workings of social life.[47] So, for Lawson, besides the discursive conscious and the unconscious realm, the mind operates at a tacit level as well, also referred to as the level of practical consciousness, and it is precisely the complex interplay between this tacit dimension and self-monitoring that accounts for the unintended reproduction of structures. It should be added, though, that not all realists are as sympathetic to Giddens's theory as Lawson is. For instance, Margaret Archer's morphogenetic approach implies a strong criticism of Giddens and, indeed, a milder one of Bhaskar. *Pace* Giddens's focus on the synchronic reproduction of structures, Archer points out that, while structure predates agency, structural elaboration or reproduction post-dates people's actions. As opposed to Giddens's fallacy of 'central conflation', Archer makes an effort to distinguish clearly structural conditions and people's agencies, and the lapse of time is central to her account of change and transformation of society. 'Structure necessarily predates the action(s) which transform it.' Also, she pays particular attention to how different structures will set different conditions and therefore lead to different effects.

There is another difference with Giddens's structuration theory. Influenced partly by the later Wittgenstein, Giddens's notion of social structure refers to shared rules and resources that are recursively implicated in people's activities. Although critical realists are also indebted to Wittgenstein and Winch, they tend to describe structure in terms of social positions. The nature of these positions is independent of the people who occupy them. For instance, students come and go, but the position of student remains more or less the same.

Likewise, a landlord might have different tenants through time, but the position of tenant is unaffected by the changes. Each position remains unaltered in that the rights and obligations, which accompany each, will be unaffected by the change in personnel. Critical realists tend to pay particular attention to 'internally related' as opposed to 'externally related' relations. In the former, positions are what they are because of the relationship between them, whereas in the latter each entity is independent of the relationship with the other. An example of an external relationship is the relationship between commuters: they are what they are independent of their relationship. In contrast, a landlord is what they are by virtue of their relationship with a tenant, and vice versa. The same applies to the relationship between teacher and student, parent and child, master and slave, and so on. Critical realists point out that a huge amount of relationships are internal, and that they are of tremendous importance for social analysis. They are significant because they embody inequality and power differentials. Each position goes hand in hand with historically given interests and resources. These interests and resources constitute an 'objective reality' that is bound to affect present and future strategies.[48]

There is a final difference with Giddens. He is sceptical of the usefulness of evolutionary thinking in sociology. His point has always been that the differences between the social and the natural world are so large that evolutionary models do not provide the same explanatory power in the social realm as they do in the natural world.[49] The explanatory gains are minimal. Critical realists have, on the whole, been far more sympathetic towards evolutionary analogies. Influenced by Richard Dawkins's interpretation of Darwin, Rom Harré has been one of the first committed realists to draw attention to the fruitfulness of evolutionary forms of explanations and Bhaskar has been following him in this regard.[50] Both have been particularly interested in Dawkins's notion of the meme as a social equivalent to the gene. But it is especially in economics that critical realists have taken on board the relevance of evolutionary thinking. Geoff Hodgson's *Economics and Evolution* has been crucial in this respect, because he has drawn attention to the importance of complexity theory and chaos theory for economics and the other social sciences, and he has managed to summarize these new developments within a coherent frame of reference.[51] In a similar vein Lawson's *Reorienting Economics* introduces a model in which both positive and negative feedback loops occupy a central position. For Lawson, the transformational model of social action is perfectly compatible with this viewpoint.[52]

Application: British politics

Critical realists have been particularly prolific at a theoretical level, but they have traditionally paid less attention to empirical research. Recently, however, some attempts have been made to demonstrate the usefulness of the new creed for social research. One such example is Bob Carter's *Realism and Racism*, which studies issues concerning ethnicity and race from the perspective of critical theory, although the book is more a contribution to social theory than an empirical study, questioning as it does the analytical usefulness of the concept of race.[53] In a similar vein, Carter and New's *Making Realism Work* is devoted particularly to demonstrating the implications of critical realism for methodology and empirical research in the social sciences.[54] More immediately linked to empirical research is Fleetwood and Ackroyd's edited collection *Critical Realist Applications in Organisation and Management Studies*, which explores the relevance of realist social theory and methodology in the domain of organizational theory and business studies.[55] Perhaps the most influential empirical research, from a critical realist perspective, is *Postwar British Politics in Perspective*, written by David Marsh and his colleagues at the University of Birmingham.[56] The sheer impact of the book and the clarity of exposition make it worth discussing in detail.

The authors argue that most work on post-war British politics has been superficial, atheoretical and ahistorical. Embedded in positivist epistemology, most of these writings remain at the surface level, dealing with various political events and political actors. Authors dealing with British politics tend to overemphasize the role of individuals, exemplified in the huge amount of literature on Margaret Thatcher's personality and leadership style. This approach provides useful empirical detail, but fails to lay down a sophisticated theoretical framework that would make sense of the multitude of recorded phenomena. Most of these writings on post-war Britain focus on specific political or social cases, but without putting them into a broader historical context. For instance, by focusing on the period Thatcher was in office, numerous books fail to account for the structural factors that contributed to her rise and success. In short, the literature on post-war British politics presents a plethora of facts but little theoretical work to account for them.[57]

In this context, Marsh et al. argue that a critical realist perspective is called for. They take a strong anti-positivist stance, maintaining that a proper explanation goes beyond the surface level of events and actions. They also plead for an interdisciplinary approach, which recognizes that various mechanisms can come into play, ranging from the economic to the cultural, some reinforcing each other, others cancelling each other out. The realist viewpoint also pays particular attention to the interplay between structural factors and individual agency. The relationship between structure and agency is portrayed as dialectical. On the one hand, agents cannot help but face or rely on structures. The structures are, to some extent, given and external. On the other hand, individuals also interpret and affect the structures. They can act strategically and reproduce or change structures, but any change is always accompanied by some element of continuity. We have to be wary, therefore, of any simplistic account of change in terms of neatly demarcated periods.[58]

This perspective is very well exemplified in the discussion of the successive Thatcher governments. The authors spell out the specific structural context in which Thatcher rose to and maintained power. They take a historical perspective and avoid one-sided analyses. One such partial explanation for the rise and popularity of Thatcher is the view that she presented a coherent response to Britain's economic crisis. The authors also reject the discontinuity thesis: that is, the assumption that Thatcher knew from the very beginning what Thatcherism was about, and that her first years in office were radically different from what preceded them. Marsh et al. employ an evolutionary viewpoint, emphasizing that Thatcherism was always changing and evolving in response to various inputs. These inputs ranged from crises in modern capitalism to New Right ideology. The authors explore how the particular economic and political situation in the UK and worldwide in the 1970s and 1980s provided particular challenges to and constraints on the Thatcher governments. From the late 1970s onwards, subsequent British governments were faced with a weakening of US hegemony and a global crisis of the Fordist modes of economic regulation. The responses of the governments were limited by the declining economic and political role of Britain in the world. Before Thatcher came to power, the Keynesian consensus was already limited because of the ongoing attempts to take care of the financial market of the City of London and to preserve the value of the pound. As such, Thatcherism did not constitute such a radical break with the past. Thatcher's responses – notably privatization, monetarism and management reform – were initially inconsistent and random. Only during Thatcher's third term and the Major government did these solutions achieve more consistency and higher levels of sophistication.[59]

In the post-Thatcher era, both the Conservative Party and Labour focused a lot of energy on issues concerning party management, and image and style. This can be explained by broader structural transformations, which go well beyond Britain. With the collapse of Soviet-style communism, politics has entered a new 'post-ideological' era: most mainstream parties are liberal democratic and agree on key issues. Centre-left and centre-right parties increasingly embrace a similar neo-liberal agenda, rejecting the social democratic orthodoxy of the earlier period. This post-ideological shift has two major consequences. First, with very few political parties differing substantially, political agents need to compete at the level of image and 'governing competence' rather than ideology. The focus of New Labour on image can be seen as an active, strategic response to these new challenges and constraints. This manifests itself in a more prominent role attached to 'spin doctors'. Second, with political parties having lost their traditional positions, there is an increasing likelihood of dissent and splits within each party. This explains the extent to which Europe (and, in particular, the Maastricht Treaty) became such a divisive issue within the Conservative Party during the 1990s.[60]

However enticing their view on post-war British politics, it is not entirely clear why Marsh et al. need the intricacies of critical realist philosophy to justify their work. To underpin this historical account, a theoretical discussion of the relationship between structure and agency would have sufficed. The further commitment of Marsh et al. to the other aspects of the philosophical programme of critical realism does not seem to add much. Moreover, any persuasive historical explanation manages to create the right balance between agency and structure, focusing on the way in which central actors make decisions in the face of structural constraints and selective pressures. Contrary to what Marsh and his colleagues suggest, other historians, writing about the same period, have done this as well and with considerable success. The authors of *Postwar British Politics in Perspective* have a tendency to put up straw men, suggesting grotesque stereotypes of other historical accounts. Very few competent historical writings about this period of British history comply with the crude positivism suggested by Marsh et al.

Evaluation

Critical realism tries to develop a normative model in that it presents guidelines about how social science ought to be conducted and how it should not be done. It occasionally justifies itself on the basis that it constructs these directives, and so the question whether it is successful in accomplishing this mission becomes an important issue indeed. As already mentioned, the task in hand is twofold: it is not simply to do with informing social researchers about the right kind of procedures but also apropos warning them where not to go. Realists are moderately convincing as far as the former category is concerned – the positive instructions, that is. They have clear instructions as to how researchers should proceed. Starting with observed stylized facts, they ought to use analogies and metaphors in order to develop plausible hypotheses about the mechanisms situated at the deeper levels of reality. These hypotheses will eventually be tested empirically, and the more explanatory power these hypotheses have, the better for us. But realists are less informative when it comes to lessons that contradict certain research practices or that at least suggest something different from what has been done hitherto. With the exception of economics, most mainstream social research complies with the intricate procedures suggested by the realist agenda. Critical realists often point at the spectre of positivism, the extent to which social research has been impregnated with the remnants of logical positivism. But this is not entirely correct. It is simply not the case that contemporary social researchers are satisfied with a mere recording of regularity conjunctions; they look for mechanisms that account for *how* the regularities are brought about. Critical realists articulate that which most social researchers have been doing for a very long time.[61]

Another problem with the realist perspective is its reduced notion of knowledge acquisition – its diminished sense of the multitude of types of knowledge available to the human investigator. Critical realists tend to regard the aim of social science is to explain and depict the outer world as accurately as possible, and there is little attention to other reasons why people might feel motivated or inspired to investigate their social surroundings. They do occasionally mention self-emancipation and societal critique but it is unmistakable that their philosophical and methodological investigations are geared, not towards those aims, but towards explanatory power and faithful portrayal. Critical realists adopt a limited view of what knowledge can be about partly because they are caught within a 'scientistic' perspective, by which I mean a view in which a particular model of the natural sciences looms large over any investigation into the nature of knowledge acquisition. It is in this respect that critical realism resembles the philosophical doctrines against which it reacts in that Hume's empiricism, Hempel's logical positivism and Popper's falsificationism all share a scientistic bias too. It is of course true that, in contrast with these philosophical positions, Bhaskar et al. suggest a different notion of what science is about, or a distinct view of what scientific explanation means in the natural sciences. But their overall outlook is not very different from say Hume, Hempel or Popper in that they still operate with a notion of knowledge acquisition set within the restricted contours of how some natural sciences operate.

Even if we were to accept this limited notion of knowledge acquisition, it is not entirely obvious whether the critical realist agenda would enable explanation or depiction to be achieved at all. Given its own premises, it remains unclear how the critical realist guidelines will enable the social researcher to uncover the various mechanisms and powers that are not immediately accessible to observation. One of these assumptions is that most systems are open systems and that social systems are among them. This notion of open systems has initially been used to criticize the regularity notion of causality, according to which the regular conjunction between phenomena is both a necessary and a sufficient condition for causality. Realists rightly point out that, once we acknowledge the openness of most systems, the regularity notion breaks down because there might be a lack of synchrony between the deep and the observational realm. So we cannot rely on the observational realm to infer law-like generalizations of the kind that hard-core empiricists purported to identify because of the openness of systems and therefore the fact that various mechanisms interfere with the observational level. But if this is the case, then it is equally problematic to expect social researchers to be able to gain access to the deeper level in the way in which realists claim they can, for references to the empirical realm would be contaminated by the interferences of various mechanisms or powers. Likewise, the critical realist reliance on demi-regularities and stylized facts seems odd given their insistence on the lack of synchrony between the observable and the deep. It is remarkable that critical realists do not acknowledge the far-reaching consequences of their own presuppositions. If they are right in claiming that most systems are open in the way in which indeed social systems are, and if scientists operate according to the principles of critical realism, then it follows that most scientific explanations cannot be properly justified philosophically. This is, of course, not necessarily a sufficient reason for dismissing their cognitive validity, but it would imply a far more sceptical position than the one adopted by critical realists.

Critical realists have a tendency to put up straw men so as to strengthen their argument and hint at its revolutionary nature. They thereby simplify the views of others and possibly stereotype them, placing diverse theoretical positions under the heading of one ideal-typical construction. One example of this is the way in which Bhaskar opposes voluntarism and determinism or, in sociological parlance, action-orientated and structure-orientated theories. For Bhaskar, the former goes back to Max Weber's individualist position, the latter to Durkheim's collectivist outlook, and both present an incomplete and ultimately unsatisfactory picture. Therefore, the juxtaposition needs to be transcended if we are to represent the social more comprehensively and accurately. The problem with Bhaskar's argument is that very few theories would lend themselves to belonging to either of those extreme categories. Most theories are more sophisticated than either type, recognizing and honouring the sheer complexity and ambiguity of social life and the intersection between the social and the individual. Surely, the theoretical perspectives of Georg Simmel, G. H. Mead or Talcott Parsons cannot be reduced to either voluntarism or determinism. Parsons's point was precisely to integrate some of the fruitful insights of Weber about purposive action with the sobering truths of more systemic approaches, and he subsequently managed to do so by linking the pattern variables (which represent choice) to his functional analysis (which represents systemic constraint). Furthermore, there is a lack of clarity in postulating that there is a contradistinction between approaches that emphasize individual agency and those that stress structure, because there are at least two ways in which either agency or structure can be accentuated. We might be holding a methodological position or making an ontological assertion, and one does not necessitate the other. It is perfectly possible to believe in methodological individualism while holding on to ontological collectivism, and vice versa. Bhaskar's tendency to conflate the two makes his argument considerably less compelling.[62]

Bhaskar's attempt to transcend the opposition between voluntarism and determinism reveals another unspoken presupposition that characterizes his thought and indeed that of most critical realists. The assumption is close to what Dewey called the 'spectator theory of knowledge'.[63] Critical realists implicitly adopt the spectator theory of knowledge in that they assume that the aim of social research is to map the social world as accurately and completely as possible. While prediction is no longer considered a plausible aim on account of the incurable openness of most systems, what is now at stake in research is the mirroring of the outer world. This notion of the social researcher as a would-be cartographer fuels the desire to go beyond both 'one-sided' and 'incomplete' perspectives, to recognize that there is not just action but also structure, and to realize that where there is society, there is also agency. It also underscores the urge to point out that structures are not simply constraining but also enabling, that they are not just an impediment for people to do something, but also at times help them to accomplish things and exercise agency. And it is the very same notion of cartography that underlies their attempts to pay attention to insights from hermeneutics. Given the pre-interpreted nature of social reality, the capturing of people's meanings and beliefs is regarded as a prerequisite for a reliable representation of what is going on in the social realm, and it is precisely because positivist methods purposefully ignore the meaningful dimension of social life that they will ultimately fail to depict truthfully. But the spectator theory of knowledge is problematic on several levels. Firstly, while it makes perfect sense to see language and knowledge as some of the sophisticated tools which the human species employs so as to adjust itself to the external world, it would be far-fetched to argue that people's cognitive functions had been altered so much that they are now able to mirror the world and represent it as it really is.[64] In chapters 5 to 7, it will be argued that it is more fruitful to conceive of knowledge acquisition as a way of coping with, rather than copying, the external world. So knowledge ought to be seen as active rather than representational – an action rather than a picture. Secondly, rather than seeing the interpretative method as a stepping stone towards unravelling previously unacknowledged mechanisms and gaining access to hitherto inaccessible levels of reality, it makes more sense to treat interpretation and understanding in the way in which Gadamer wrote about them. The Gadamerian view of understanding will be explored in subsequent chapters, but it is worth mentioning here that one of its implications is that culturally specific presuppositions are a *sine qua non* to any act of interpretation, and that therefore it is misleading to defend the interpretative method on the basis that it would facilitate the representation of social things as they really are.

In what follows I will be developing this non-representational view of knowledge further and, in doing so, will adopt a position that is very different from, if not diametrically opposed to, the realist view of science. I will draw on American pragmatism, a philosophical tradition that is in many respects antithetical to realism. One of the central ideas of my proposal is that, in the light of recent philosophical and historical insights, the search for a methodological strategy which supposedly unites the social and the natural sciences becomes increasingly tenuous. Pragmatism heralds a new direction in social research, in which knowledge is no longer conceived as mirroring or depicting the outer world, but rather as intimately related to practical achievements. Critical theorists have been particularly receptive to pragmatism; Jürgen Habermas relied heavily on Peirce, Mead and other pragmatists. Therefore, the next chapter deals with critical theory and pays attention to the way in which it has incorporated pragmatism. This sets the stage for the discussion of Rorty's ideas in chapter 6 and for my outline of a pragmatist philosophy of the social sciences in chapter 7.

Further reading

Among the predecessors of the realist movement are Mary Hesse and Rom Harré; their interest in the role of models and analogies struck a chord with critical realists. To get acquainted with Hesse's ideas, I suggest her *Forces and Fields* and *Models and Analogies in Science.* Harré's *An Introduction to the Logic of the Sciences* explored similar themes. Roy Bhaskar is one of the leading members of the critical realist movement, and both his *A Realist Theory of Science* and *The Possibility of Naturalism* are regarded as foundational texts. The first of these proposes the outline of a realist philosophy of science; the second presents a realist view of the *social* sciences. Both books are a difficult read mainly because of Bhaskar's elusive prose rather than the complexity of the arguments presented. Those struggling with the texts might find solace in the fact that Bhaskar's most recent books are even more impenetrable and that Andrew Collier's *Critical Realism* is a remarkably simple introduction to Bhaskar's thinking. An equally accessible, though less systematic, exposition of realism can be found in Peter Manicas's *A History and Philosophy of the Social Sciences.* Lawson's *Economics and Reality* might be even more appropriate for those unacquainted with the critical realist literature. Large sections of the book deal with economics, but chapters 2, 3, 5 and 6 constitute an excellent introduction to critical realism. For those interested in a more advanced introduction, Lawson's *Reorienting Economics* follows on from the previous book. For an introductory review of the relationship between realism, critical theory and hermeneutics, see Outhwaite's *New Philosophies of Social Science,* an outstanding overview, though I remain sceptical of the way in which Outhwaite wants to merge Habermas's consensual theory of truth with a realist notion. For a convincing articulation of the realist critique of the Humean notion of causality, see Harré and Madden's *Causal Powers.* Another contribution to the philosophy of science that is close to critical realism is Nancy Cartwright's *How the Laws of Physics Lie.* Realist views on social theory are expressed in Keat and Urry's *Social Theory as Science,* Bhaskar's *The Possibility of Naturalism* and Archer's *Realist Social Theory.*

5
Critical Theory

Introduction

Critical theory refers to an intellectual tradition that attributes epistemological priority to the notion of critique. Critical theorists emphasize that social research does not simply have to aim at describing or explaining things. Other objectives are worth considering. Research may aim at criticizing a situation; it may point at inequalities or injustices; it may present us with a normative yardstick, something to aim at or to strive for. Critical theorists wish to link social research to a progressive political agenda, and they think it is imperative to reflect on the ideology underlying social research. They disagree with the view that research is, can or should be value-free. Whether intended or not, research always assumes and reinforces certain values. Critical theorists are particularly hostile to the way in which social research is often used for conservative purposes, for identifying malfunctions or problems of social order.

Many academics today call themselves critical theorists or have sympathy with critical theory. Initially, however, the term 'critical theory' was associated with the work of a small group of neo-Marxist intellectuals who worked in the interdisciplinary Institut für Sozialforschung (Institute for Social Research) in Frankfurt in the 1920s and early 1930s. The institute was founded in 1923 with the aim of developing Marxist-inspired social research. The Frankfurt School (as they became known) included Theodor Adorno, Walter Benjamin, Erich Fromm, Carl Grünberg, Max Horkheimer, Leo Löwenthal, Herbert Marcuse, Friedrich Pollock and Franz Neumann. Grünberg was the first director, and in 1930 Horkheimer took over. Besides Marx, they were also deeply influenced by Friedrich Nietzsche, Max Weber and Sigmund Freud. Their work mixed philosophical discussions with empirical research on a variety of topics, ranging from the family to political economy. Because of the political events in the early 1930s, the Frankfurt School dissolved and most of its members moved to other countries of Europe or to the United

States. After World War II, some of them returned to Germany. Jürgen Habermas and Alex Honneth are among the most prominent members of the second generation of the Frankfurt School. Whereas the first generation was still deeply embedded in German philosophy, Habermas and Honneth have incorporated insights from Anglo-Saxon philosophy to a much greater extent.

In traditional philosophy of social science, little attention was given to critical theory. Social research was conceived mainly as an explanatory endeavour – not a basis for critique. The focus was on how to make social research properly *scientific*, and critical theory seemed a deviation from the scientific path. Also, the elusive writing of the members of the Frankfurt School did not help. Their publications were dense and convoluted, whereas the dominant analytical school prided itself on its precision and clarity. From a pragmatist point of view, however, it is worth paying close attention to the Frankfurt School for two reasons. Firstly, the work of the early Frankfurt School has helped us move away from the narrow notion of social science as solely a descriptive and explanatory device. Adorno and Horkheimer were able to conceive of social research in broader terms. They also developed a critique of contemporary epistemology. Secondly, Habermas was able to follow up this perspective by incorporating insights from pragmatism. Whereas the early Frankfurt School pointed at the dangers of the Enlightenment and of positivist epistemology, Habermas took a more balanced view. He emphasized the radical potential within the emergent bourgeois society of the early nineteenth century and his critical theory is based on that potential.

The early Frankfurt School

The members of the Frankfurt School conceived of themselves as neo-Marxists. They were inspired by Marx and often referred to him. However, they also wanted to move beyond Marx and Marxism. They felt that Marxist research often shared some of the epistemological presuppositions of bourgeois science: it was often based on a narrow positivist model of science. Positivism was one of their *bêtes noires*, and I shall return to this theme shortly. Suffice it to say, at this stage, that positivists wished to model the social sciences after the natural sciences, underplayed the interpretative dimension of social life, and conceived of science as primarily a predictive endeavour. So-called vulgar Marxists were prone to slip into a positivist outlook because they were preoccupied with the way in which the economic base determined other aspects of society. The early Frankfurt School wanted to move away from what they regarded as monistic materialism. Monistic materialism reduces various phenomena to one factor: the material base. The Frankfurt School realized that the determinism embedded in vulgar Marxism was inappropriate for understanding social processes. They wished to resurrect the Hegelian aspects of Marx. Above all, they realized that an understanding of society today required an in-depth analysis of its non-economic aspects. This brings us to the interdisciplinary nature of their work.

The early critical theorists promoted unequivocally interdisciplinary research and were highly critical of the segmented and specialized nature of the contemporary academy. Interdisciplinarity was central to the research programme of the early Frankfurt School, and it played a prominent role in Horkheimer's inaugural address.[1] This position tied in with their sceptical stance *vis-à-vis* atomistic approaches to the social sciences. In philosophy, atomism considers the whole as reducible to its component parts. In the case of the social sciences, this leads to what is known as 'methodological individualism', which reduces the social to an aggregate of individual actions. The members of the Frankfurt School preferred a holistic approach. Holism advocates the irreducibility of the whole. The Frankfurt School argued that the interdependency of various parts of society necessitated the collaboration of psychologists, economists and sociologists. In a discussion with Popper, Adorno explained this point in relationship to his own study on *The Authoritarian Personality*.[2] This book attempted to identify the personality traits of people with extremist political leanings, but Adorno was keen to point out that the book was not intended to suggest that fascism could be explained exclusively in social-psychological terms. To explain the rise of National Socialism, we need to take into account the social structure, politics and economy of the Weimar Republic.[3] The use of different disciplines also underlay Adorno and Horkheimer's treatment of contemporary culture. This is already obvious from the terminology they used. They talked about the 'culture industry' rather than, say, 'mass culture' or 'popular culture'. 'Culture industry' showed how intertwined culture, personality and the economy had become. Economic forces dictated the content of the cultural products, while these products were imposed on people and affected them considerably. This phenomenon could not be studied adequately in isolation. Adorno and Horkheimer's writings about the culture industry explored in depth the psychological mechanisms at play and analysed the economic conditions in which it operated. They also put these cultural shifts within a broader perspective about the spread of instrumental rationality in modern society.[4]

These critical theorists opposed a positivist conception of social research. At the time, positivism occupied a relatively prominent position in social research. Positivist social research tried to apply the methodology of the natural sciences to the social realm, searching for laws or law-like generalizations. For positivist research, a good explanation predicts accurately and may eventually allow us to control our social surroundings. Critical theorists acknowledged the historical achievements of positivism. It had helped us to emancipate ourselves from metaphysics and theology, by substituting sensory experiences for abstract and religious notions. It also provided a basis for a critique of organicist and totalitarian views of society.[5] Organicist social science portrayed social systems by drawing on analogies with biological systems. Organicist views of the social had sometimes been used to justify conservative or non-democratic politics, and this explains why the early Frankfurt School was sympathetic to the positivist critique of organicism. However, Adorno and others saw some serious drawbacks to positivism. Positivism was particularly problematic because it had become such a dominant force. Whereas positivism was initially a progressive movement, it had turned into a new form of totalitarianism. It was unable to stand back and properly question itself. It was incapable of grasping its own limitations and of conceiving of other forms of knowledge acquisition. In short, it had become yet another ideology. It reduced any knowledge to the empiricist type of knowledge; no other type of knowledge was considered to be meaningful. This position of the early Frankfurt School – that knowledge should not be reduced to an empiricist type of knowledge – would also play a central role in the work of the second generation of critical theorists, notably Habermas.

Critical theorists regarded positivist epistemology, in its extreme form, as yet another manifestation of the spread of instrumental rationality.[6] Influenced by Weber, they regarded the omnipresence of instrumental or means–end rationality as characteristic of the shift towards modernity. Instrumental rationality refers to a particular orientation in which cost–benefit analysis plays a central role. It is different from substantive rationality, which refers to the ability to reflect on and assess the objectives that are being pursued. Weber noticed how the emergence of Protestantism was accompanied by the predominance of rational capitalism and rationalization of culture. This rationalization manifested itself in various ways, from the increasing use of a methodical and efficient approach to things to the decline of magic and ultimately the demise of religion. Weber's analysis hinted at a possible contradiction between instrumental and substantive rationality: for instance, bureaucrats are trained to operate effectively but not to reflect on or assess what they are trying to achieve. Critical theorists paid particular attention to this contradiction: it explains the vigorous and effective pursuit of irrational objectives in, for instance, Nazi Germany. For critical theorists, instrumental rationality spread on a massive scale in late capitalism, even affecting what we regard as knowledge.[7] Influenced by Husserl, critical theorists regarded modern science and positivism as the epitome of the rationalization process. Positivism implied a remarkably narrow notion of what knowledge is about, and it disregarded theoretical and critical reflection as metaphysical or normative residues of a previous era. As a consequence, the remit for the social sciences had become ridiculously narrow. Positivism conceived of social research as a tool for technical mastery of the social, for restoring social order and avoiding malfunctions in the system. Auguste Comte's dictum 'to know in order to predict and to predict in order to control' (*savoir pour prévoir et prévoir pour saisir*) sums up this restricted conception.[8]

One of the reasons for such a narrow remit is that positivists tended to take a phenomenalist position. As the name suggests, phenomenalism attributed epistemological primacy to observable facts. 'Here, only experience, purified experience in the strict sense it has received in natural science, is called knowledge.'[9] Phenomenalism is hostile to *a priori* thinking. *A priori* thinking refers to any reliance on reason with the hope of establishing basic principles prior to observation. For Adorno and Horkheimer, phenomenalism shunned critical or theoretical reflection, dismissing them as unfortunate residues of a metaphysical or theological era. In contrast, critical theorists held a Hegelian view, according to which it is inconceivable to have an object independent of a subject. Theories are necessary to make sense of the 'scattered facts'. Positivism held on to an untenable distinction between theoretical and observational language as if it is possible to talk about observable facts independent of theory. Adorno pointed out that, whereas in philosophy this view had been discredited a long time ago, sociologists still held on to this outdated notion. In contrast, critical theorists argued that it is only because we have theories that we can select and process information about the outside world. Only because we hold theoretical presuppositions can we observe.[10] It is important to become self-conscious of what we cannot avoid: the fact that we use theory. It allows us to take up a more critical attitude to the various presuppositions we might take on board.

There is another reason why the early Frankfurt School felt uncomfortable with phenomenalism: it failed to attribute reality to features that are not immediately accessible to observation. Critical theorists wished to acknowledge the existence of a reality beneath the surface level. They regarded it as the task of sociology to uncover the underlying mechanisms, structures or powers that affect the observable sphere. Genuine sociology does not simply search for regularity conjunctions and it is not solely about recording people's perceptions, accounts and beliefs; it delves further and explores mechanisms and powers that may account for the regularities or for people's views. This is not to say that people's opinions ought to be ignored, but it is not sufficient simply to record them. They need to be put in relation to the underlying objective structures. In this respect, critical theory has affinities with critical realism. It too points at the need to uncover mechanisms and powers that are not immediately observable.

The early critical theorists argued that positivism restricts *what* is being investigated. Rather than studying the objective mechanisms underneath the observable level, positivist research embarked upon an objective study of subjective features: beliefs, perceptions and experiences.[11] Researchers employed highly sophisticated techniques to find out how people experience and feel about their work, leisure or home life. The sociological work on alienation is a good example of this.[12] Sociologists have redefined the concept so that it no longer refers to an objective condition but to *perceptions* of an objective condition. It no longer refers to the absence of autonomy or loss of power but to the *perception* of this lack. It no longer refers to isolating features of the capitalist mode of production but to the *feeling* of being isolated. This is not to say that this research, or so-called opinion research, ought to be ignored. Nor is it to say that perceptions are irrelevant; they often reflect crucial changes in the underlying structure. For research to retain its critical potential, it ought to be able to assess the validity of these perceptions. 'Empirical research itself becomes ideology as soon as it posits public opinion as being absolute.'[13]

Critical theorists such as Adorno and Horkheimer also confronted the positivist insistence on value-neutrality. Value-neutrality refers to the Weberian position that the values of the researcher should not interfere with the research process. It may affect the choice of the research object but should not interfere with the investigation itself. From a critical theory perspective, it is wrong to assume there can be such a neat distinction between what is and what ought to be. The values and political views of researchers always interfere with their research, even if they make an effort to remain neutral. Research is a human activity and as such is embedded in a normative framework.[14] Moreover, it is wrong to conceive of methods and theories as simply technical devices for studying the social world. In themselves they imply and reinforce particular values. For instance, functionalist explanations are not simply explanations; they also assume and reinforce the view that a cohesive, conflict-free and well-integrated society is desirable. Finally, the very stance of value-neutrality is in itself a normative position. It is often used to justify not making a judgement and to legitimize standing back when faced with obvious inequalities and injustices.[15]

These critical theorists also criticized another aspect of the notion of value-neutrality: the position that social research is not a critical but a descriptive and explanatory endeavour. For critical theory the research in itself ought to make a judgement and take a position.[16] There is no point in simply describing or explaining phenomena; the research ought to give us an indication about how self-emancipation has been impeded and how it can be achieved. Not taking such a position means reinforcing the existing order; the obsession with representing reality erodes our imaginative capabilities. This type of sociology 'supports what exists in the over-zealous attempt to say what exists. Such sociology becomes ideology in the strictest sense – a necessary illusion.'[17] In an intellectual exchange with Popper, Adorno clarified this position. For him Popper's notion of 'critical approach' restricts itself to mere self-criticism. It is critical only in so far as it suggests scientists continually assess their scientific theories on the basis of empirical evidence. For Adorno, the critical approach should be broader; it ought to involve a 'critique of the sociological object'.[18] This is not to say that there cannot be any critical value in traditional forms of research, settling as they do matters of empirical validity, but this critique is of limited value. It is not geared towards self-emancipation.[19]

The critique of the positivist emphasis on value-neutrality goes even further. The members of the Frankfurt School maintained that there is something deeply conservative in the positivist insistence on empirical observations. The preoccupation with facts leads to a reduction of the role of the political imaginary. Auguste Comte's philosophy and Durkheim's sociological research programme are prime examples of empiricist projects that undermine the role of political philosophy. For Comte and Durkheim, we cannot simply search for the ideal society. Instead, we should search for the law-like regularities that dominate social life; politics can only be conceived of within the boundaries of these regularities. Within this perspective, social research becomes the handmaiden of an incremental type of social policy in which small alterations are achieved within the boundaries of sociological laws. Politics loses its substantive focus. Its imaginary component is subordinated to the tyranny of 'sociological facts'. These facts and laws are portrayed as given, external to us and immutable, and, because they are so invariable, politics needs to be subordinated to them.[20]

Critical theorists felt that positivist sociology paid too much attention to research methods and techniques at the expense of an in-depth understanding of the material covered. Whereas the statistical techniques might be extremely sophisticated, the same cannot be said about the level of analysis, which was often remarkably superficial. Positivists had a narrow notion of what can be studied; the method affects what is being investigated rather than the other way around.[21] Again, the sociological study of alienation proves the point. The concept has strong philosophical roots. In its Hegelian or Marxist definition, it would not fit positivist research, but it has been redefined so that it can be measured and incorporated within the orthodox realm of empirical research. Whereas it formerly referred to the objective condition of powerlessness within the capitalist mode of production, it now refers to the *feeling* of powerlessness. From the point of view of critical theory, methods are only means; they should not dictate the research agenda. It is, again, indicative of the heavy emphasis on means–end rationality in contemporary culture that methods play such an important role in social research.[22]

Positivist research tended to reduce the agency of individuals to a minimum. It portrayed people as passive recipients of external forces, as powerless atoms confronted with a ubiquitous and overwhelming society.[23] This was especially the case for research inspired by Durkheim. For Durkheim-informed research, social facts are explained by other social facts – not by individuals pursuing their goals. This form of research failed to acknowledge that people are capable of reflecting upon their conditions and of acting in accordance with that knowledge. Ironically, this model of human behaviour mirrored the conditions of contemporary society, in which people were very much passive consumers of the products of the culture industry. This does not mean, however, that positivism has been vindicated. It is representative of a time- and culturally specific condition, one that was thoroughly alienating and by no account representative of the human condition. The error of positivism was to take this view as the base for a model about human behaviour *in general*.[24]

There are other ways in which positivist research was unable to distance itself from contemporary society: it was uncritical of the various categorizations and representations that people employ in society. Moreover, it used the very same representations and, by doing so, reinforced them.[25] It employed various dichotomies that were in operation in society and replicated them, for instance, in interviews and questionnaires. Whereas research should aim at questioning and deconstructing the distinctions and concepts people employ, this positivist research, so-called opinion research, reinforced and legitimized them. This is yet another way in which this form of research maintained the status quo. From the point of view of critical theory, empirical researchers should realize that the generalizations they obtain should not be attributed simply to reality but also partly to the method itself.[26] Critical theory promoted such a reflexive attitude on the part of the researchers, ready to question the presuppositions that guide their research and methodology.

The Frankfurt School was particularly hostile to the excessive use of quantitative analysis. There is a place for quantitative methods, but not at the expense of other methods. Quantification goes hand in hand with the emphasis on factual observations and the distrust of theory. 'Every other kind of scientific statement which does not offer a deposit of facts in the most familiar categories and, if possible, in the most neutral form, the mathematical, is already accused of being theoretical.'[27] Critical theorists traced the preoccupation with the use of mathematics back to the Enlightenment vision of science so vividly expressed by Poincaré and Descartes. In this view, the ultimate aim of science was to be able to reconstruct a multitude of phenomena in terms of basic mathematical and logical principles. The simplicity of mathematics and pure logic proved particularly enticing.[28] Critical theorists, however, had serious reservations about this view. In contrast with the homogeneity of the object of 'classical natural science', human life is complex. It is varied. It contains inconsistencies and contradictions. People are able to reflect on their surroundings and regularly act on the basis of the knowledge gained. Statistical analysis fails to do full justice to this complexity. It reduces complexity to the false homogeneity of the 'law of large numbers'.[29]

Positivist philosophers overemphasized the formal nature of the intellectual enterprise. They tried to find atemporal foundations of scientific knowledge so as to provide universal recipes for successful social research. They may have reflected on various issues, ranging from the nature of scientific method and truth to the distinction between science and non-science, but they did not pay much attention to how scientists *actually* proceed, nor did they take into account the social structure in which research is conducted. A closer look showed that actual research never operates according to the algorithm set out by these philosophers. In contrast critical theorists tried to be sensitive to the actual workings of scientists and to the way these practices tied in with the social structure in which they found themselves.[30] More importantly, critical theory conceived it as its task to be critical of the institutions and structures in which scientists, including social scientists, operated, for these institutional settings influenced the research that was being produced. Hence critical theorists showed a keen interest in the sociology of science, although they remained sceptical about the way in which this area of research had been turned into conventional social science.[31]

The early Frankfurt School has been valuable in several ways. At a time when logical positivism dominated philosophy and the social sciences, Adorno and others provided a valuable counter-position. They warned us against the way in which sociology had often become a handmaiden to a conservative social policy agenda. At the time, little attention had been paid to how social research itself can be complicit in maintaining the status quo. They were right to point out that value-free social science is an unfeasible objective: whether intentionally or unwittingly, research necessarily draws on and promotes certain values. They pointed out the restricted scope of a lot of positivist sociological research: it tended to be descriptive and remained at the surface level. They tried to define research more broadly: it is not simply about explaining or predicting but ultimately ought to fulfil a function of critique. They drew attention to the necessity of a reflexive social science – that is, a social science that reflects critically on its own presuppositions and workings.

There are, however, some serious limitations to their work. Their training and expertise was in continental philosophy and their knowledge of sociology was limited. They were 'armchair sociologists', pondering over various phenomena without actually doing systematic research. Their comments about sociology were ungrounded; their 'observations' on the nature of social research reflected gross ignorance. They exhibited a tendency to portray social research as a homogeneous enterprise, as if most empirical studies comply with the cataclysmic image they portrayed. Their writings cast an unnecessary slur on the reputation of empirical sociology, as if it is simply a mindless fact-finding mission without direction, let alone theoretical assistance. Social research has always been a more multifaceted enterprise than the members of the Frankfurt School were willing to acknowledge. To apply, as they did, the label of positivism is to use a broad brush; very few pieces of research conform to positivism in its pure form. For instance, Durkheim is often depicted as the archetypal positivist sociologist but, as I pointed out earlier, he deviated substantially from the positivist creed. He was, among other things, not satisfied with simply recording regularity conjunctions; he wanted to delve deeper and uncover mechanisms that bring about the observed regularities. Also, Adorno's critique of quantitative analysis now finds less resonance than when he was writing. We no longer think in terms of opposition between quantitative and qualitative methods. We see them as complementary: each provides what the other is lacking. It is therefore not surprising that, when Adorno embarked on empirical research (in *The Authoritarian Personality*), he decided to forgo his prejudices and employ statistical analysis.

Critical theorists adopted an ambiguous relationship to functionalism. Functionalist explanations account for the persistence of social phenomena by indicating how they contribute to the maintenance or stability of the system in which they are embedded. On the one hand, critical theorists were hostile to functionalist explanations, maintaining that they have often been used to vindicate existing social arrangements. On the other hand, critical theorists themselves exhibited a tendency to use functional explanations. Adorno and Horkheimer's critique of the culture industry relied on a functionalist logic: they tried to show how the entertainment industry contributes to the reproduction of the capitalist mode of production by sedating people's passions and critical faculties. They also employed a similar type of explanation when they attributed conservative features to social research, indicating that it supports the existing political order. However, most, if not all, social practices can be reconstructed as if they play a part in producing social order. This poses two problems. Firstly, it exposes the questionable logic underlying Adorno and Horkheimer's critique of social research. If any set of recurrent practices can be reconstructed as such, the value of the functionalist critique of social research must be seriously compromised. Secondly, it is equally feasible to attribute stabilizing functions to their critical theory – for instance, by arguing that it contains the potentially explosive notion of critique within the safe haven of the ivory tower, or that it reaches such levels of abstraction that it is devoid of any practical value.

Those who belonged to the early Frankfurt School used a similarly questionable functionalist logic to justify their hostility to and disregard of American pragmatism. They argued that pragmatism legitimized and contributed to the status quo of American society: it fitted the liberal agenda underlying the capitalist mode of production. Their hostility was partly based on ignorance and on a misguided reading of pragmatist texts. The members of the Frankfurt School erroneously equated pragmatism with an empiricist and positivist outlook and they mistakenly portrayed it as hostile to both theorizing and critique. They conceived of pragmatism as complicit with capitalism and its logic of instrumental reason. They were dismayed by the pragmatist emphasis on instrumental value, which, for them, was yet another expression of the dominance of instrumental rationality in contemporary society. It is remarkable that the Frankfurt School, in particular those members who moved to the United States, retained such a mistaken view of American pragmatism and remained oblivious to the progressive and critical dimension of this philosophy. In this respect, the second generation of the Frankfurt School made huge progress. Not only did they show a more sophisticated knowledge of pragmatism and treat it more fairly, they also properly engaged with it and incorporated many of its ideas. This is especially the case for the most prominent member of this second generation: Jürgen Habermas. It is to his work that attention will be drawn in the next section.

Jürgen Habermas

After Habermas studied various subjects in the humanities at the universities of Göttingen, Zurich and Bonn, he joined the Institute for Social Research in 1956 as Adorno's assistant. He was to stay there for a number of years, and after a couple of other appointments (Heidelberg and the Max Planck Institute) he returned to take up the chair in sociology and philosophy at the University of Frankfurt. It would have been surprising if the formative years at the institute had not influenced Habermas's intellectual development, and indeed he has always had quite a lot in common with the early Frankfurt School. Like them, Habermas's main objective has been to contribute to a critical theory of contemporary society. Social research should do more than simply explain phenomena. It is also about assessing and criticizing the contemporary constellation. It is about providing a normative yardstick to make this critique possible. It is about thinking of socio-political alternatives. Like his predecessors, Habermas was critical of the unnecessarily narrow lens through which positivist social science looks at reality. He disagreed with the way in which positivism denigrates other forms of knowledge and asserts its authority over them.

However, Habermas also helped move critical theory in a very different direction. The most obvious difference between Habermas and the early Frankfurt School lies in their attitude towards the Enlightenment project. Early on, Habermas disagreed with how the early Frankfurt School portrayed the transition towards modernity. While he agreed with Adorno and Horkheimer that the shift from the pre-modern to modernity goes hand in hand with the spread of instrumental rationality, he emphasized that there is also a more benevolent side to modernity. Adorno and Horkheimer made the mistake of equating the rationalization process to the omnipresence of means–end rationality. Modernity also brings about a different kind of rationalization: communicative rationality. Communicative rationality refers to procedures of open debate and criticism. With the transition towards modern society comes the implementation of these procedures. For instance, in *Structural Transformation of the Public Sphere*, Habermas showed how in the course of the eighteenth and nineteenth centuries a 'public sphere' emerged: citizens openly discussed significant social and political events.[32] The public sphere was later eroded, partly because of the commercialization of the media. This example shows, however, that the advent of bourgeois society should not be conceived solely in negative terms. Liberal democracy also heralds a new era, referring to the radical potential of non-coerced debate among equals. Not only ought critical theory to acknowledge this 'discursive will-formation', it should also base its critical theory on it.

Habermas has also deviated from the early Frankfurt School in another way. He has explicitly drawn on American pragmatism. The early Frankfurt School was very much embedded in German philosophy, notably Hegel, Marx and Nietzsche. Habermas has also been influenced by a wide variety of Anglo-Saxon sources, ranging from G. H. Mead's theory of social behaviour and Charles Peirce's 'pragmaticism' to Talcott Parsons's sociological theory and Austin and Searle's theory of speech acts. Charles Peirce had a significant impact on *Knowledge and Human Interests*.[33] Habermas used Peirce to explore the relationship between types of knowledge and *a priori* interests. Cognitive interests are basic orientations that tie in with fundamental conditions of reproduction and self-constitution of the human species. Although Habermas's two volumes of *The Theory of Communicative Action* heralded a radical departure in his intellectual development, pragmatism still occupied a prominent place.[34] His theory of universal pragmatics focused on the practical use of language. Habermas relied on Austin and Searle's theory of speech acts to move away from a Cartesian 'philosophy of consciousness' (*Bewusstseinsphilosophie*) and explore the relationship between linguistically mediated interaction and rationality. This theory of communicative action drew partly on a reconstruction of G. H. Mead's social psychological account of symbolic interaction. Habermas has gone a long way towards reconciling the European strand of critical theory with the American pragmatist tradition.

In *Knowledge and Human Interests* Habermas reacted against the way in which science and a particular view of science has been portrayed as 'absolute knowledge' or as the only valid form of knowledge. For him the dominant positivist type of social research is only one type of knowledge. Philosophy ought never to abandon its critical reflection. It ought never cease to reflect on the kind of knowledge that is being produced. Positivist philosophy did precisely that. It tended to equate knowledge with science, and so abandoned any critical reflection on science. Positivism disregarded the edifying components of social research. Self-edification (*Bildungsprozess*) refers to the process by which knowledge about the social world enables individuals to grow, helping them to become aware of who they are and of who they want to be.[35] In their own ways, Hegel and Marx managed to see through the scientism that was so prominent in their time, but it took a combination of Dilthey's hermeneutics and Charles Peirce's pragmatism to provide a philosophical platform that enabled the exploration of the relationship between types of knowledge and cognitive interests.[36] This brings us to what Habermas set out to achieve. He developed a classification of types of knowledge based on a demonstration of the relationship between 'logical-methodological rules' and 'knowledge-constitutive interests'. His starting point was that people's knowledge ought to be put within the context of the 'natural history of the human species'. It does not follow, however, that knowledge is merely an instrument for adaptation. Knowledge can be adaptive, but other types of knowledge transcend mere self-preservation. Habermas arrived at three forms of knowledge. Each is linked to a particular means of social organization: work, language and power. Whereas 'empirical-analytical sciences' tie in with work and exhibit a technical cognitive interest, 'historical-hermeneutic sciences' are connected to language and have a practical interest. Finally, 'critically orientated science' is tied to power and is directed towards self-emancipation.[37]

Let me briefly explain the three types of knowledge. The empirical-analytical type of knowledge produces 'nomological' knowledge. 'Nomos' means law. Nomological knowledge, therefore, purports to obtain laws, universal statements or law-like generalizations. Empirical-analytical knowledge consists of theories from which, with the help of initial conditions, empirical hypotheses are deductively inferred.[38] Emile Durkheim's work on suicide provides a good example of what Habermas had in mind. Durkheim relied on general assumptions and initial conditions, from which he inferred empirical hypotheses. For instance, he assumed that people find it more difficult to cope with stressful situations when they are not properly integrated, and he noticed that divorcees and widowers are less integrated than married people and that Protestants are less integrated than Catholics. From this he deduced that, on the whole, divorcees and widowers have higher suicide rates than married people, and Protestants are likely to have higher suicide rates than Catholics.[39] Controlled empirical observations are used to check the cognitive validity of the hypotheses. The most controlled of these observations is the experiment, but if this is not possible (and often it is not in the social sciences) then we may rely on quasi-experiments such as comparative research or multivariate statistical research. In both comparative and statistical research we are able to ascertain a causal link between variables by controlling other variables. Habermas noted that, within the empirical-analytical tradition, observations are often wrongly portrayed as 'objective representations' of facts. Actually, these so-called objective facts are constituted within the organizational boundaries of instrumental action. Be that as it may, once the hypotheses have been corroborated, they are supposed to allow for prediction. They predict because they are always of the structure: 'B will occur (or B is more likely to occur) if A occurs'. It should be clear that these predictions also allow for control: if we know that B will occur (or that B will be more likely to occur) if A occurs, then we can decide to bring B about (or to increase the likelihood of B) by creating A. For instance, if research shows that workers tend to be more productive if they are involved in decisions, then we may want to increase workers' productivity by consulting them. This explains why Habermas insisted that this form of knowledge ties in with a technical cognitive interest. It allows for control and prediction.[40]

The historic-hermeneutic sciences operate differently. The cognitive interest is no longer of a technical kind. It establishes understanding and, in particular, mutual understanding. Access to facts is no longer obtained through observation; it is achieved through understanding of meaning. Some historicist authors assume that the understanding of meaning is unproblematic, that we can, for example, access another culture 'as it really is'. This assumes that we are like a blank sheet, able to immerse ourselves totally in a different setting. Nothing is further from the truth. Following Hans-Georg Gadamer, Habermas insisted that our presuppositions are a *sine qua non* for any understanding. For instance, by reading a book, we do not gain access to the text 'as it really is'. We read books in our own way, drawing on our particular concerns, experiences and values. This explains why Habermas emphasized that hermeneutic knowledge 'is always mediated through this pre-understanding, which is derived from the interpreter's initial situation.'[41] It follows that different people might attribute different meanings to what they encounter. We might read Balzac's *Colonel Chabert* as a book about personal identity, or about sincerity and insincerity, post-Napoleonic France, or the transition from a society of honour to a society in which money reigns. Depending on our own tradition, on where we come from, we will have a different take on the book. Through the process of interpreting, however, our own world becomes clarified. By reading books, we are confronted with our own presuppositions and reassess and re-evaluate them. Therefore, the process of understanding is not a one-way process; it brings about communication between different worlds. This is why Habermas talked about hermeneutics being directed towards 'mutual understanding' rather than just 'understanding'.[42]

Critical social science is different again. It does not simply search for invariants, nor does it merely attribute meaning. Its cognitive interest is of a practical and emancipatory kind. It wishes to establish whether theoretical statements refer to invariants or to 'ideologically frozen relations of dependence'. The former cannot be transcended, but the latter can. Critical social science makes people conscious of the mechanisms that have hitherto affected their lives. Making people conscious of the 'hypostatized powers' contributes to making these inoperative. Critical social science combines empirical-analytical and hermeneutic knowledge, with the aim of self-emancipation. Psychoanalysis is an example of critical social science.[43] The psychoanalyst uses various hermeneutic techniques to understand patients so as to uncover causal mechanisms that inhibit their further development. The psychoanalytic use of these hermeneutic devices does not assume that the patient is always fully aware of his or her internal logic. Sigmund Freud's 'depth hermeneutics' pays attention to the way in which, via everyday activities or dreams, people both express and conceal self-deceptions. Habermas argued that we should extend the psychoanalytic model to the societal level and ascertain how power and ideology make for distorted communication. Whether at individual or societal level, the ultimate aim of critical social science is not to understand, or to control or predict. The ultimate objective of psychoanalysis, for instance, is to bring about self-emancipation: the uplifting of the causal mechanisms that inhibit the mental and emotional growth of the patient. Hermeneutic and causal-mechanical knowledge are simply means of obtaining this objective.[44]

Since the publication of *Knowledge and Human Interests* Habermas has been receptive to criticisms against it. Initially, he thought that it was perfectly possible to overcome the criticisms within the book's general frame of reference. For instance, it has been pointed out that, throughout *Knowledge and Human Interests*, he used the term 'reflection' ambiguously, oscillating between the Kantian notion of critique (as a reflection upon the conditions of possibilities of knowing) and the Hegelian notion of *Bildung* (as reflection upon unconscious or hypostatized constraints). Habermas agreed that the distinction is important. He called the latter self-criticism and the former rational reconstruction. Later, however, he realized that, in other respects, the overall framework is problematic. He felt that the book was still too much embedded in what he calls a 'philosophy of consciousness' (*Bewusstseinsphilosophie*). A philosophy of consciousness conceives of isolated subjects and ignores the social dimension of communicative practices. From the 1970s onwards Habermas has developed a new account of rationality that goes well beyond a philosophy of consciousness. This intellectual shift is known as Habermas's 'linguistic turn' because of his focus on communication and language. For this he has drawn on 'reconstructive sciences', such as Chomsky's generative grammar, Kohlberg's account of moral development and Piaget's theory of cognitive development. Reconstructive sciences reveal the implicit rules that govern our pre-theoretical 'knowing how'. They are empirical sciences and therefore fallible and subject to methods of empirical testing. This intellectual enterprise has culminated in his theory of universal pragmatics and theory of communicative action.[45]

To understand the rationale behind the theory of communicative action, it is important to revisit the differences between Habermas and the early Frankfurt School. I mentioned that, in comparison with Adorno and

Horkheimer, Habermas has paid a lot of attention to the 'radical potential' of the Enlightenment project. This already transpired from his earlier work on *Structural Transformation of the Public Sphere*, in which he argued that the emergence of a bourgeois society brought about the implementation of procedures of open discussion and criticism. For Habermas, the transition towards modernity is characterized not only by instrumental rationality, but also by communicative rationality. Communicative rationality refers to procedures of unconstrained debate and criticism between equals, and is gradually spreading in various spheres. This is not to say that our current society has embraced communicative rationality entirely, but it has moved more in that direction than, say, pre-modern Europe. For instance, compared to the one in the late Middle Ages, our current legal system provides more of a transparent structure in which the accused can properly defend themselves against allegations made against them. Likewise, knowledge is no longer legitimized through tradition or religion. Instead, academic journals and conferences provide a platform for an open discussion of the latest scientific findings. Not only did Habermas believe that communicative rationality is becoming more prevalent, he also deemed it worth defending. Communicative rationality was actually so important for him that it became the central pillar of his critical theory.

Habermas elaborated on this by developing his 'theory of universal pragmatics', in which the notion of competence is crucial. 'Competence' refers to the skills people have that allow them to draw various distinctions. People are able to distinguish between action orientated towards success and action directed towards 'understanding' (*Verständigung*). Action orientated towards success can be either instrumental or strategic: the former refers to a relationship with nature, the latter to a relationship with people. Digging for oil in Alaska is an example of the former, work relations depicted by Marx an example of the latter. Like strategic action, communicative action is directed towards people but differs in that it is aimed at understanding and agreement – not success. Habermas's critical theory focused on this communicative action. But it also assumed that people are able to make another distinction, namely between three different worlds: external nature, society and internal nature. The realm of external nature involves issues of factual representation; the realm of society deals with issues of moral rightness of social rules; and the world of internal nature deals with issues of sincerity. What, then, is the link between communicative action and the three worlds? Habermas argued that communicative action is orientated towards understanding regarding what he called 'validity claims', and these validity claims depend on the distinction between the three worlds.

To explain this, Habermas drew upon speech act theory. Speech act theory pays attention to the things we accomplish or do by saying something. Habermas argued that, whenever people are involved in a conversation, four 'validity claims' are presupposed: 'intelligibility' (*Verständlichkeit*), 'propositional truth' (*Wahrheit*), 'moral rightness' (*Richtigkeit*) and 'sincerity' (*Wahrhaftigkeit*).[46] Whenever we speak, the very act of speaking presupposes that what we say is intelligible, that it is true, that we are justified in saying it, and that we are not saying it in order to deceive anyone. If I attend an academic seminar, for instance, I constantly make validity claims. Implicit in my speaking is the assumption that what I say is not gibberish and that I am speaking the truth. Also implicit is that I am morally justified in saying what I am saying, and that I am not saying it in order to deceive. This does *not* mean that I *am* clear and am understood, nor does it mean that I *am* speaking the truth, that I *have* the right to say everything I say or that I *am* always sincere. My interventions might well be unclear or I might say things that are plainly wrong. Some of my utterances might be outrageous and inappropriate – I might well be insulting my colleagues – and I might be a fraud. Habermas's point is not that the four validity claims are correct, but that, whenever we converse, the validity claims are *presupposed*. It is worth noting that, with the exception of intelligibility, the validity claims correspond to different worlds: truth corresponds to the objective world, moral rightness to the social world and sincerity to the internal realm.

Habermas talked about 'undistorted communication' whenever people can openly criticize and defend each other with regard to the validity claims. It occurs when there are hardly any barriers to open debate. Habermas coined 'ideal speech situation' (*ideale Sprechsituation*) to refer to the ideal-typical situation in which there are no such barriers at all. Everybody is entitled to argue their case, to question what others have said and to raise new topics. The ideal speech situation is entirely dominated by the principle of the 'force of the better argument'. Let us take the example of the academic seminar again. We are facing an ideal speech situation if all participants are allowed to question and criticize what other participants say, and if all are equally free to defend themselves. In this situation, everything I say is open to criticism. The other participants have the opportunity to ask for further clarification when they think I am being vague or incoherent. They can point out my mistakes, or they can argue that some of my statements are inappropriate or morally repugnant. Finally, they can question my sincerity, for instance, by arguing that I am not addressing the relevant issues that should be covered in the seminar. Of course, I can criticize others as well; in the ideal speech situation there are no obstacles to criticism. Conversely, I (like anybody else) can openly defend myself against criticisms. Nobody can penalize those who criticize their arguments, and, likewise, nobody should be penalized for defending their position. The absence of sociological obstacles, such as negative sanctions and power, is necessary for the ideal speech situation, but it is not sufficient. In addition, internal, psychological obstacles need to be lifted.

We do not have an ideal speech situation, for instance, if some of us are too shy to speak out in public or are easily impressed by others.

Needless to say, the ideal speech situation never exists in reality. Sanctions are always somehow in operation; people always exhibit psychological features that do not fit the model. The ideal speech situation is an ideal type in the Weberian sense of the word. What, then, is the value of this construction? For Habermas, it is a 'counterfactual' ideal that can operate as a yardstick for judging real-life situations and for comparing between them.[47] As a benchmark, it is a basis for a critique of distorted communication. Hence, Habermas's critical theory is distinct in that he proposed a *procedural* notion of rationality, giving us, not a foundation, but procedures for reaching decisions. Not every validity claim can be redeemed via discourse: for instance, sincerity can only be redeemed through subsequent action. But truth and moral rightness *can* be redeemed via discourses that approximate ideal speech situations. Note that Habermas's notion of truth is also a procedural one. It does not provide absolute foundations of knowledge, only procedures for reaching knowledge. Habermas's consensus theory of truth refers to consensus among equal participants in an open debate. Knowledge, therefore, is temporal, to be preserved until a better argument comes along and forces the community to take a different view.

In conclusion, what has been Habermas's contribution to the philosophy of the social sciences? To what extent has his critical theory been an improvement compared to the work of the early Frankfurt School? I see Habermas's contribution as twofold. Firstly, he has presented a pragmatist-inspired account of knowledge, showing the extent to which knowledge ties in with human interests. In this view, the dominant empirical-analytical type of knowledge is only one type of knowledge, aiming at prediction and control. Other types of knowledge aim at different cognitive interests; Habermas mentioned hermeneutics (directed towards understanding) and critical theory (directed towards self-emancipation). In this context, he developed a sophisticated account of critical theory as a combination of hermeneutic and empirical-analytical types of knowledge and directed towards self-emancipation. Secondly, he has convincingly shown how critical theory can be grounded in a pragmatist understanding of language and conversation. In this view, critical theory does not present foundations, but *procedures* for reaching decisions. In the process of developing his critical theory, he has managed to point out the value of unrestrained debate among equals and thereby to soften the criticisms of the Enlightenment project. At a time when Enlightenment philosophy had come under intense scrutiny by postmodernists and other sceptics, Habermas made a passionate appeal not to throw out the baby with the bath water. He identified communicative rationality as the link between various modern institutions, ranging from the legal system to the academy. He regarded this principle of communicative rationality as the core of modernity and as worth defending.

What are the limitations of Habermas's project? While *Knowledge and Human Interests* paid attention to the various cognitive interests that may guide social research, it failed to pay sufficient attention to how self-referential knowledge can be a legitimate and feasible research aim. By self-referential knowledge, I refer to the knowledge we may acquire about the presuppositions that are central to our culture. Habermas mentioned self-understanding but only in so far as it is a corollary of the pursuit of the understanding of others. Like Gadamer, Habermas conceived of self-understanding mainly in *ontological* terms: in the process of understanding other people, other texts or cultures, we end up reassessing ourselves, our own setting and presuppositions. Some form of self-understanding necessarily accompanies understanding. Habermas failed properly to conceive of self-understanding in *methodological* terms, namely as a research objective in itself, worth pursuing and worth the thought about how it should be pursued. A critical theory of society ought also to focus on self-referential knowledge, for it allows for the assessment of hitherto implicit assumptions and for the awareness of alternative socio-political scenarios.[48] It fulfils the function of critique, not in the sense of pointing out errors or inconsistencies in our views, or in the sense of transcending causal obstacles to self-emancipation, but in the sense of confronting us with new perspectives and broadening our outlook. What we need, therefore, is a reflection on the various research strategies that employ the confrontation with 'difference' to obtain this self-referential type of knowledge acquisition. This intellectual task is central to my pragmatist proposal, outlined in the final chapter, which shows that self-referential knowledge has already been pursued with success in a number of social sciences: archaeology, anthropology and history.

Habermas's assertion that communicative action is *verständigungsorientiertes Handeln* is problematic. *Verständigung* means both understanding and agreement. So the statement means that communicative action is directed towards reaching not only understanding but also agreement. This is precisely where the problem comes in. While it is certainly not impossible to imagine scenarios in which communicative action between people involves the understanding of each other's positions, it is more difficult to think of situations in which communicative action would actually imply agreement between the parties involved. The problem becomes more obvious when the different people involved in the conversation belong to quite different cultures. It is difficult enough to see how, in those situations, individuals would reach an understanding of each other's positions. Reaching agreement would be even more problematic. Habermas's innocuous 'force of the better argument' will not always present the role of arbiter that he hoped for. Even in settings where the cultural differences are minimal, that which constitutes a convincing argument does not go without contention. The stronger the differences, the more unlikely there will be a consensus about what amounts to a superior argument. For atheists, for instance, references to religious texts may not constitute credible arguments; for strong believers, they do. Of course, we could take a Habermasian response and argue that the force of the better argument should also be open to unrestrained discussion. It goes without saying that this reply would not solve our problem, for we would be entering a vicious circle in which the decision about what is a valid argument depends on argumentation that necessitates further argumentation, and so on.

The next chapter explores a more radical use of pragmatist insights through the writings of the American philosopher Richard Rorty. Compared to Habermas, Rorty, a self-declared pragmatist, takes the insights of pragmatism to a totally different level. He uses the work of John Dewey and other pragmatists to provide a compelling critique of epistemology and of the view that knowledge accurately represents the external world. A critical assessment of Rorty's writings will allow me to build the foundations of my pragmatist proposal for the philosophy of the social sciences.

Further reading

To understand Adorno, Horkheimer or Habermas, it is advisable to have some acquaintance with the history of the Frankfurt School. Marvin Jay's *The Dialectical Imagination: A History of the Frankfurt School and the Institute of Social Research, 1923–1950* is an excellent introduction to the early Frankfurt School. Equally informative is David Held's *Introduction to Critical Theory: Horkheimer to Habermas*. Compared to Jay, Held also incorporates later intellectual developments. For a philosophical introduction to the various issues raised by critical theory, I suggest Raymond Geuss's *The Idea of a Critical Theory*. William Outhwaite's *Habermas: A Critical Introduction* manages to provide an accessible account of Habermas's writings without compromising the material covered. Maeve Cooke's *Language and Reason* is a comprehensive and critical account of Habermas's pragmatics. With regard to primary sources, I would suggest Horkheimer's essay 'Traditional and Critical Theory' and Adorno's 'Sociology and Empirical Research'. Some other contributions to *The Positivist Dispute in German Sociology* could be useful, although the tone of the debate remains remarkably tame throughout the book (with the exception of the final chapter, written by Popper). For those readers interested in Habermas's theory of cognitive interests, I suggest his *Knowledge and Human Interests*. Ironically, it is best to start with the postscript. For those interested in his later work, *The Theory of Communicative Action* consists of two volumes, but it is a difficult read.

6
Richard Rorty and Pragmatism

Introduction

American pragmatism had been marginalized in philosophical circles for a long time, but it has recently been revived. This is partly because of Richard Rorty's philosophical writings: he wants to resuscitate pragmatism. Rorty gained notoriety with his ground-breaking *Philosophy and the Mirror of Nature*, in which he argues that we should relinquish any transcendental forms of inquiry that supposedly provide atemporal foundations for aesthetic, ethical and knowledge-related claims; it is simply impossible to 'step outside history' because any position, whether about beauty, morals or knowledge, is 'situated'. His *Consequences of Pragmatism* elaborates on this view, and shows it to be indebted to pragmatist philosophers such as William James and especially John Dewey. Like James and Dewey, Rorty suggests that we forsake philosophical debates if they do not have visible consequences; he targets especially what he sees as pointless arguments about the inner nature of things, which fail to yield any way of deciding between the competing views. Rorty believes that it would also be better if we dropped the numerous attempts at defining truth or presenting theories of truth if by truth is meant something unconditional or a correspondence to an absolute reality. Taking a leaf out of James's book, he maintains that we should retain a notion of truth only if it is defined in terms of successful consequences. Rorty urges that we abandon the 'spectator theory of knowledge', according to which knowledge is about representing the essence of an outer world; it is highly misleading to conceive of knowledge as mirroring the inner nature of the external realm. Like Dewey, he suggests that we treat knowledge as a type of action, as a way of meeting our desires. Denouncing the conspicuous position of epistemology in contemporary philosophy, Rorty proposes instead an edifying form of philosophy, partly inspired by Gadamer's hermeneutics, in which we no longer search for atemporal foundations, but redescribe ourselves in conversation with others.

Richard Rorty is inspired not only by American pragmatism. I have already mentioned Gadamer's impact. Rorty integrates pragmatism with very different traditions such as analytical philosophy, post-positivist philosophy of science and French structuralism. He is convinced that developments in analytical philosophy and the philosophy of science herald the end of philosophy as traditionally conceived. Rorty uses a Wittgensteinian metaphor when he argues that Anglo-Saxon philosophers such as Quine, Davidson and Sellars help us to climb the ladder of analytical philosophy all the way and then kick it away.[1] The upshot of this is that we have to abandon the idea that philosophy is able to develop a 'final vocabulary' that can override all other vocabularies. Rorty points out that Dewey had already articulated this view one century ago and developed a new conception of philosophy that was similar to Derrida's philosophical agenda. Rorty also draws on aligned disciplines such as literary theory and sociology. It is unsurprising that he has not held a formal appointment in a philosophy department since the early 1980s, not only because he preached 'the end of Philosophy' (by 'Philosophy' he means the foundational project that presents a final vocabulary), but also because he treated literary works as being on a par with philosophy, and cut across disciplinary boundaries. Many of his contributions of late have been in the area of literary criticism or have at least drawn on the study of literary texts.[2] With these ideas, Rorty was bound to become a philosopher for non-philosophers. While they stopped short of making analytical philosophers unemployable, his writings were dismissed by some of them as sloppy.[3] The less welcome he was in American philosophy departments, the more widely read and admired Rorty was in faculties of literature and cultural studies.

I will focus on Rorty's relevance for the philosophy of the social sciences. He has not written a huge amount about the social sciences, but he has provided some commentary, and his more general reflections on the role of philosophy have significant repercussions for the philosophy of the social sciences. Towards the end of this chapter, I will try to explain what these repercussions are and at the same time assess the validity and fruitfulness of Rorty's intellectual programme. This critical assessment sets the stage for the concluding chapter, in which I elaborate on the potential of a pragmatist philosophy of the social sciences.

American pragmatism and Rorty

Pragmatism is, in many respects, an American product. Whether they belong to the select category of pragmatist 'classics' (C. S. Peirce, William James, G. H. Mead and John Dewey) or to what I call 'second-wave' pragmatism (Donald Davidson, Willard Quine, Hilary Putnam and Richard Rorty), most significant pragmatists are Americans born and bred. They also proudly acknowledge the extent to which their philosophy is intrinsically linked to the country in which they grew up. They do so by arguing that the particular narrative of the United States may account for some of the distinctiveness of pragmatist philosophy, and that the pragmatist method of inquiry is particularly well suited to some American issues. But however truly American pragmatism might be, some qualifications ought to be made. First of all, several European philosophers, such as Friedrich Nietzsche and Henri Bergson, developed ideas that were remarkably close to pragmatism. Among European sociological classics, both Durkheim and Weber engaged with William James's work. More recently, Jürgen Habermas drew heavily on the work of Peirce and Mead. Contemporary European theorists, such as Hans Joas, show an increasing interest in the history of American pragmatism and in its recent developments.[4]

Furthermore, American academia has not always been immersed in pragmatism. Pragmatism might have occupied a relatively dominant position in philosophy departments until the 1930s, but within a decade pragmatists were swept away by an influx of refugees from Europe who were steeped in logical positivism. While this was originally predominantly a phenomenon of Cambridge and Vienna, logical positivists such as Otto Neurath and Moritz Schlick had laid the conceptual foundations for what was to become the dominant analytical approach in American philosophy. It was, of course, still possible for *historians* of philosophy to study pragmatism, which was henceforth seen as a quaint, outdated speculative theory, worthy of some attention. However, few self-respecting philosophers would have espoused pragmatist views; even fewer would have called themselves pragmatists. It took almost half a century for pragmatism to be rediscovered. Even the impact of that rediscovery on American philosophy should not be overestimated. It was the achievement of only a handful of people (among whom Rorty and R. J. Bernstein probably stand out), and with fewer followers in philosophy departments than in literary circles.

Finally, American pragmatism is a broad church that includes rival factions and is constantly evolving. There have been so many differences, even among the founding fathers, that Peirce felt the need to coin a new term (the unfashionable 'Pragmaticism') so as to distinguish his views from those of others.[5] In a similar vein, Arthur Lovejoy felt entitled to write about the 'thirteen Pragmatisms',[6] and Schiller went even further by intimating that there are as many pragmatisms as there are pragmatists.[7] It is thus not surprising that a significant part of the secondary literature on pragmatism attempts to conceptualize the major splits or divisions within pragmatism.[8] Some commentators focus on the juxtaposition between Peirce's attention to the intersubjectivity of a community of inquirers and James's focus on individuals' thought processes; others to the difference between those pragmatists who still hold on to some notion of objectivity of truth and those who have abandoned that search altogether. Others mention the contrast between pragmatists, such as Sidney Hook, who wish to impose scientific rationality on other aspects of culture, and those, such as Rorty, who do not wish to attribute more rationality to science than to art, politics and religion.[9]

Still, different pragmatists have a lot in common. There might not be a pragmatist party line that all have to toe, but there are a number of key ideas that most pragmatists, including Rorty, have in common. I suggest four ideas that are central to Rorty's thought and that make it pragmatist. The first idea, which most pragmatic philosophers share, is a distrust of what John Dewey called the 'spectator theory of knowledge'.[10] The spectator theory of knowledge sees knowledge as predominantly, if not exclusively, a way of representing the inner nature of an outer world as accurately as possible. In contrast, pragmatism wishes to break with this metaphor of vision. Inspired by Darwinian evolutionary theory, it expounds a truly 'anti-representationalist' view; knowledge acquisition is seen as active in that it is a way of coping with life's demands. Darwinism taught pragmatists that it is perfectly possible to explain how the human species developed language as one among many sophisticated methods of survival, but it is difficult to see how human beings would have acquired the capacity to represent the universe as it actually is. It would, in the light of biological evolution, be an extraordinary coincidence if people's cognitive functions were so radically transformed as to allow for adequate representation.[11] In the work of Dewey and Mead, therefore, knowledge is seen as a tool that makes possible the continuation of a previously inhibited course of action.[12] For Dewey pragmatism builds upon modern science and, in contrast with ancient conceptions of experience and science, experimental science underscores the active processes, the doing, in knowledge acquisition. For rationalists reality is ready-made, complete and waiting to be discovered; for pragmatists it is always in the making. Knowledge is not about copying but coping.[13]

Most pragmatist writings are hostile to any transcendental form of inquiry that supposedly grounds aesthetic, ethical or cognitive claims. For a long time philosophers thought their discipline consisted of doing precisely that. While non-philosophers were able to articulate the historically and culturally specific, philosophers assumed they were able somehow to provide atemporal foundations. They differed in how to arrive at the foundations. Some appealed to intuition, some to self-inquiry, others again relied upon reason, or a combination of all these, and so on. But what they had in common was the belief that their philosophical quest would ultimately enable them 'to step outside history' and provide the groundwork. Pragmatists, on the other hand, argue that the validity of this project has been compromised. Transcendental forms of inquiry are problematic because they have never worked: none of the attempts so far have proved to be successful. They are also problematic because contributions to analytical philosophy by Quine, Goodman and

Sellars have seriously compromised some of the assumptions that accompany that search. Pragmatists therefore talk about the 'agent's point of view', referring to the fact that people cannot escape using a conceptual system. But recognizing the situated nature of human inquiry need not imply that people's knowledge is merely subjective (if by subjective we mean that this knowledge somehow fails to correspond to the inner nature of reality).[14]

Most pragmatists try to settle theoretical disputes by gauging what effects they have. They are particularly dismayed by the extent to which philosophers and scientists get involved in pointless debates. These discussions often concern the 'inner' nature of things, alleged 'necessities' or 'first principles'. Pragmatists such as James argued that many disputes of this kind are merely 'specious' or 'verbal'. To know whether a debate is worth having, so their argument goes, we should simply ascertain whether it makes any difference to take up one position or another, and we should abandon the debate if there are no observable consequences of taking one position or another. James put it crisply: 'there can be *no* difference anywhere that doesn't *make* a difference elsewhere.'[15] Which 'differences elsewhere' do pragmatists regard as significant? It obviously depends on our values, and pragmatists may differ on this. In science pragmatists tend to argue that *empirical* effects matter; in the social sciences other effects (such as repercussions in terms of social policy) may be considered. Let me take the pragmatic treatment of the 'tautomerous' in chemistry as an example. Scientists used to argue endlessly about the inner constitution of certain bodies called 'tautomerous'. The evidence provided seemed insufficient to decide whether an unstable hydrogen atom fluctuates in the tautomerous or whether it is an unstable mixture of two bodies. Influenced by pragmatism, Oswald asked what empirical differences would occur if one position or another were true. The answer is none. For Oswald, it follows that the difference is meaningless. Scientists may discuss the inner nature of the tautomerous *ad infinitum*, but it is a pointless exercise.

For centuries philosophers have been preoccupied with providing a theory of truth. Philosophers have also been inclined to treat scientific progress as a gradual progress towards truth (though never attaining it). In contrast, some contemporary pragmatists are sceptical towards any philosophical search for the meaning of 'truth'.[16] To ascertain whether an idea or a theory is true is a pointless exercise if by 'true' is meant something unconditional or a correspondence to an absolute reality. As Putnam pointed out, any claim that a belief corresponds to reality calls for the question: ' "reality" under which description?' Pragmatists feel they have nothing interesting to say about truth; that is, they have nothing significant to say about that which all true statements share. If pressed, they might say that 'truth' is simply a name attributed to the feature which all true statements share. When confronted with the tautological nature of that answer, they would reply that this is the best they can do.[17] For pragmatists, what is more important is whether the idea or theory is successful: that is, whether it accomplishes what we want to achieve. So they might be willing to retain the notion of truth in so far as it is defined in terms of successful consequences: 'Ideas . . . become true only in so far as they help us to get into satisfactory relation with other parts of our experience.'[18]

The myth of the scientific method

In *Philosophy and the Mirror of Nature* Rorty questioned the assumption underlying epistemology that all contributions to a particular object of inquiry are 'commensurable'. To assume commensurability is to presuppose that it is possible to detect a set of rules that allow us to judge between conflicting knowledge claims. Epistemologists may of course differ in where they locate that common ground. Cartesians may think that this common ground lies in the mind, those following Kant will position it in the categories, while analytical philosophers may point at language. In contrast, hermeneutics promotes conversation as an exchange between different positions. Like epistemology, it entails the hope for agreement but without the assumption that there is a common ground prior to the conversation. The traditional view is that epistemology and hermeneutics cover different aspects of culture: epistemology provides a secure base for the superior, objective aspects of culture, whereas hermeneutics deals with its lesser, 'non-cognitive' manifestation. In this view, epistemology and hermeneutics seem to carve up culture between them: epistemology is about detecting the key to the success of the 'natural' sciences, while hermeneutics is happy to assist the poetry, rhetoric and vision that make up the humanities. Rorty's point is that there is no one-to-one relationship between the type of philosophy and domain of inquiry. There are certain periods when hermeneutics is perfectly applicable to the natural sciences and epistemology to poetry. It all depends on whether the discourses are 'normal' or 'abnormal'. Normal discourse is one in which there is a consensus about how to adjudicate between conflicting claims – an agreement that is entirely missing in periods dominated by abnormal discourse. When confronted with the latter, hermeneutics is our best hope for agreement. In the case of the former, epistemology is the answer.[19]

In the light of the above, it is not surprising that Rorty is sceptical of those attempts to uncover the 'reliable method' of science, let alone 'the one reliable method for reaching the truth about the nature of things'. This is not to say that he does not subscribe to an experimental, fallibilist attitude to science. He does, but he feels that it is impossible to identify *the* method that epitomizes (or does most justice to) this attitude.[20] To take an experimental, fallibilist attitude is not to assume that empirical evidence or 'hard facts' provide final answers when deciding how to describe the world. From Quine and

Putnam (and, to some extent, Kuhn), Rorty learns that new pieces of evidence are incorporated in existing webs of belief. They might, of course, eventually lead to readjustment of these webs of belief, and Rorty actually suggests that the researchers consider reweaving the web of beliefs in the light of the new beliefs acquired.[21] But the point is that, according to the holistic form of pragmatism advocated by Rorty, new pieces of evidence do not simply impose themselves on the researchers; they are always interpreted in the light of what is already known. Notice also that Rorty insists that his cautious guideline (that it might be useful to see whether conceptual adjustment needs to be made in the light of new insights) is not another call for the 'one reliable method'. 'The one piece of advice would only entail the other if experience had shown that having a conscious epistemological view were always an efficient instrument for readjusting old beliefs to new. But experience does not show this, any more than it shows the opposite.'[22]

In his mission against the myth of the reliable method, Rorty finds inspiration in the work of Thomas Kuhn. Rorty has always had a great admiration for Kuhn's *The Structure of Scientific Revolutions*. He regards Kuhn not simply as a historian of science, but as a philosopher, mainly because Kuhn managed to make us think in a novel way about science and scientific activities. In this new view, natural scientists do not have a privileged access to reality or to truth.[23] The Platonic distinction between logic and rhetoric is undermined, because scientific revolutions do not subscribe to some neutral, universal algorithm; with every revolution the criteria of relevance and truth are being adjusted. Rorty is, however, not an unqualified admirer of Kuhn, and he spends some time assessing the validity of Kuhn's critics. His verdict is a balanced one. On the one hand, Rorty regards the core of the controversy between Kuhn and his critics as centring on the question whether the forms of argumentation in science are different from patterns of argument regarding 'practical' or 'aesthetic' matters. He points out that Kuhn's writings suggest that there is no difference, and Rorty certainly argues so himself.[24] On the other hand, like Kuhn's critics, Rorty distances himself from the more idealist passages in *The Structure of Scientific Revolutions* where scientists are portrayed as perceiving a different world after a scientific revolution. For Rorty, this portrayal is unfortunate because it has meant that most commentators have failed to appreciate the importance of the overall argument of the book.[25]

Kuhn's work leads in itself to a paradigm shift; it makes certain questions redundant. We should no longer be preoccupied by questions such as 'Which method is intrinsic to science?' and *mutatis mutandis* by queries such as 'How can we model the social sciences on a scientific footing?' Some have tried to answer the first question by claiming that science allows for accurate predictions, and surely what we now call 'science' does precisely this. But we should not conflate its current meaning with some putative essence. All that has happened is that over the centuries the ability to make successful predictions has become a more important criterion for adjudicating scientific research.[26] A slightly more convincing answer to the same question, but still a flawed one, is to say that what distinguishes scientific from other activities is that their knowledge claims rest upon a consensus among non-coerced inquirers about who has succeeded and who has failed. However, Kuhn has shown that the criteria of successful research change in time, and that there is sometimes a lack of a clear single criterion. We also know that the larger the number of criteria of success and the less clarity about what are significant criteria, the less agreement there is about what counts as success. The solution lies in recharting our culture. Rather than mapping culture in terms of a hierarchy between the objective natural sciences and the defective humanities, it makes more sense to describe culture in terms of a spectrum ranging from the non-consensual to the consensual. The natural sciences are often on the consensual side of the spectrum, but during revolutionary periods they veer to the other side. Not every discipline can be categorized as either consensual or non-consensual for ever: in contrast with today, seventeenth-century philosophy and physics very much lacked agreement, and literary criticism was precisely the opposite.[27]

Rorty's reading of Kuhn has significant repercussions for the social sciences. Since the Enlightenment, and especially since Kant, the practice of the natural sciences was considered to be a model for acquiring secure knowledge, one to be emulated by the rest of our culture.[28] From J. S. Mill to Popper, philosophers of science tried to uncover the key to the success of the natural sciences, the method that underlies their activities, that distinguishes them from other forms of knowledge acquisition, and that guarantees their continual progress. They suggest the social sciences follow the very same methodological guidelines that secured such significant advancement in the natural sciences, or alternatively that, given the different ontology between the social and the natural, the social sciences follow different guidelines that nevertheless ensure equally 'objective' knowledge. Assuming Rorty is right that there is no neutral algorithm in the natural sciences save a *post factum* and a Whiggish one (that is, an epistemology congruent with the winning sides of scientific debates),[29] then the pursuit of a similar ideal in the social sciences seems to be ill-conceived. Assuming Rorty is right that Kuhn showed convincingly that there is no single unifying method which underscores all successful scientific activities and distinguishes them from other, lesser activities, then the question whether social scientists employ the 'right' methods and are 'scientific' enough seems to be less pressing. Rorty recognizes this himself, and writes about 'Kuhnianization' to refer to the process by which there is a growing acceptance that there is no single method for success and that the criteria for good work change through time. This is as visible a trend in the social sciences as it is in philosophy.[30]

Rorty discusses at great length the *Methodenstreit*, the struggle between naturalist and anti-naturalist approaches. His reconstruction of that dispute, which took place at the end of the nineteenth century, is close to the way in which it has traditionally been presented. There are, first of all, those who argue that historians and social scientists should emulate the natural sciences. This means, in practice, promoting the shibboleth of value-neutrality: the values of the historian or sociologist should not interfere with their investigations. Instead they ought to aim at describing the social entirely in descriptive terms so as to infer predictive generalizations. There are, secondly, those who argue that the nature of the social is different from that of the natural and that, by virtue of that difference, the *Geisteswissenschaften* require a method distinct from the one adopted by the *Naturwissenschaften*. The ontological features of the social call for the use of the 'hermeneutic' method, which does not assume value-neutrality. More recently, it has been fashionable to rephrase the juxtaposition of naturalist and anti-naturalist approaches in terms of 'explanation' versus 'understanding', but Rorty is of the opinion that, although an improvement, it does not make a huge difference. The assumption is still that there is a valid dispute about the right kind of method.[31]

This is precisely where Rorty disagrees with both sides of the debate. For him the controversy is an ill-conceived one, because it is not actually about method. Debates about method would require a common goal, and this is absent here. It would be preposterous to hold that naturalist and anti-naturalist 'readings' of the social have the same objective; they obviously do different things. Whether either position is a plausible route to take depends on what we want to achieve. If we want to predict and control, naturalist approaches will do; if we want to treat human beings as moral individuals, then surely anti-naturalist approaches are called for.[32] The two approaches, the naturalist and the anti-naturalist, share the erroneous view that accomplishing one is a stepping stone for achieving the other. Naturalists assume that to predict and control helps to make moral judgements; anti-naturalists believe that to treat humans in a moral and just way facilitates steering and predicting. Both are wrong, however. There is no intrinsic link between the two requirements, one does not entail the secret password to the other, and it is therefore foolish to debate whether explanation or understanding is more appropriate without specifying what aims we want to achieve.[33]

Some authors make the case for a hermeneutically inspired social science by pointing out the ontological differences between nature and the social. They argue that the social realm is governed by meaning in ways in which nature is not, and that these ontological differences are so vast that they call for methodological differences. Rorty objects to this way of reasoning. The gist of his argument is that it is not possible to invent an appropriate vocabulary for the social that cannot also be used effectively for treating the natural world, and that the interpretative methods have been employed with success in the natural sciences.[34] For instance, although it is convincing to say, as hermeneutics does, that we learn about people and cultural items by looking at their relationship with other people or artefacts, it is equally plausible that we find out about a puzzling fossil by investigating its relationship with other fossils. It is precisely this interpretative method that paleontology employed before the discipline became 'normalized'. Researchers in the natural sciences have, in the past, often relied on 'intepretative' methods in that they invoked a vocabulary that made intelligible new objects by relating them to more familiar objects. Only later, when normal science came into play, did the natural scientists abandon these holistic interpretative methods. The hermeneutic assumption that somebody's own vocabulary is the best one for understanding what he or she is up to is just another version of the widespread fallacy that science ought to adopt the same vocabulary as the one which the universe employs to explain itself to itself. Against hermeneutic authors such as Charles Taylor who search for people's own explanations for their actions, Rorty insists that people's accounts could be so obviously false that they are to be dismissed. This is not to say that it is unwise to ask people about their motives. We should ask them, not to find some 'true meaning', but simply because the people might be able to provide an adequate vocabulary; if so, asking them would save time compared to designing a vocabulary ourselves.[35]

The New Left and the Cultural Left

Rorty is highly critical of Marxist theories of society, and this is apparent in two recent publications, 'The End of Leninism, Havel, and Social Hope' and 'Failed Prophecies, Glorious Hopes'.[36] Rorty recognizes that Marx inspired many significant political movements, which in turn have achieved a great deal. But he remains sceptical of Marx's thought on two accounts. The first critique relies on the pragmatist view of history. He laments the extent to which Marxism is embedded in the nineteenth-century Zeitgeist, in particular its attempt to uncover iron laws of societal evolution and its quasi-religious belief that knowledge of historical patterns will empower people to anticipate the future. Rorty is highly critical of the view that the past holds the magical key for a better future and that the laws of history will hold for ever as they have always done in the past. In this context, he is obviously influenced by the pragmatist view of history, which entails what G. H. Mead so aptly called the notion of the 'incurable contingency of the future'. Almost a century ago, Dewey and Mead introduced their pragmatic notion of history as antithetical to any eschatological view of history. Armed with notions such as the 'emergent present' and 'novelty', the pragmatic view of history was meant to oppose Hegelian attempts at 'world history', and, likewise, Rorty feels there is very little to be learnt from these all-embracing theories of history. Rorty's second critique seems indebted to Popper and Fukuyama, although it is still compatible with a pragmatist view of the world. This critique of Marxism focuses on its empirical refutations; it has a philosophical and a practical component. The philosophical component is exemplified by the extent to which Rorty is alarmed by the irrefutable nature of Marx's prophecies. Like Popper, he is convinced that a theory that hardly excludes anything ultimately fails to explain properly. But Rorty pays more attention to the practical dimension. It would be irresponsible to disregard the empirical fact that, in practice, Marxism has led to various unpleasant regimes. Like Popper and Berlin (and, of course, like Dewey), Rorty believes that these totalitarian states cannot be dismissed as mere aberrations, unfortunate accidents of history, but are indicative that there is something wrong with the theory itself. Fukuyama is right to point out that the fall of the Berlin Wall was the final blow to the belief that a centrally planned society, as envisaged by Marx, was a workable model. Of course, pragmatists do not need elaborate theoretical constructions to rebuff Marxism. The fact that history has shown Marxist theories not to work is a sufficient reason to abandon them.[37]

Rorty is not saying that *The Communist Manifesto* and other writings by Marx are archaic documents and can be discarded. We should still read his works, and we should do so thoroughly. We should still teach Marx to our students; there is a lot of depth in his work. He was remarkably perceptive in uncovering and explaining the exploitation and alienation intrinsic to the capitalist mode of production. He was able to show how religion and other ideologies managed to mask the vast inequalities of contemporary society and thereby attempted to justify the unjustifiable. His writings have led people to act and to pursue various worthwhile goals, which in turn have led to more equality and justice in society. So, Marx is a pivotal intellectual figure, whose work, for all its misuses, has helped to shape society for the better.[38] The question, then, is not whether to read his writings but *how* to read them, how to read them in the light of our experiences today. The question is not who the real Marx was but which Marx is relevant for today. Rorty makes two suggestions. Firstly, instead of seeing *The Communist Manifesto* as an attempt at a faithful depiction of historical processes, we should read it as a magnificent expression of hope for a more humane future. Rather than treating Marx as someone who purported to have found the key that opens the door to both our history and destiny, we should extract the utopian elements and the humanity from his work. Secondly, Rorty describes the transition towards a modern society as accompanied by a tendency to treat the past and present as discontinuous – to imagine neither what is present nor what has ever been. This view of modernity is indeed a recurrent theme in American pragmatism, one articulated vividly by Mead in his *Movements of Thought in the Nineteenth Century* and *Philosophy of the Present*. Rorty points out that, from this perspective, *The Communist Manifesto* is a transitional work. On the one hand, it epitomizes this new philosophy of hope. It is a magnificent example of the realization that the future is not closed, but made by people, and that people cannot escape the responsibility to make the future more just and equal than the past. On the other hand, the *Manifesto* also incorporates some outdated notions of history as if the future owes something to the past, as if people's agency pales into insignificance against the iron laws of history.[39]

Rorty's critique of Marxism is consistent with what he regards to be a viable agenda for the 'American Left'. Rorty describes the twentieth-century history of the American Left in two stages, with first the 'Reformist Left', and from the 1960s onwards the 'New Left'. The former category refers to enlightened liberals such as John Dewey, the latter to Marxist-inspired intellectuals such as C. Wright Mills and Christopher Lasch.[40] Given his reservations *vis-à-vis* Marxism, it is not surprising that Rorty's sympathies lie with the Reformist Left. For Rorty, Dewey and other representatives of this strand represent tolerance and exude liberal and democratic values, whereas most members of the New Left were Marxist and doctrinaire. The New Left ignored the political and intellectual riches brought by the previous generation and they therefore failed to acknowledge the radical potential in American culture.[41] Instead, they advocated a culture of self-loathing and 'knee-jerk liberalism': the United States was portrayed as the source of injustice and inequality across the world. Rorty is at pains not to be seen as underestimating the achievements of the New Left. He reckons that if the New Left had not been as effective as it was, if people had not demonstrated and rallied as they did, the Vietnam War would have gone on for much longer.[42] There are many other achievements. But the failure of the New Left was to be oblivious to the American tradition of a 'Deweyan, pragmatic participatory Left', and this explains why it was never able to appeal to a broader liberal constituency. It is, then, not entirely surprising that the New Left culminated in the 'Cultural Left', an odd blend of Marxist theory and postmodernism that impregnated literature and cultural studies departments. Members of the Cultural Left draw on the work of a number of French theorists, in particular Jacques Derrida and Michel Foucault, and they see themselves as a new progressive force, as vanguards of an imminent politico-cultural revolution. In reality, they are anything but politically vibrant. They use a highly self-referential discourse devoid of any social or political significance. Their works are ridiculously abstract, meaningful only within a narrow academic context, and ultimately without political vision, without hope.[43]

Rorty is even more sceptical of the Cultural Left than the New Left, and he puts forward two types of criticism. Firstly, whereas the New Left was politically active, most contemporary literary and culture critics are mere spectators. The Cultural Left tends to 'Gothicize' the social world in that they invoke preternatural forces, all-embracing Foucauldian power networks that people cannot recognize, resist or avoid. While the belief in these ubiquitous power relations jeopardizes any urge to act politically and reduces the intellectual to the role of spectator, the Cultural Left takes its Derrida-inspired readings as political acts. However, these deconstructionist readings, the ones that 'problematize' or 'call into question' 'traditional concepts and distinctions', are anything but political acts. Any practice of some complexity contains internal tensions, but there is no point in displaying them unless there is an attempt to resolve them. These postmodern readings are, if anything, symptomatic of the paralysed nature of the Cultural Left, inward looking as it is, unable to reach out, incapable of operating effectively in the political arena.[44] Secondly, Rorty has serious reservations about the value of the intellectual products. He is scornful of the way in which literary critics routinely read texts through a rigid lens with the sole intention of illustrating the applicability of their framework and with the undesirable effect of reiterating the very same frame of reference.[45] Whether the lens is deconstructionism or queer theory, feminism or Foucauldian, the interpreter is never surprised or affected by what is being interpreted. Acts of interpretation have become ritualistic acts in which the text, rather than being a source of inspiration or novelty, is merely a medium through which the framework gets reproduced. In opposition to this cynical game, Rorty pleads for 'unmethodical criticism', which 'uses the author or text not as a specimen reiterating a type but as an occasion for changing a previously accepted taxonomy, or for putting a new twist on a previously told story.'[46]

Evaluation

It is difficult not to have sympathy with Rorty's social and political views expressed so vividly in *Achieving our Country* and related works. Who would rebuff Rorty's ideal of a 'cooperative commonwealth, . . . which ensures equality of opportunity as well as individual liberty'[47] or his plea for a 'struggle against avoidable misery'?[48] A closer look finds his views wanting, however, even for those who are sympathetic to neo-pragmatist philosophy. Whitman's romantic vision of American society was notoriously obscure, Dewey's political platform was not particularly lucid either, and Rorty does not seem to add much to these nebulous political agendas. Rorty does not specify how these pragmatist ideas are supposed to provide a base for a critical account of society, nor does he explain why this pragmatist agenda is chosen over the sophisticated theories of J. S. Mill and other progressive liberals. He fails to clarify why a progressive agenda for Americans ought to be steeped mainly in an American intellectual tradition and why it needs to exhibit a self-consciously patriotic outlook. In the global world of today, it seems anachronistic to develop a progressive political platform that is beholden to a narrow national agenda. Rorty is probably right that we need to have pride in ourselves in order to be positive and constructive political actors, and it is equally plausible to argue that an allegiance to a collective entity is a *sine qua non* for individual self-esteem. But it remains unclear why this entity ought to be a nation.

Equally problematic is his view that the New Left made a fatal mistake in embracing Marxism. It is, of course, unfortunate that some factions of the New Left flirted with the totalitarian, non-democratic features of Marxist thought, but only a minority did, and the fascination of the New Left with Marxist philosophy was on the whole intellectually well founded. Marxist theory provided a perspicacious economic and sociological theory of society, unmatched by any pragmatist contribution to date, and crucial in providing both the intellectual structure and motivational energy for political action. It is true that philosophy, educational science, social psychology and micro-sociology would have been poorer without the contributions of Dewey and G. H. Mead, but their theoretical insights into the workings of modern society do not begin to compare with those of Marx. In combination with psycho-analysis, neo-Marxism provided imaginative and penetrating analyses, as can be gleaned from the work of Herbert Marcuse and Erich Fromm. Their writings fuelled political action. These ideas might no longer appear as innovative or persuasive as they once did, but this should not take away their value at the time. Rorty suggests that, until a new meta-narrative emerges, Marxist vocabulary should be replaced by a non-theoretical one with concepts such as 'greed', 'selfishness' and 'hatred',[49] but it is difficult to see what would be gained by doing this. Rorty's knowledge of Marx is limited, as he acknowledges himself in *Philosophy and Social Hope*.[50] The essay 'Failed Prophecies, Glorious Hopes' is a glaring example of Rorty's unfortunate tendency to reduce Marx's thought to the schematic and prophetic *Communist Manifesto*. Like Karl Popper, Rorty diminishes the corpus of Marx to a monstrous alliance of historicism and totalitarianism. Like Popper, he downplays the enormous depth and breadth of Marxism, and fails to recognize properly what a powerful framework it provides for analysing and eventually transforming society. At least Popper wrote his political pamphlets against Marxism in a highly charged socio-political context.[51] The fact that Rorty writes these polemical pieces against Marxism in a very different climate, one in which capitalism has been victorious, makes the lack of subtlety in his reading all the more surprising.

In spite of these lacunae, there are more positive sides to Rorty's philosophy. With some modifications, his neo-pragmatist insights form a stepping stone towards a fruitful agenda for the philosophy of the social sciences. First, his neo-pragmatism helps to demonstrate the limits of 'methodological naturalism'. By methodological naturalism I refer to a particular approach to the philosophy of science that searches for the methodological principles (or 'logic of discovery') that underscore both the social and the natural sciences. This notion is shared by otherwise very different philosophies of the social sciences, ranging from Durkheim's 'scientific rationalism' and Popper's falsificationism to the more recent wave of critical realism. Methodological naturalists direct their efforts mostly towards uncovering this unifying methodology and applying it to the study of the social realm. They may try, through reasoning, to detect the essence of scientific inquiry, that which makes it distinctive and superior to other forms of inquiry; they may, by studying the history of the natural sciences, attempt to infer the method adopted by scientists which led to their empirical success. Or, they may combine both strategies, and argue that the essence of science is also embodied in the practice of the natural sciences. In the face of mounting historical counter-evidence, however, it becomes increasingly implausible that there is such a perennial set of methodological guidelines that guarantees scientific success. Pragmatists such as Rorty are probably right to argue that there is no 'ahistorical metavocabulary in terms of which to formulate algorithms for theory choice',[52] since any attempt to discover such a meta-vocabulary has so far been remarkably unsuccessful.[53] This flagrant lack of success is not surprising given that methodological naturalists embark on a delicate balancing act, so delicate that they are bound to trip over. If the guidelines are too strict, the danger exists that there have been scientific activities that proved successful and deviate from these norms. If they are too vague, then it becomes difficult to gauge how they could possibly have the positive effects that are claimed for them. Logico-positivist guidelines are examples of the former, critical realist prescriptions of the latter. More importantly, not only is it doubtful that an identical formula underscores a wide range of disciplines (do, say, paleontology and astrophysics have that much in common?), the same method may have different consequences at different points in time. There is no reason to hold that a *modus operandi* that has hitherto been successful in a particular field will remain so in the future. Also, it remains unclear why a methodological strategy that has so far been proven to have *some* empirical success is, for that very reason, recommended for the future. There seems to be a conflation between what is deemed optimal and what has hitherto been fruitful. There is no guarantee that there are no other strategies that are more satisfactory.

Secondly, there is significant value in the pragmatist view that knowledge is a form of action, which, like any action, brings changes to the world. James rightly defined 'the Pragmatic method . . . as an indication of the ways in which existing realities may be changed.'[54] It follows that a pragmatist perspective is sensitive to the multitude of cognitive interests that may underlie social research. It rightly regards methodological strategies as at least partly dependent on the objectives that guide the research in a move similar to Nietzsche's refusal to accept the notion of truth as independent from interests and needs.[55] This pragmatist position can be clarified by juxtaposing it with another viewpoint, one that has recently been portrayed as an alternative to methodological naturalism. Influenced by the philosophical project of hermeneutics, social phenomenology or the later Wittgenstein, some social scientists, such as Anthony Giddens, propound that the ontology of the social (and its differences with the natural realm) makes for the necessity of a distinctive interpretative method.[56] It is thought that, unlike the natural realm, the social is made up of a complex layer of signs, and, in order to unravel these, the researcher has to gain familiarity with the various language games and semantic fields in which social practices participate. To acquire this familiarity is to acquire knowledge of the social rules and assumptions that make up these games or fields. These authors assume that the objective of social research is to employ concepts that allow for as accurate mapping of social reality as possible and interpretative procedures are regarded as being fundamental to the delicate art of social cartography. I leave aside the issue of whether this assertion is, as these sociologists argue, implied in or consistent with the philosophies, such as Wittgenstein's, in which they find inspiration. (I do not think it is.) What I want to point out instead is that, from a neo-pragmatist perspective, these anti-naturalists commit the 'ontological fallacy': that is, the erroneous assumption that references to ontology would be sufficient to settle methodological disputes. From a neo-pragmatic angle, ontological assertions can never suffice, as methodological options are at least partly dependent on what is to be achieved. It would be erroneous to hold that there is something intrinsic to the social that necessitates a single method of inquiry because this would be tantamount to making the blatantly absurd assertion that a single method serves all cognitive interests.

This is not to say, of course, that the choice of a methodological path is simply to be reduced to a matter of cognitive interests. Rorty seems to commit this 'instrumentalist fallacy' when he suggests that questions of methodology cannot be grounded in ontology.[57] *Pace* Rorty, there are differences between various substantive fields to the extent that it is possible that a particular methodology allows for the accomplishment of an objective in one field of inquiry but not in another. It is not impossible either that the nature of a particular object of study makes some objectives unobtainable. In short, while methodology is a matter of choice in so far as it is dependent on our objectives, it remains a *bounded* choice in that the ontology of our object of research limits what can be achieved and how it is to be accomplished. For instance, the field of fossils does not allow for interpretative understanding in the way in which the social world obviously allows for it. Rorty's attempts to demonstrate the contrary are misleading because they rely on an elastic notion of the interpretative method. He defines the interpretative method as a holistic method by which new objects are made intelligible by relating them to other more familiar objects,[58] but this is a remarkably nebulous description as apt for structuralism as for the interpretative method. For instance, while it is not wrong to describe Weber's concept of interpretative understanding as simply constituting 'webs of meaning', it is imprecise. Weber creates *specific* webs of meaning, by attributing goals and reasons to people's actions, in the hope of explaining why people have done what they have. This is an impossible aim in the field of paleontology for the simple reason that fossils do not attribute meanings to their surroundings in the way in which people do. As for Rorty's other objection to hermeneutics, he is, of course, right that the accounts of the people involved should not have epistemological priority over those of the social scientist, but Taylor and other hermeneutic authors have rightly replied that they never said so in the first place. They are not talking 'about subjective meanings, the property of one or some individuals, but rather intersubjective meanings, which are constitutive of the social matrix in which individuals find themselves and act.'[59] Therefore, it is wrong to say that Taylor is identifying the meaning of the activities of individuals with their descriptions of these activities.

This brings me to my third and final point. From a pragmatic angle, naturalists and anti-naturalists have a lot in common in that they take for granted or are oblivious to the plethora of goals that guide social research. Whereas naturalists presuppose that legitimate social research aims at explaining and possibly predicting an outer world, the anti-naturalists discussed above assume social inquiry aims at mirroring the social as accurately and completely as possible. Neither takes seriously into account the other cognitive interests that may underlie social research, and in particular both disregard the idea that self-knowledge may be a legitimate aim for investigating the social realm. By self-knowledge I refer to the process by which research into different forms of life, rather than giving way to an unmediated access to an outer world, is seen as an opportunity for rearticulating our selves and our own culture. What I have in mind is close to Hans-Georg Gadamer's notion of *wirkungsgeschichtliches Bewusstsein*, which is at the centre of his hermeneutic project, and which is characterized by an interest, not in what happened in history as such, but by how the past enables us to express ourselves differently.[60] Just as Rorty conceives of post-analytical philosophy as edifying and directed towards *Bildung*,[61] this self-referential form of knowledge would enable people to make discursive what was previously unquestioned in their culture, to challenge deep-seated beliefs about it, and to imagine socio-political scenarios other than the ones that are currently present. Whereas both Gadamer and Rorty treat self-knowledge as primarily a philosophical concept, it has also manifested itself as a fruitful methodological strategy in different fields of inquiry, ranging from the critical turn in cultural anthropology to genealogy as a method for historical inquiry.

The notion of self-referential knowledge ties in neatly with some passages in *Achieving our Country* and *Philosophy and Social Hope* devoted to the current state of the humanities, in which Rorty exposes the sterile, repetitive scholarship that is often conducted under the banner of 'theory' or 'critical theory'. These reflections are relevant not only to literature departments, because 'theory' is used and misused in similar ways in sociology and other social sciences. The system of research grants, as currently in place in several countries, is partly constitutive of the problem identified by Rorty in that, from the outset, researchers are requested to commit themselves to a theoretical framework that is supposed to 'guide' or 'inform' the research. 'Guiding' or 'informing' unfortunately often implies a blinkered way of seeing things – reading the social so as to reinforce the very presuppositions that fuel the research. Researchers are encouraged to use recognizable frameworks, associated with names of celebrated theoreticians. Whether the theory is Lacanian or inspired by Anthony Giddens, whether the object of research is contemporary French cinema or the dwindling welfare state, the unspoken assumption is that the success of a piece of research is proportionate to how conclusively the framework has been shown to be applicable. Whereas research in the humanities should enhance our imaginative capacities, open up new futures, this form of 'theory-inspired research' does precisely the opposite: it closes off new experiences. However risqué or avant-garde this research would like to present itself as being, it is in the end intellectually deeply conservative, using the object of study not to learn something new, but to reinforce what is already presupposed.

Rorty is right to believe that a plausible solution to the impasse may lie in pragmatism, but he is plainly wrong when he suggests that this answer means abandoning theory altogether.[62] Even if we tried to do so, we would not be able to because, as Rorty and other pragmatists have pointed out, our pre-suppositions are *sine qua non* to any knowledge whatsoever. It is better to be aware of what theory we use rather than deny what cannot be denied: that we are holding one. A coherent pragmatist response, for me, culminates in the view that it ought to be intrinsic to the vocation of researchers always to remain sufficiently open-minded that their presuppositions and expectations can be affected by the studies they embark upon. Success is then no longer measured by the extent to which a theory has been shown to 'fit' the data neatly, the extent to which the various components of the theory are shown to weave easily into the myriad of empirical experiences. Instead, it is the ability to see things differently, to form a *Gestalt* switch, which ought to be viewed as a sign of success. As I indicated before, Nietzsche had already anticipated this Gadamerian view when he explained the rationale behind his proposal for a genealogical method of history. What is the point of working away in archives from dawn to dusk, Nietzsche asks fellow historians, if the data collected do not somehow affect the present, if they do not help to invigorate us? Pre-empting Rorty's own appeal for a conversational and edifying philosophy,[63] genealogy confronts the past so as to help create distance from our present presuppositions, so as to help people imagine future alternatives to present conditions. Foucault aptly called this approach a 'history of the present' in that the confrontation with an unfamiliar past is used to gain access to and erode a familiar present.[64] When Rorty criticizes Foucault for writing 'from a point of view light-years away from the problems of contemporary society',[65] he has obviously failed to realize the affinity between the history of the present and the Deweyan view that language and knowledge, rather than acts of representation, allow people to increase the range of human possibilities. Genealogical history is perfectly consistent with Rorty's dictum that an anti-representationalist view of inquiry should be 'open to the encounter with other actual and possible cultures, and to make this openness central to its self-image.'[66] To help people to estrange themselves from themselves, in the way in which the history of the present manages to do it, is precisely to achieve this Deweyan ideal: to enlarge people's potentialities.

This brief journey through pragmatism and Rorty's writings has led to an insight into what precisely a pragmatist proposal for the philosophy of the social sciences might look like. It involves a very different way of thinking about social research. It implies, among other things, scepticism towards the value of assuming that there is something like an essence of scientific inquiry. The kind of pragmatist view I have been proposing also implies a non-representational outlook, in which knowledge is seen as a dialogue. In the concluding chapter I will move away from Rorty and elaborate fully on this pragmatist proposal. I will show that this pragmatist viewpoint is not simply a philosophical construction, and that it has already been implemented in various forms of social research, notably in archaeology, anthropology and history. These applications have led to a number of stimulating research programmes.

Further reading

Rorty's *magnum opus* is undoubtedly *Philosophy and the Mirror of Nature*, but some parts of the book are hard to read for those unfamiliar with some of the debates in analytical philosophy. I would recommend the accessible third part of the book, which explores the consequences of Rorty's new perspective on philosophy. Rorty's views on Kuhn's philosophy of science are developed in chapter 7, 'From Epistemology to Hermeneutics', whereas chapter 8, 'Philosophy without Mirrors', explores the relationship between Rorty's views on the one hand and those of Sartre and Gadamer on the other. For those who are not familiar with Rorty's work or with philosophy in general, I suggest starting with *Philosophy and Social Hope*, an easy-to-read collection of articles aimed at a wider audience. The introduction to that volume, entitled 'Relativism: Finding and Making', provides an excellent chance to become acquainted with some of Rorty's ideas. I would then suggest moving on to 'Introduction: Pragmatism and Philosophy', in *Consequences of*

Pragmatism; it provides a comprehensive overview of the main themes in Rorty's philosophy. There are several excellent edited collections about Rorty, among which Malachowski's *Reading Rorty* and Brandom's *Rorty and his Critics* discuss the philosophical sides of the argument. The contributors to the Malachowski collection focus virtually exclusively on *Philosophy and the Mirror of Nature* and *Consequences of Pragmatism*, whereas *Rorty and his Critics* covers a far wider range of Rorty's writings. Rorty wrote a reply for every chapter of Brandom's volume, as well as for those in Festenstein and Thompson's *Richard Rorty*; this edited collection is different from Brandom's in that the contributors discuss mainly issues of social and political theory. Rorty's views on the implications of pragmatism for the philosophy of science can be found in 'Pragmatism without Method', in *Philosophical Papers*, vol. 1: *Objectivity, Relativism and Truth*. Equally important is his essay on Kuhn in *Philosophy and Social Hope*. For Rorty's views about the philosophy of the social sciences, see his essay 'Method, Social Science, Social Hope', in *Consequences of Pragmatism*. A more complex version of the same argument is developed in 'Texts and Lumps', in *Objectivity, Relativism and Truth*. For those interested in Rorty's appeal for a piecemeal reformist agenda and in his critique of Marxism, I suggest going through *Achieving our Country*. One of the essays in *Philosophy and Social Hope*, 'Failed Prophecies, Glorious Hopes', originally published in the same year as *Achieving our Country*, continues the critique of Marxism and explores its similarities with Christianity. 'The End of Leninism', published in *Truth and Progress*, the third volume of *Philosophical Papers*, makes a similar argument. Some sections of 'Habermas and Lyotard on Postmodernity', published in *Philosophical Papers*, vol. 2: *Essays on Heidegger and Others*, are also relevant to the philosophy of the social sciences.

7
A Pragmatist Philosophy of the Social Sciences

Outline of a pragmatist view

The influence of pragmatist philosophy on philosophy of the social sciences has been limited. Of course pragmatism had a substantial effect on the way in which social science unfolded in the course of the twentieth century, especially in the United States. John Dewey's legacy is the development of a progressive, praxis-driven theory of education, while G. H. Mead is remembered for having broken with a Cartesian concept of an isolated, non-social self. Both have contributed successfully to the construction of an interactionist theory of society that has been influential in sociology, educational science and social psychology.[1] It should also be acknowledged that the Chicago School was heavily embedded in American pragmatism, as were a number of subsequent social scientists and critical commentators such as C. Wright Mills.[2] Recently, there has been a growing recognition that pragmatist social science is not exclusive to North America, and a fruitful dialogue between pragmatism and European social theory is developing.[3] These examples, however, are restricted to the practice of social science and social theory; the interest in pragmatism, on the whole, does not extend to the philosophy of the social sciences. With some exceptions, philosophers of social science have tended to overlook pragmatism or express hostility.[4] Although the recent rediscovery of the pragmatist tradition by Richard Rorty, Richard J. Bernstein and others has undoubtedly had a significant impact on philosophy and literary studies,[5] its influence on the philosophy of the social sciences is negligible in comparison. The point of this chapter is to fill this vacuum, to pull the threads of this book together and indicate what pragmatism, and especially its recent development, has to offer to the philosophy of the social sciences. This is not to say that pragmatists are the only ones who hold the views that I am promoting, and some philosophers, situated in a hermeneutic framework, have articulated similar ideas.[6] My point is simply that pragmatism provides a coherent and appealing framework to express these ideas.

Let me clarify what I will be arguing and what I am not trying to say. First, my suggestions are in line with *recent* contributions to pragmatism, specifically Rorty and Bernstein. I am not arguing that my views are necessarily consistent with those expressed by earlier generations of pragmatists. Some of them are, some are not, but a discussion of this lies outside the scope of this chapter. Second, my outline is *inspired* by neo-pragmatism rather than derived from it. What follows is not a reconstruction of the views self-proclaimed pragmatists hold. The gist of my argument, however, is perfectly in line with the philosophical outlook of neo-pragmatism.

What are the main ideas put forward here? What constitutes my proposal for a pragmatist philosophy of social science?

1 Methodological diversity characterizes science

I follow the pragmatist scepticism towards foundational philosophical projects. Charles Peirce, John Dewey, Richard Rorty and other pragmatists have already articulated enmity towards the view that there are firm, unchangeable foundations to knowledge. These pragmatists rejected the view that philosophical insight would carve a secret path that ultimately leads to these foundations.[7] However, I am interested less in the broader philosophical debate and more in the way in which foundationalism has managed to permeate contemporary philosophy of science. It is present in the ongoing attempts to uncover the 'essence' or 'logic' of science – the logic of inquiry that all successful scientific activities purportedly have in common – and it is this form of foundationalism that I reject. The pursuit of the ontological and methodological unity of science was characteristic of the Vienna Circle, testimony of which are the numerous volumes of the *Encyclopedia of Unified Science* edited by Rudolph Carnap, Otto Neurath and Charles Morris.[8] The idea of ontological unity was quickly abandoned, but falsificationists and critical realists further developed the search for methodological unity. While recognizing essential differences between the social and the natural sciences, both Popper and Bhaskar have searched for what these fields of inquiry methodologically have in common.[9] The history of the natural sciences has shown, however, that any such reconstruction is highly contentious. It is difficult to see what various disciplines within the natural sciences have in common that would make it defensible to treat them as belonging to one category with a single method. Different disciplines in the natural sciences function according to very different procedures unless the logic of inquiry is spelled out at such a high level that it loses any meaning. Recently, for instance, there has been a growing awareness that, contrary to the neo-positivist reconstruction of the natural sciences, biology does not fit the pattern of most aspects of physics and chemistry.[10] The nature of the subject matter of biology seems to make for the inapplicability of the 'metaphysics of modern science'. Whereas the latter postulates the existence of structures that are law-governed, deterministic and entirely comprehensible, the former confronts us with the opposite, or what Dupré coins 'the disorder of things'.[11] Biological complexity surpasses our computational and cognitive capabilities so that a complete account cannot be accomplished. It is not surprising, then, that physicists and chemists try to uncover the underlying structure of the physical realm whereas biologists operate in a more practical, instrumental fashion.[12] If biology is so different, surely the idea of a methodological unity of science is fictitious. Dupré's work is indicative of a growing body of literature that questions the assumption of the unity of science. It becomes increasingly apparent that those who believe in this unifying methodology erroneously generalize from a few sub-disciplines (mainly in physics) in which the procedures apply.

There is another reason for abandoning the search for the essence of science: the belief that a neutral algorithm underscores all scientific activities rests on a selective and distorted view of science as an accomplished and neatly demarcated activity. Numerous publications in the sociology of science over the last couple of decades have revealed how incorrect this view is. There has recently been a growing interest in the social practices of scientists, which culminated in what is known as the 'strong programme of sociology of science'.[13] The strong programme differs from Mannheim's sociology of knowledge. For Mannheim, sociology accounts for the humanities and the social sciences and for why scholars deviate from the rational course of action.[14] Sociologists such as Harry Collins and Barry Barnes extend the scope of the sociology of knowledge so that it can also account for practices in the natural sciences and mathematics. For them, sociology is as successful at explaining scientific success as it is at accounting for failure. With this growing interest in the social construction of science, the view that there is a fixed notion of science (which distinguishes it from other activities) comes into question. The closer we look at science, the more blurred the distinction between science and non-science becomes. The more we study how scientists actually operate, the more contentious their products appear to us. In *Science in Action*, Bruno Latour shows how scientists use various props or rhetorical devices to persuade others. We quickly learn that using the 'right scientific method' is not sufficient for scientists to make a mark. They have to publish in the right journals, and they manage to do so only if they write in an appropriate fashion, backing up their own claims with equally contentious references, further referring to other articles, and so on *ad infinitum*. Scientists not only employ as much rhetoric in science as do people in daily life; their own empirical research is far messier than was ever acknowledged by neopositivist philosophers. Research results may look uncontroversial and authoritative when they finally appear in neat articles in prestigious scientific journals, but a detailed ethnography of actual empirical research that led to the 'findings' shows how problematic and fabricated these findings can be.[15] In a similar vein, Paul Feyerabend has shown that the Church's initial objections to Galileo were not so irrational. The Church's arguments were partly scientific, partly ethical, but, either way, they made sense against the background of the assumptions at the time.[16] It could be counter-argued that these assumptions were wrong, but the point is that no scientific judgement can be made without reliance on broader presuppositions, most of which cannot be evaluated empirically. There were no compelling reasons at the time to question the dominant conventions that guided scientific research. Furthermore, Galileo hardly worked in ways that modern textbooks would regard as scientific: he held on to his theory in spite of repeated falsifications, and he used 'propaganda' and 'psychological tricks' to persuade his audience.[17] From afar he may represent the trinity of science, reason and truth conquering prejudice (that is how he has entered modern mythology), but a detailed historical account shows that, by any standard of what science is about, he was the one who was breaking the rules.

Lack of methodological unity in science is not simply about methodological differences across disciplines. Lack of unity also creeps in *within* disciplines. Historians of science such as Thomas Kuhn and Paul Feyerabend have demonstrated that in physics, for example, no overarching methodological set of rules guides successful scientific research.[18] There is a pattern, the *longue durée* of normal science being followed by short bursts of scientific revolution; Kuhn's work is particularly well known for the cyclical picture that he described so majestically. This pattern, however, should not be confused with the recurrent use of a single method.[19] With every new paradigm, the methodological rules are altered irrevocably and to such an extent that it is possible to talk about epistemological discontinuities. It also brought to light the impossibility of explaining these ruptures without resorting to sociological concepts, without referring to the complex interplay of social practices and communal interests. It is legitimate to say there is no neutral algorithm to science in the sense of there being no overarching set of rules (applicable to all paradigms), except for the most bland and uninformative propositions. In the same vein, Feyerabend showed that, within a discipline, a particular logic of inquiry that is perfectly successful at one time and context might not be so in another. The emergence of a new institutional and societal setting might make for the inapplicability of what used to be a highly successful research strategy, and, likewise, what used to be a lost cause might suddenly become a winning strategy. Furthermore, detailed studies of scientists at work have shown the 'locality' of scientific research: different cultures, countries and laboratories operate differently. As such, there is a growing interest in the differences between 'research schools' spearheaded by historians such as G. L.

Geison.[20] Even within disciplines, such empirical evidence suggests there is not necessarily a single method at play.

2 The social sciences gain from methodological pluralism

It is problematic to infer methodological guidelines for social research from the purported logic of inquiry in the natural sciences. Any attempt to do so risks falling victim to several logical flaws. Firstly, there is a tendency to reduce the multitude of cognitive interests that underlie social research to only one: explanation, possibly leading to prediction. Reducing knowledge to this form of 'empirical-analytical knowledge', as Habermas has already pointed out, is a logical error committed by several authors associated with positivist epistemology.[21] Without wishing to commit myself to other aspects of Habermas's argument in *Knowledge and Human Interests*, he is certainly right when he argues that the distinctive nature of the social makes it possible to pursue other cognitive aims. The notion of 'cognitive interest' is more fundamental than so-called criteria for theory selection to which philosophers of science often refer. For instance, when Kuhn mentions accuracy, consistency, scope, simplicity and fruitfulness as criteria,[22] he still assumes that research explains the outer world, and the criteria indicate how good the explanation is. Cognitive aims of social investigation include the critique of society (which ties in with self-emancipation or the lifting of past restrictions), understanding (which comes down to the attribution of meanings to texts or practices) and, as I will stress, self-understanding. Secondly, the tendency to put the social sciences in a methodological straitjacket that barely fits the natural sciences is even more problematic. Underlying the use of the natural sciences as a role model is the assumption that all branches of the natural sciences have something significant in common. If, as I have argued, this assumption is problematic, then the methodological dictum that the social sciences should emulate the natural sciences becomes a confused request. Thirdly, just as it is questionable to categorize the various natural sciences as a single entity, it is equally problematic to treat the social sciences as a unified enterprise. It could easily be argued that, in terms of methods, demography has more in common with some disciplines in the natural sciences than with, say, linguistics. Even within each branch, it is dangerous to assume methodological unity, as has been pointed out in great detail in the case of psychology.[23] In the case of sociology, this lack of consensus can be highly constructive. Sociology lacks the level of methodological unity that is found in contemporary economics, but this is not necessarily an impediment. It allows for an ongoing awareness among researchers of the precise presuppositions that underlie their research, and for their recognition of the alternative scenarios that can be sketched. The strength of sociology today lies precisely in its ability to break with previously established assumptions and regularly to introduce new angles on a given topic. The multitude of methodological options cultivates a sense of self-awareness, which is desirable and to which I will turn shortly.

Although this pragmatist alternative is antithetical to naturalism, the argument is different to that of most hermeneutic or interpretative approaches. Hermeneutic philosophers of the social sciences also oppose naturalism, but they fail to challenge the naturalist assumption that the natural sciences share a single method. At its base, the hermeneutic critique of naturalism argues that the nature of the social realm eludes the method of the natural sciences. Hermeneutic philosophers of the social sciences argue that the social world is different, that people attribute meaning to their surroundings and act accordingly. The social realm is *so* different that the methods adopted by natural scientists simply do not work or distort what is quintessentially social. The pragmatist view I advocate questions if it makes sense to talk about a single scientific method in the first place. It becomes problematic to assert that the social sciences differ from the natural sciences once it is acknowledged that the natural sciences are not as unified as is often assumed. From this view, naturalists and anti-naturalists make a similar mistake: each assumes that there is something that the natural sciences have in common. Each adopts a misguided textbook account of what scientists do.

3 The spectator theory of knowledge is inappropriate for social research

I take issue with the view that the main objective of social research is to map the social world as accurately and completely as possible. Various philosophers and social theorists, such as Roy Bhaskar and Anthony Giddens, assume that social research depicts the social realm, and their position ties in with their rejection of an instrumentalist view of science. Whereas instrumentalists would tend to make a case that predictive power is essential to science, Bhaskar and Giddens play down the importance of this criterion. Bhaskar contends that predictive power is less important because of the openness of systems in general and social systems in particular.[24] Giddens argues that people's accounts and knowledge of the social feed back into the social, making for the unpredictability of the social.[25] Both Bhaskar and Giddens maintain that research should aim at accounting for or depicting the social rather than pursuing the lure of prediction. Both thinkers implicitly assume that an ontologically grounded social theory provides the necessary conceptual apparatus to make the portrayal of the social possible. They fit what John Dewey ironically described as the 'spectator theory of knowledge', a view of knowledge as mainly, if not exclusively, representing the intrinsic nature of an external world.[26] In a sociological context, James Rule talks about the 'theory as objective mapping', a view of theory as mirroring the outer world.[27] It is not surprising that Giddens regards structuration theory as primarily concerned with 'ontological' issues: his bridging of the gap between objectivism and subjectivism is an attempt to avoid the shortcomings of each so as to construct conceptual tools that allow for a more authentic and extensive portrayal of social reality.[28] The sociologist, then, becomes a self-declared social cartographer who sets out to draw the social map as accurately and comprehensively as possible. This explains why Derek Layder, who draws on realism and structuration theory, recommends that sociologists pay attention to the various dimensions of the 'research map' and draw as complete a chart as possible.[29] An understanding of the subjects' shared interpretative procedures is a prerequisite for a faithful representation of the social. The methods of the natural sciences ignore the meaningful dimension of social life and, as a consequence, do not allow for accurate depicting of the social. For instance, notions such as reflexivity, concept-dependency or practical consciousness are introduced to indicate the extent to which people's definitions or accounts are constitutive of what they are reporting. Positivist approaches allegedly fail to capture this 'double hermeneutic', and it is precisely because they fail to be isomorphic to the outer world that they are regarded as incurably deficient.[30]

These spectator theories are not convincing. The very reasons these authors give for the necessity of the interpretative method help to explain why faithful picturing can never be achieved. Consistent with Quine's notion of the 'agent's point of view', sociologists such as Layder are right to assume that people draw upon shared, interpretative procedures to make sense of their surrounding world. They are also justified in asserting that this pre-interpreted nature of the social calls attention to the merits of the interpretative method. In practice, however, sociologists such as Layder fail to attribute similar interpretative mechanisms to researchers. While Bhaskar and Giddens consider the social as pre-interpreted, those who rely on them often recommend that social researchers renounce their prejudices, as if their metamorphosis into 'thin' culture is necessary for gaining access to the 'thick' culture of the researched. By doing so, they attribute a mysterious capacity to individual researchers to 'step outside history', to assume what Quine called a 'God's eye view', stripped from their own culture, while subjects being investigated are portrayed as necessarily drawing upon a culturally specific framework to make sense of the world. This position implicitly postulates a curious 'ontological asymmetry' in that two mutually exclusive ontological positions are taken, one applicable to the researcher and one to the researched. In contrast, pragmatists conceive of presuppositions as *sine qua non* to any form of inquiry. As such, they assume researchers must reflect on the nature of their presuppositions.[31]

4 Social research is a conversation

My fourth claim affects social theory more broadly. I question what Steven Seidman and Jeffrey Alexander aptly call 'foundationalism' in the social sciences.[32] In philosophy, foundationalism refers to the systematic search for an epistemology (or other basis) that supposedly grounds cognitive (or ethical and aesthetic) claims. Earlier forms of pragmatism criticized foundationalism in this sense. Like Seidman and Alexander, I use foundationalism in a broader sense. Seidman and Alexander refer to a dominant way in which social theorists conceived of their discipline during most of the twentieth century. As their task, these theorists seek to uncover unchanging foundations of an all-embracing framework or science of the social. Foundationalism probably finds its purest expression in critical realism, but it comes in many other shapes and forms, ranging from Parsons's structural-functionalism and Giddens's structuration theory to Luhmann's system theory and Habermas' theory of communicative action. More recently, rational choice theory (or rational action theory as some prefer to call it) has come to the fore. Although some of its presuppositions are remarkably different from those of preceding theoretical programmes, it shares the same foundationalist aspirations. Foundationalism, then, can postulate individual agency or structural constraint, take a politically conservative or radical position, be positivist or hermeneutically inspired. The unifying feature of foundationalism is the belief that theory provides an objective base for a powerful frame of reference, one that is applicable to different, if not all, settings, cultures and times. In the philosophy of social science, foundationalism is accompanied by ongoing analytical debates about the relative virtues and defects of holism versus individualism, functional versus intentional explanations, and so on. These philosophical questions supposedly settle the controversies between the various foundationalist projects.

This is not the place to embark on an elaborate philosophical argument against foundationalism in social science and theory. Indeed, others have already done so with considerable aplomb.[33] The pressing question for pragmatists, instead, is what the community of social researchers has gained from foundationalist projects. The answer is very little. We are not any nearer to the question as to which of these projects or theories would be more convincing. Rather, one of the upshots of foundationalism has been the institutional separation into different schools and, with this, the entrenchment and growing intellectual rigidity of these schools. Most researchers refer to other members of their school and build on them; some schools even have their own journals or book series. In short, members of opposing camps tend not to acknowledge each other's positions. When they do, they employ what Richard J. Bernstein called the 'adversarial' or 'confrontational' style of argumentation.[34] In this form of academic exchange, assertions of the opposite school are targeted and criticized with the aim of demolishing them. The views of members of opposing academic tribes are shown to be false, incoherent or insignificant. Those engaged in this form of debate do not attempt to learn from other viewpoints, nor do they use the opportunity of academic exchange to reflect upon and question some of their own presuppositions. Foundationalists build and defend intellectual fortresses while destroying rival constructions. Instead, I suggest a movement beyond the era of foundationalism to regard academic exchange as what Bernstein calls a 'dialogical encounter'.[35] In a dialogical encounter people do not wish to score points by exploiting the weaknesses of others; they try to listen to them by understanding them in the strongest way. They strengthen their arguments so as to make them most credible and to learn from them. Academic communication, then, becomes more like a proper conversation, which encourages the participants to think differently. The ultimate aim is not to defend or refine a particular system but to use academic conversation to enhance our imaginative faculties.

5 Knowledge is action

One way forward is to conceive of knowledge, not as representational, but as a form of action, as something active. As William James rightly pointed out, 'the Pragmatic method . . . appears as an indication of the ways in which existing realities may be changed.'[36] Knowledge, then, ties in with 'cognitive interests'; the philosophy of the social sciences ought to reflect on the various objectives that underlie social research and examine how each objective can be achieved. In this view, no cognitive interest can take *a priori* precedence over the others. To take pragmatism seriously, therefore, is to avoid the 'ontological fallacy', the mistaken assumption that methodological questions can be reduced to matters of ontology.[37] Against this assumption, I argue that questions of method always entail questions of aims and, as such, that the method used depends at least in part on what the research wants to achieve. No reference to the ontology of the social can ever be sufficient to settle matters of social methodology; there is nothing essential about the social that compels the use of a particular method. However, this is not to say that methodology is *simply* an issue of aims. Indeed, Rorty seems to commit this 'instrumentalist fallacy' when he writes that methodology cannot be grounded in ontology at all.[38] Contrary to Rorty, it is possible that a certain methodological path might lead the way towards a particular objective in one field of inquiry but not in another. It is equally possible that the nature of a particular object of study excludes the possibility of obtaining a particular objective altogether. Furthermore, social theorists or philosophers are probably well placed and perfectly able to identify ontological features of the social that may be useful to methodological qualifications of this sort. In short, although methodologi-

cal choice is always limited, it is not infeasible for us to identify the ontological constraints put upon that choice.

6 Self-understanding opens up alternative scenarios

I suggest that we take self-knowledge seriously as a cognitive interest. This
ties in with an appeal to conceive of understanding in a Gadamerian fashion.[39]
By this I mean that understanding ought to be seen as an encounter, firstly, in
which we rely upon our cultural presuppositions to gain access to what is
being studied, and, secondly, through which we articulate and rearticulate
the very same presuppositions. The notion of 'hermeneutic circle' refers to a
recursive process by which our assumptions are both preconditions of and
affected by the encounter. Gadamer uses this notion of understanding mainly
in ontological terms. I suggest that we employ it also as a methodological
device. It might well be true that understanding always implies the conversational model, but I argue that there is a lot to be gained from actively pursuing the dialogue. The notion of dialogue has already been used fruitfully in
ethics and political theory, as can be gleaned from the influential writings of
Alasdair MacIntyre.[40] For him and many others who use the dialogical model,
the pursuit of a universal theory of justice disregards the fact that ethical positions are situated in ethical traditions. Rather than trying to step outside a tradition and obtain a neutral vantage point, it is important for us to acknowledge
the cultural specificity of our views while being sensitive to other traditions.
This sensitivity can be achieved through a conscious effort to remain open to
other traditions and learn from them. This openness and willingness to learn
from other traditions is central to the way in which the dialogical model can
be employed in the philosophy of the social sciences.

The notion of hermeneutic circle has three significant ramifications for the
methodology of social research. The first implication of this recursive notion
is that it fully acknowledges that people cannot obtain a view of the world
that does not in some way reflect their interests and values. Just as pragmatists insist that philosophy should free itself from what Nietzsche called a 'true
world', the notion of hermeneutic circle suggests that understanding can only
take place in the context of the quotidian or *Lebenswelt*. Just as Stanley Fish
has convincingly pointed out that it is erroneous to believe that we can
abandon the force of the 'interpretative community' and somehow go 'back-
to-the-text', it is equally problematic to hold that the right interpretative
method would allow us to touch upon the 'reality-out-there'. The second
consequence of the notion of hermeneutic circle is that, as this concept of
understanding is so radically dissociated from any traditional notion of correspondence, it becomes problematic to judge different accounts of social
reality based on which of them best mirrors the outer world. However, to deny

the suitability of this yardstick is not to argue that there are no standards at all. One such obvious yardstick refers to the extent to which a piece of research sheds new light on what is being studied – new, that is, in relation to an existing consensus. The third ramification of the notion of hermeneutic circle is that 'understanding' is closely linked to 'self-understanding': encountering new social settings can allow us to redescribe and reconceptualize our selves, our culture and our surroundings. Again, my proposal becomes clear in opposition to other conceptions of social research, such as the view that the primary aim of social research is to portray an outer social world faithfully. Inspired by Rorty's proposal for an 'edifying' philosophy, my pragmatic view promotes the importance of 'self-referential' forms of knowledge acquisition in which individuals learn to see themselves, their own culture and their own presuppositions from a different perspective, and to contrast this reinterpretation with alternative forms of life.[41] Another way of putting it is to say that self-referential knowledge attempts to articulate and question the very same presuppositions that make the encounter with difference possible in the first place.

Whereas Rorty is still preoccupied with philosophy, I think that the social sciences (and not philosophy) have a central role to play in this self-referential type of knowledge. In the social sciences, encountering difference can affect people's self-knowledge in three ways. There is, firstly, the 'conceptualizing effect' in that the encounter with different forms of life may allow people to articulate and conceptualize their own culture. Research into different forms of life allows individuals to verbalize their unconscious presuppositions, and articulate the interpretative procedures by which they have hitherto made sense of their surroundings. There is, secondly, the 'emancipating effect' in that encountering difference may allow people to question some of their deep-seated beliefs about their own culture or about some cultural artefacts in general. For example, the confrontation with a different setting may enable people to distinguish the necessary from the contingent, the essential from historical specificity. Whereas people generally tend to experience their taken-for-granted cultural surroundings as universal, the awareness that things are done differently may question this experience or undermine it altogether. There is, thirdly, the 'imaginative component' in that facing difference may allow people to envisage alternative futures. People's expectations and imaginative faculties tend to be shaped and constrained by the taken-for-granted world that they inhabit, and encountering a different setting may enable them to distance themselves from their own culture so as to explore new worlds. It empowers people to develop their imaginative abilities in that they become able to conceptualize what is not present.

These proposals for a pragmatic philosophy are not simply philosophical constructions; they have a direct bearing on empirical research. A growing body of research in the social sciences operates along these lines. I will give examples of research from three different disciplines to illustrate my argument. One of these illustrations is drawn from cultural anthropology, one from archaeology and, finally, one from history (and historical sociology). These examples allow me to demonstrate applications of my pragmatic outlook and identify some of its possible theoretical and methodological pitfalls and how they can be circumvented.

Cultural anthropology

The notion of a 'critical turn' in social and cultural anthropology was first introduced in two books: Marcus and Fischer's *Anthropology as Cultural Critique* and Clifford and Marcus's edited collection entitled *Writing Culture*. Some anthropological pieces of research preceded this movement, for instance, Paul Rabinow's *Reflections of Fieldwork in Morocco*,[42] but *Anthropology as Cultural Critique* and *Writing Culture* have been able to summarize and consolidate this new movement. Since then, anthropologists have developed these ideas further, and this new wave has been disseminated partly through new journals such as *Cultural Anthropology*, *Public Culture* and *Positions*. Central in this perspective is the idea of 'experimentation' (the subtitle of *Anthropology as Cultural Critique* is *An Experimental Moment in the Human Sciences*), which refers to a period of intellectual eclecticism.[43] There is no dominant theoretical or methodological orientation during this 'experimental moment', no obvious party line that needs to be toed. There is no dominant view about what constitutes the subject matter of anthropology; anthropologists increasingly recognize that they can study their own society as well as the 'exotic'.[44] The experimental moment allows anthropologists to explore various avenues, to reflect critically on hitherto dominant paradigms and to evaluate the practice of anthropology itself. The critical turn exhibits a similar liberal attitude towards methodology. The key focus is not on methodology but on writing (hence the title of the Clifford and Marcus collection). There are different styles of writing at the anthropologist's disposal. Given the increased awareness of the constructed and contested nature of knowledge, writing is no longer merely an issue of method. The concern with writing style in anthropology reflects an awareness of the competing rhetorical and linguistic devices that are in operation, recognizing that academic and literary genres overlap substantially. There is no good reason to attribute epistemological priority to traditional academic forms of writing over other genres.[45]

The critical turn tries to explore how anthropology can challenge common sense and help reassess our implicit presuppositions. It also considers the role of anthropology *vis-à-vis* various societal processes such as colonization and globalization.[46] Anthropology has always tried to deal with both, but advocates of the critical turn assert that both objectives need to be considered in light of recent philosophical developments. One such development is what Marcus and Fischer call the 'crisis of representation', which refers to the absence of a dominant theoretical framework.[47] A consensus about the kind of theory that should guide our research no longer exists. The crisis of representation, then, ties in neatly with the concept of experimentation. Instead of regarding the crisis of representation as an obstacle to the construction of fruitful anthropological knowledge, the exponents of the critical turn conceive the absence of a dominant theory as an opportunity for developing new forms of anthropological research. The crisis of representation heralds an era of intellectual liberation, where anthropologists are no longer tied to a canon and use anthropological fieldwork to engage in a dialogical relationship with the researched. This explains the importance attached to ethnographies and the insistence that 'ethnographic truths are . . . inherently *partial* – committed and incomplete.'[48] Influenced by Gadamer's hermeneutics, this new form of anthropological research explores the possibilities of communication and exchange between cultures. As Rapport rightly pointed out, this form of anthropology is modelled around what Michael Oakeshott called 'conversation'. 'It is the diversity, the manifold of different voices speaking in different idioms or modes, that "makes" conversation.'[49] Like Oakeshott's notion of conversation, the critical turn respects the voices of different people in different positions, some of whom do the research, some are being studied, some might be academics, others literary figures. There is no *a priori* hierarchy between these different voices.[50]

The critical turn, then, goes hand in hand with the substitution of discursive metaphors (knowledge as 'cultural poetics', as an interplay of voices) for visual ones (knowledge as the observing eye).[51] Within this perspective, research is no longer merely an account or explanation of what is out there. Rather, it uses an encounter with difference as an opportunity, firstly, to reconsider some of our own presuppositions and, secondly, to reflect on the extent to which the position of anthropology in a broader socio-political context affects the kind of cognitive claims it makes.[52] The first objective is exemplified by anthropological research on the notion of identity and selfhood. The encounter with radically different notions of selfhood enables us to reconsider our own taken-for-granted concepts, to make them explicit and to realize that they are not necessarily universal.[53] The second objective refers, for instance, to an increasing attention to the ways in which anthropology has been intricately linked to the history of colonialism, and the extent to which this might still affect tacit epistemological assumptions today. Both objectives tie in with the notion of critique in that, in both cases, knowledge is about challenging and questioning our own culture, including the very discipline of anthropology itself.[54] Each objective ties in with the neo-pragmatist notion of edification. Whereas systematic accounts of reality aim to arrive at 'universal commensurability', edifying accounts suggest we open ourselves up to new experiences while never giving up on conversation.[55]

Almost two decades have passed since the idea of a critical turn was first introduced. Since then, various anthropological researches have been conducted under this new banner. In that period, many societal changes have occurred: for instance, the gradual erosion of homogeneous nation-states, partly through huge demographic shifts, partly through the strengthening of supranational organizations and corporations. The rise of new forms of technologies and the way they affect contemporary communication patterns are other examples. The critical turn stresses the dialogical nature of knowledge and the relevance of knowledge for our own society. As such, anthropology must face these new challenges and topics, some demanding a greater reliance of interdisciplinary research and others challenging presuppositions that underlie the critical turn.[56] For instance, some cross-disciplinary research explores the local effects of global forces, drawing upon insights, not only from anthropology, but also from geography, sociology and history. The changes that are taking place also affect the epistemological level, however. The idea that anthropologists simply explore the 'other' (as a relatively homogeneous and unproblematic category) is now inappropriate. Increasingly, anthropologists face empirical realities that are already interpreted and represented by many others: journalists, historians, previous anthropologists and the people involved themselves. Those operating within the critical turn take these representations as part of what is being studied, as social facts. There is a growing awareness that any social reality is multifaceted and that many representations coexist.[57] This in turn has contributed to further discussions about reflexivity. There is, for instance, a growing interest in the extent to which the autobiographies of anthropologists affect not only the kind of fieldwork they do, but also which conclusions they reach.[58]

To sum up, many social and cultural anthropologists have recently opted for a methodological path that is perfectly in line with the pragmatist stance I have been advocating. The pragmatist incredulity towards foundational projects finds its practical manifestation in the anthropology of 'cultural poetics' and its respect for the multiplicity of voices. Not only do contemporary anthropologists tend to reject the naturalist research programme that dominated anthropology for a good part of the twentieth century, they are also sceptical of the notion that anthropology faithfully copies or represents foreign cultural settings. They take seriously the view that any anthropological account ties in with multiple layers of interests and normative orientations, and from this they infer the need for anthropologists to be vigilant and to be ready to be self-critical. The pragmatist notion of 'dialogical encounter' captures the core idea underlying this critical turn: rather than simply accounting for what is being studied, anthropology embarks on a conversation that ultimately may enhance our imaginative faculties. This dialogical encounter may challenge us to reflect not only on the presuppositions of the discipline but also on the wider cultural constellation in which we find ourselves.

Archaeology

To understand the rationale behind 'post-processual archaeology', we need to understand the project of 'processual archaeology'. Processual archaeology, or 'new archaeology' as it is sometimes called, emerged in the 1960s and 1970s. It imported the methods of the natural sciences into archaeology as a reaction against cultural history and normative archaeology. These new archaeologists broke with what they saw as the impressionist amateurism that had characterized previous generations of archaeology. It was thought that archaeology could become more scientific by employing sophisticated statistical techniques and information and system theory in order to find law-like generalizations similar to those in the natural sciences. Drawing on Hempel's deductive-nomological model, these archaeologists tested middle-range theories about the way in which different societies create different types of material culture. Middle-range theories were supposed to form the right balance between abstract theory and data; they are neither too broad nor tied to the empirical realm. Ultimately the theories purported to explain how the material artefacts allow people to adjust themselves to their surroundings. Agency, the extent to which individuals attribute meanings to their surroundings and actively reproduce or transform things, did not play a significant role. The focus, instead, was on the extent to which the various material artefacts functionally fit within the broader system in which they are situated. The substitution of the rigour of science for the humanism of history was to have clear benefits. Archaeology was no longer a gentle excursion into a distant past; it gathered hard data vital to our present concerns. By uncovering generalizations, the new archaeology would allow us to help control things in the present.[59]

Post-processual archaeologists argue that people attribute meanings to their surroundings: 'it is ideas, beliefs and meanings, which interpose themselves between people and things.'[60] These attitudes and meanings undermine the plausibility that archaeologists can find generalizations of the kind the new archaeology thought it was able to uncover. It is naïve to believe that testing is unproblematic. Any observation relies upon theoretical observations and, as such, is highly fallible. The social world is 'polysemous': any social act or material product can be interpreted in different ways.[61] Post-processual archaeology wishes to revitalize its link with history. It is characterized by a renewed interest in the complex mechanisms of diffusion, reproduction and transformation of culture. This implies paying attention to the various sense-making practices through which people contribute to stability and change.

This interest goes hand in hand with the import of insights from social and critical theory, ranging from Marxism and structuralism to hermeneutics and critical theory.

Post-processual archaeology pays particular attention to the relationship between past and present. Firstly, it emphasizes that there is not a right and a wrong way of establishing meaning in the past. Of course, some interpretations are undoubtedly more valuable than others, but frequently archaeologists arrive at different conclusions and there is no neutral algorithm on hand to judge between them. One of the reasons for this uncertainty is the theory-laden nature of observations, the fact that observations always take place against the background of a theoretical framework or web of beliefs.[62] Influenced by these considerations, archaeologists open excavations to educate the public about the constructed nature of archaeological knowledge.[63] Post-processual researchers reject the earlier distinction between theory and fact: the reconstruction of the past is irrevocably tied to a viewpoint in the present, and, moreover, any archaeological narrative about the past is tied to power interests today. Hence there is a growing interest in the intricate mechanisms of power and ideology not simply in relationship to artefacts, but also to the work of the archaeologist.[64]

The fact that the notion of heritage occupies such a central role in contemporary society might have contributed to this reflexive turn in archaeology. In an age in which heritage and preservation of the past have become such powerful features of the cultural landscape,[65] there is bound to be a growing awareness of the cognitive frailty of any reconstruction of the past. The 'heritage crusade' may also encourage archaeologists to pay attention to how vested interest groups are served by competing narratives, the extent to which power struggles in the present extend to claims about the past. It is in this context that post-processual archaeology criticizes the traditional notion of the museum, which reduces visitors to passive observers and displays a unique storyline with the help of 'indisputable' findings.[66] Archaeology has been forced to reflect upon some of its own assumptions, to question some of its beliefs. Faced with a growing uncertainty regarding the cognitive validity of the various claims regarding the past and aware that these claims are necessarily 'tainted' by interests, archaeologists have become more open to reflecting critically upon their own work and to reconsidering their presuppositions. For instance, Western archaeological narratives are challenged through indigenous archaeologies, and feminist-inspired archaeologists challenge the extent to which Western views of sexual division of labour are unconsciously attributed to other societies.[67] The awareness of the contingent nature of knowledge has meant that archaeology must reconsider its own intellectual products. This brings me to my next point.

There is a second way in which post-processual archaeologists reconsider the link between past and present: they stress that archaeology can be employed *deliberately* to challenge and criticize the present, and to challenge our deep-seated assumptions. Although post-processualists recognize that any archaeological narrative is inevitably linked to and dependent on interests and ideologies in the present, they also believe that it is possible for the archaeological researcher to employ the object to set his or her own cultural assumptions at a distance.[68] This perspective underlies the research on identity formation carried out under a feminist post-processual umbrella with the aim of challenging some of the dichotomies that keep us captive today.[69] Likewise, post-colonial anthropology may show the creole and hybrid nature of colonized societies so as to question some of the well-known presuppositions that underlie current legal debates.[70] Notice the difference with the earlier point that the confrontation with other views has forced archaeologists to reconsider their presuppositions: the past is now employed *intentionally* to question the present. Hence Tilley's dictum that 'archaeologists have so far interpreted the past; they *should* undertake to change it in service of the present.'[71] This explains why post-processualists are hostile to any call for an empiricist strand of archaeology, not only because the notion of a safe haven of theory-free observations is illusionary, but also because it reduces the *métier* of the archaeologist to a mere fact-finding mission. There is more to archaeology than simply recording data; it is also about creatively employing the data to confront the present.[72] This also explains why post-processualists criticize the new archaeology for not recognizing the distinctiveness of the past, for reducing it to a mirror of the present. It is only by honouring the discontinuity between the past and the present that the former can be employed successfully to challenge the latter.[73] Critiquing the present may operate at two levels, one internal to the discipline, the other external. It refers first of all to the questioning of the assumptions of the theoretical frameworks employed by archaeologists themselves. Secondly, it refers to the questioning of some of the categories or principles of organization in society today.[74] Post-processualists are particularly concerned with the societal significance of their work. As such, they are ultimately more interested in the societal than the disciplinary level.

In sum, many contemporary archaeologists have embarked on a methodological path that is congruent with the pragmatist agenda I have been advocating. Whereas processual archaeology was very much embedded in a naturalist agenda, post-processual archaeology moves beyond naturalism. Post-processual archaeology acknowledges that people attribute meanings to their surroundings and that archaeologists in turn make sense of these sense-making activities. Rather than representing or mirroring the social 'as it really is', attributing meaning to sense-making activities is a more creative process. Although influenced by hermeneutics and interpretative sociology, these contemporary archaeologists go further than simply acknowledging the meaningful nature of the social. They adopt a pragmatist stance, emphasizing how their method of inquiry may alter the present constellation of meanings. Knowledge is no longer conceived as something passive, but it is more like an action: it affects things. Like the pragmatist method, these archaeologists explore how their discipline can be used to confront and alter some of our dominant views today.

History and the social sciences

Influenced by Foucault's rediscovery of Nietzsche's genealogical approach to the study of history,[75] many contemporary historians and sociologists have adopted the genealogical method and apply it widely. This has led to a variety of sophisticated historical analyses, for instance, of 'governmentality', modern notions of selfhood, and the treatment of the poor.[76] Like the critical turn in anthropology and post-processual archaeology, genealogy aims at self-referential knowledge acquisition. Rather than gaining access to the unfamiliar past, genealogy articulates and illuminates the familiar present. The past then becomes a means to access the present, deracinate traditional foundations and challenge the assumption of continuity.[77] For genealogists, historical research has little value unless it feeds into 'life and action', unless it helps us to rid ourselves of our own constructions and see through our own imprisonment: 'knowledge is not made for understanding; it is made for cutting.'[78] History makes sense in so far as it *does* something to the present, undermining or cutting through the present.[79] Genealogical voyages into the past can foster a critical distance towards our present condition. The genealogist demonstrates that our deep-seated presuppositions (e.g., about morality) or entrenched practices (e.g., punishment) are more historically specific than we imagine. Illuminating the historical emergence of these presuppositions or practices at a particular point in time allows us to demonstrate their relationship to specific historical contingencies or power struggles. This undermines our propensity to see these presuppositions or practices as either naturally given or necessarily progressive. Nietzsche's genealogy ties in with a critique of the metaphysical pursuit of the 'origin' (*Ursprung*). Searching for the *Ursprung* is an attempt to recover a lost essence, to retrieve those 'immobile forms that precede the external world of accident and succession.'[80] In genealogical research, there is no 'timeless and essential secret' except the awareness that such an essence does not exist and that things were not more valuable or pure when they came into being.[81] Geuss contrasts genealogy with a pedigree: whereas the latter legitimizes a person, family or other entity by disclosing a continuous and long line of succession, thus leading to a single and noble origin, the former uncovers not one but many lines of development.

The further back in time we go, the more lowly the origins seem to be.[82] Another difference between genealogy and pedigree is that the genealogist searches for discontinuity, the ruptures that occur throughout history and which make for the emergence of radically different forms of thought and being. Nietzsche talked here about effective history (wirkliche Historie), aimed at undermining the presupposition of continuity, of universals, and of essences.[83]

These reflections are theoretical, but they have strong ramifications for empirical research. Foucault's Discipline and Punish helps to clarify the relationship between genealogy and self-referential knowledge. The book is a historical account of how social control was conceived and organized since the advent of modernity. Foucault argued that until the late eighteenth century punishment was a horrific public spectacle of torture and execution before a huge audience.[84] As crimes were considered assaults on or challenges to the authority of the sovereign, public torture both reinforced and symbolized the power of the sovereign. This form of punishment targeted the body of the culprit – not the mind or soul. The efficiency of this system depended on its ability to exercise fear. This system was very different from our present penal system, but had its own logic; it was sophisticated and internally coherent. Towards the end of the eighteenth century, however, the society of spectacle ran into difficulties. Increasingly, persons about to be executed started speaking out against the sovereign. The condemned had nothing to lose, and had a large, often sympathetic, audience. As this led to considerable disorder, policy-makers and intellectuals started thinking about new forms of social control.[85]

In the eighteenth century the philosophes had already criticized the old system on humanitarian grounds, but the new system that would eventually emerge had very little in common with what the philosophes had in mind. The utilitarian reforms of the early nineteenth century led to a 'disciplinary' society with new notions of punishment. Disciplinary power focused on regular, systematic training and monitoring of individuals. The new disciplinary system was centred round incarceration, 'hierarchical observation', 'normalization' and 'examination'.[86] Hierarchical observation was epitomized by the 'panopticon', a specific organization of space in which inmates knew they could always be watched but at no point in time did they know whether they were being monitored. Underlying this system of surveillance was the idea of 'self-correction': knowing they could always be watched (and without knowing if or when they were) prisoners would end up monitoring themselves. Normalization refers to a penal accountancy system in which behaviour was rewarded or punished depending on whether it complied with or deviated from a yardstick. Increasingly, people were ranked depending on how well they conformed to the set standards. The combination of hierarchical observation and normalization led to 'examination', which drew on sophisticated techniques of documentation and classification, which in turn depended on the emerging social sciences. By the mid-nineteenth century the 'society of surveillance' was fully established. Very few traces were left of the 'society of spectacle'. Public tortures and executions were replaced by incarceration. The target was no longer the body, but the mind or soul of the individual. The focus was on reforming individuals, turning them into proper citizens.[87]

This brief excursion into *Discipline and Punish* helps establish how Foucault's use of genealogy enabled him to pursue self-referential knowledge. Firstly, by juxtaposing past and present, genealogy erodes the present constellation. The present becomes manifest and is found not to be as universal as was once thought. The opening chapter in *Discipline and Punish* is particularly telling in this regard. Foucault depicted a sharp contrast between the gruesome public execution of Damien in 1757 and the rigid time schedule of the prison regime in the early nineteenth century. This juxtaposition reveals the assumptions of both regimes. The reader realizes that the public spectacle is very different from the penal system today, and the juxtaposition makes the assumptions of the latter manifest. Secondly, Foucault's genealogical method undermines those justifications of the present that portray it as inevitable – as a necessary outcome of the past. Genealogy challenges these notions of inevitability by showing that the historical trajectory of the present was tied to a 'network of contingencies': accidents and unanticipated consequences. For example, confronted with the historical knowledge that the call for a new penal system was partly a result of the unintended chaos and social disorder of the old regime, it becomes more difficult to see the current system as enshrined in history, as the product of a necessary development. Thirdly, genealogy undermines those justifications of the present configuration that portray it as the product of a continuous progression. Genealogy shows how assumptions of continuity and progress are problematic. The past cannot be reconstructed into a continuous narrative because it is so different from the present. In genealogy, the past has its own internal logic and justification, and there is no independent yardstick with which to compare different systems or regimes of power. For example, Foucault elaborated on the internal logic of the society of spectacle, and he pointed out that the current penal system is not simply a humanitarian progression, but a different (albeit more sophisticated) form of social control. Fourthly, genealogy challenges the present configuration because it shows how various belief systems, practices and institutions, which appear innocuous or honourable, are tainted by power struggles. Foucault's historical journey in *Discipline and Punish* showed that, in spite of their rhetoric of emancipation, the social sciences were central to the rise of the disciplinary society. Likewise, whatever its good intentions, the current 'carceral system' is implicated in the contemporary disciplinary regime.

Some concluding remarks

Each example – from anthropology, archaeology and historical sociology – shows facets of the central thesis throughout the book: we have to think more broadly about what social research can offer. Researchers tend to focus on explaining, testing, predicting or mapping an outer world. Self-referential knowledge acquisition achieves something very different. It no longer craves for an accurate, full representation, or for verifying, falsifying or predicting. Whereas most social research wants to ignore the subjective (because it gets in the way of the research process), self-referential knowledge deliberately confronts us with our selves, our presuppositions and practices. My pragmatist proposal explores our blind spot, shedding light on what is normally hidden. It surprises, confronting us with a new angle or storyline. It teaches us about alternative socio-political futures, encouraging us to conceptualize and experience what is not present. Self-referential knowledge enlarges our imagination.

The three examples (the critical turn in anthropology, post-processual archaeology and genealogical history) demonstrate the potential of a research programme along the *contours* of my pragmatist proposal. They show how a self-referential form of knowledge acquisition, rather than simply a theoretical construction, can and has been applied in actual research. They set forth the wide applicability of this methodological outlook, the extent to which it can be put into operation in a multitude of disciplines. But there is more to these examples. These research strategies have been around for a couple of decades now, so it ought to be possible to learn from them about the new concerns this pragmatist scheme might entail and about how to deal with these issues. There are four problems that any researcher, in pursuit of self-referential knowledge, ought to address. They refer to the danger of enhanced self-reflexivity, to the nature of otherness, to the problem of relativism, and to the relationship between knowledge and political action.

The first issue confronts the potential dangers of increased self-reflexivity. Some reflexive anthropologists and post-processual archaeologists have been criticized for their preoccupation with their respective disciplines at the expense of an in-depth analysis of the subject matter. There is truth in the allegation that their writings read more like meta-theoretical treatises than actual research reports. With the critical turn in social anthropology, for instance, the pendulum has swung too much in the opposite direction. The exasperation of some critics is justified. The sheer volume of writings about the epistemological foundations of the discipline, as well as the alleged complicity of anthropology in pernicious socio-political developments, threatens to outweigh traditional research altogether. Such critics have a point when they argue that social anthropology ought to deal with social phenomena, rather than with the *study* of social phenomena. These exaggerations, however, do not take away from the importance of the critical turn. Firstly, self-referential knowledge acquisition does not only focus on the internal mechanisms of the discipline. This type of knowledge also reflects upon the broader cultural settings to which researchers, and possibly readers, belong. This enables them to reassess and re-evaluate their own point of view. Self-referential knowledge provides a critical commentary on issues much broader than ones confined to the discipline. Secondly, while the criticisms point out the dangers of particular uses of self-referential knowledge acquisition, this type of knowledge lends itself to other, more constructive, usages. If properly conducted, self-referential forms of knowledge are not antithetical to informative discussions about the social world. On the contrary, reflections of this kind help to re-evaluate the external realm in new, imaginative ways. It is precisely the openness towards the social world that is so vital in self-referential knowledge. What these criticisms do show, however, is that researchers in pursuit of self-referential knowledge ought to make a concerted effort to exhibit this openness. If not, social research easily descends into a paralysing metatheoretical debate.

The second question concerns the status of the 'other', an issue that has prompted heated debates in a wide range of subjects, from sociology and cultural studies to history and social anthropology. Contemporary anthropologists, cultural historians and literary critics are perfectly justified in warning that the 'other' ought not to be treated as an *a priori* homogeneous and fixed entity. This concern about the nature of the 'other' is relevant to social research in general, and indeed it is one that has played an important role in debates around various topics, ranging from gender to colonial and post-colonial experience. For instance, the Lacanian feminist argument that women's experience is distinct from that of men has been rightly criticized for ignoring the empirical differences among women or for uncritically appropriating the category of 'woman'. Not only do these experiences differ according to class and ethnicity so that it becomes difficult to appeal to womanhood as a unified category, but the very notion of 'woman' as distinct from 'man' (and indeed of 'man' as different from 'woman') has been shown to be unstable and politicized.[88] In a similar vein, Said and Homi Bhabha have pointed out the extent to which various Western accounts of otherness, such as those of the Orient, 'essentialize' what is actually a heterogeneous entity.[89] To essentialize a certain category is to assume that all or most members of that category have certain features in common by virtue of some inherent quality. For Said, Orientalism is the type of discourse that promotes this distorted view of the 'other' as a unified item. The danger, then, just as in the case of 'womanhood', is that various empirical differences within the category are wrongly discarded. The problem is even more pressing if, as is the case of the examples given earlier, the study consists of *deliberate* encounters with difference and if these encounters are a crucial component of the investigation. Researchers within this tradition need to make sure they avoid treating the objects of investigation as a uniform, undifferentiated entity. It is essential, then, that the pursuit of self-referential knowledge acquisition goes hand in hand with a commitment to reassess regularly any presuppositions that tie in with how the 'other' is conceived.

The third issue concerns the charge that these types of research are relativistic. Some post-processual archaeologists and reflexive anthropologists argue that any reconstruction of data is merely an act of interpretation, a narrative among many narratives. Nietzsche made similar suggestions when he appealed to 'perspectivism', according to which any history is portrayed as simply a history *from* the present.[90] For Nietzsche, 'a fact, a work is eloquent in a *new* way for every age and every new type of man. History always enunciates *new* truths.'[91] Such assertions are notoriously vague; no wonder they have been interpreted as relativist in a way that is self-defeating. I do not believe, however, that they *have* to be interpreted in ways that warrant these labels. The power of this stance is that no neutral algorithm exists which can judge and compare between the various narratives; decisions of this kind can be arrived at only through open dialogue between experienced researchers. The stance *is* problematic if it implies that no such judgements can ever be made and that, consequently, any narrative is as valid (or as implausible) as any other. The latter position not only opposes common sense and is self-contradictory, it is also irreconcilable with what was coined the emancipating effect of self-referential knowledge. Indeed, the position that any narrative will do seriously undermines our ability to question our beliefs or assumptions, for instance regarding the fixity or universality of certain concepts. It contradicts an essential part of Nietzsche's genealogy of morals. But the former position, the one I am advocating, would not contradict it. It simply acknowledges that it is impossible to set out guidelines prior to an open conversation between peers. This position is perfectly in line with the pragmatist insistence on the social nature of the self and the communal aspect of any form of inquiry, according to which 'it is only by submitting our hypotheses to public critical discussion that we become aware of what is valid in our claims and what fails to withstand critical scrutiny.'[92]

The fourth and final issue concerns the ethics involved in social research. The pursuit of a self-referential type of knowledge raises new ethical concerns and responsibilities for the researcher. This is particularly obvious in the case of Foucault's history of the present. Within the contours of traditional history, the primary aim is to account for the past, so there is no burden on the researcher to suggest how to act politically. Foucauldian historians do carry this responsibility. They seek to unsettle the present, so the onus is on them to indicate how to proceed subsequently.[93] Foucault's response to this dilemma was to present himself as a 'new intellectual' as opposed to the 'traditional intellectual'. Whereas the latter preaches from above and tries to impose a worldview, the former simply provides tools to allow people to establish a distance from their taken-for-granted world and see things differently.[94] From my pragmatic perspective, Foucault's response is only partly convincing. He is persuasive in so far as he is sceptical about attempts to ground critique on a timeless footing, and about the idea that any change necessarily implies progress. The problem still remains, however, that, once the present is disturbed in the way Foucault intended it to be, the researcher is responsible for providing guidelines about what needs to be done. It is not surprising that Foucault was politically active; he tried hard to improve the penal system in France. Self-referential knowledge acquisition must go hand in hand with a strong commitment on the part of the researcher to act. This stance is, of course, perfectly in line with the pragmatist suggestion that knowledge, rather than mirroring an outer world, is about making a difference. The earlier generation of pragmatists, including G. H. Mead and John Dewey, were very much involved in social policy and intervention and paid particular attention to the interplay between scientific discovery, ethics and political action.[95] Self-referential knowledge needs to be set in the context of this pragmatist tradition, in which the pursuit of knowledge goes hand in hand with a responsibility to bring about change.

Notes

Introduction

1 This tradition has led to some outstanding contributions: for instance, Doyal and Harris (1986), Fay (1996), Flew (1991), Hollis (1994), Kaufmann (1978), Martin and McIntyre (1994), Papineau (1978), Pratt (1978), Ryan (1970) and Trigg (1985).

2 Excellent overviews of this kind can be found in, for instance, Kincaid (1996), May and Williams (1998), McIntyre (1996), Rosenberg (1995) and Williams (2000). Some authors focus and promote one such theoretical framework: e.g., Elster (1989), Bunge (1998), Jarvie (1986) and Phillips (2000).

3 See, for instance, Gordon (1991). His history of the philosophy of the social sciences is not meant to be constructive in any way: 'I am not convinced that knowledge of the history of a science improves one's ability to practise it, and I am even more skeptical of the claim that current research would be facilitated if scientists were to pay close attention to the issues that are the philosophers' stock in trade. Study of the history and philosophy of science can be strongly recommended, but for a different reason: because of the contributions they can make to one's understanding of modern Western civilization' (Gordon 1991, ix).

4 Just as Manicas's (1987), Outhwaite's (1987) and Potter's (2000) historical reconstructions tie in with the development of a realist alternative, mine is linked to a pragmatist proposal.

5 Other interesting proposals for a non-naturalist philosophy of the social sciences include, for instance, Doyal and Harris (1986), Flyvbjerg (2001) and Taylor (1985).

6 In this respect, my pragmatist proposal is sympathetic to the attention that the philosophy of the social sciences has recently given to critical theory and its attendant notion of cognitive interests. Examples include Bentz and Shapiro (1998, 146–59), Bohman (1991), Crotty (1998), Delanty and Strydom (2003, 207–76), Fay (1987, 1996), Flyvbjerg (2001) and Outhwaite (1987).

Chapter 1 Emile Durkheim's Naturalism

1 Durkheim (1982a), henceforth RSM.
2 Durkheim (1989), henceforth S.
3 Durkheim (1984), henceforth DL.
4 Durkheim (1978a), henceforth CS.
5 Durkheim (1965b), henceforth MSS.
6 Durkheim (1982c), henceforth SSS.
7 See, for instance, Halfpenny (1982), Keat and Urry (1982).
8 RSM, pp. 33, 159.
9 Durkheim (1983, 1), henceforth PS.
10 MSS, pp. 3–14, 50.
11 RSM, pp. 159–60.
12 Durkheim (1953, 59–62), henceforth DMF.
13 Concerning the ambiguous relationship between Durkheim and Comte, see, for instance, Gane (1997).
14 CS, pp. 47–8.
15 CS, p. 48.
16 DL, pp. 13–14.
17 PS, pp. 89–90.
18 RSM, pp. 64ff., 108–9, 139–41; SSS, pp. 176–82.
19 S, p. 36.
20 Durkheim (1982d, 215).
21 MSS, pp. 11–12.
22 S, pp. 148–51.
23 Durkheim (1982b, 170–2), henceforth MCH.
24 MCH, pp. 172–4.
25 This is mainly because members of the Vienna Circle embraced atomism.
26 RSM, pp. 143–4.
27 Durkheim (1965c, 83).
28 RSM, pp. 85–6.
29 DL, p. xxvii.
30 RSM, p. 104.
31 DL, pp. xxvii–xxviii.
32 CS, pp. 44–5.
33 CS, pp. 45–8.
34 CS, pp. 47–50.
35 DL, pp. xxv–xxvi, 5–6; DMF, pp. 35–8; CS, pp. 66–8.
36 SSS, pp. 175–80.
37 PS, pp. 89–91; CS, pp. 50–4.
38 SSS, pp. 180–4; CS, pp. 54–61.
39 RSM, p. 75.
40 CS, pp. 57–8.
41 CS, p. 54.
42 PS, pp. 1–2.
43 PS, pp. 66–7.
44 PS, pp. 66–8.

45 PS, p. 68.
46 SSS, pp. 192–6.
47 SSS, pp. 196–7.
48 SSS, pp. 197–9.
49 SSS, pp. 202–6.
50 S, p. 36.
51 MSS, pp. 3–7.
52 RSM, pp. 128–9, 259.
53 RSM, pp. 125–7; DL, pp. 26–7, 39–41, 179–99.
54 RSM, pp. 125–35.
55 MSS, p. 3.
56 CS, pp. 44–61.
57 RSM, pp. 50, 59.
58 RSM, p. 52.
59 RSM, pp. 50–5.
60 RSM, pp. 52–6.
61 RSM, pp. 54–7.
62 RSM, pp. 60–3.
63 RSM, pp. 63–6.
64 RSM, pp. 66–9.
65 RSM, pp. 69ff. See also S, pp. 37–8.
66 See, for instance, MSS, pp. 3–4.
67 RSM, pp. 69–72.
68 RSM, pp. 73–83.
69 MSS, pp. 7–8, 17–18, 44–9.
70 RSM, pp. 85–7.
71 RSM, pp. 88–95; DL, p. xxvii.
72 RSM, pp. 94–7.
73 RSM, pp. 108–18.
74 DL, pp. 291–309.
75 DL, pp. xxxi–lix.
76 MSS, pp. 40–4.
77 RSM, pp. 119–25.
78 DL, pp. 12–13.
79 RSM, pp. 119–25.
80 S, pp. 57–103, 123–42.
81 RSM, pp. 125–35.
82 MSS, pp. 36–49.
83 RSM, pp. 135–44; DL, pp. 200–25.
84 MSS, pp. 50–2.
85 RSM, p. 150.
86 S, pp. 146ff.
87 RSM, pp. 152–3.
88 S, pp. 37–9.
89 See also S, p. 46.
90 S, pp. 51–2.
91 S, p. 42.

92 S, p. 44.
93 S, pp. 57, 81.
94 S, pp. 77–81.
95 S, pp. 82–93.
96 S, pp. 94–103.
97 S, pp. 104–9.
98 S, pp. 109–22.
99 S, pp. 123–37.
100 S, pp. 137–40.
101 S, pp. 137–42.
102 S, pp. 152–70.
103 S, pp. 171–208.
104 S, pp. 197–216.
105 S, p. 225.
106 S, pp. 217–20.
107 S, pp. 221–7.
108 S, pp. 228–40.
109 S, pp. 241–58.
110 S, pp. 259–76.
111 S, pp. 297ff.
112 DL, pp. 11–30.
113 For example, DL, pp. 24ff.
114 Filloux (1977).
115 DL, pp. 269–88.
116 DL, pp. xxxi–lix.
117 PS, pp. 89ff.; SSS, pp. 178–82.
118 Durkheim (1978b, 247–8); DL, pp. 291ff.; RSM, pp. 143ff.
119 Durkheim (1982e, 246–7).
120 Nagel (1986).

Chapter 2 Max Weber's Interpretative Method

1 Weber (1948, 134–6), henceforth SV.
2 SV, p. 135.
3 SV, pp. 135–8, 150–1.
4 Weber (1949b, 67–71), henceforth OSS.
5 OSS, pp. 100ff.
6 Weber (1964, 102–7), henceforth FCS.
7 Weber (1975), henceforth RK.
8 OSS.
9 Weber (1949c), henceforth LCS.
10 FCS.
11 Weber (1949a), henceforth MEN.
12 OSS, p. 111.
13 OSS, pp. 72–9.
14 OSS, p. 76.

15 OSS, p. 82.
16 Oakes (1975, 9ff.).
17 OSS, pp. 78–81; RK, pp. 63–4.
18 OSS, pp. 91–3; RK, pp. 64–6.
19 OSS, pp. 104–5.
20 MEN, pp. 10–12.
21 MEN, pp. 13–15.
22 OSS, pp. 83–4.
23 OSS, pp. 110–11.
24 OSS, pp. 96–9.
25 LCS, pp. 175–7.
26 LCS, pp. 177ff.
27 MEN, pp. 1–2; SV, pp. 134–56.
28 OSS, pp. 51–2; MEN, pp. 18–25.
29 MEN, pp. 27–39.
30 MEN, pp. 18–19; SV, pp. 150–2.
31 OSS, pp. 52–7.
32 OSS, pp. 110–11; MEN, pp. 18–25; SV, pp. 152–6.
33 MEN, p. 19.
34 OSS, pp. 105–7.
35 OSS, pp. 76–80; RK, pp. 62–6.
36 RK, p. 180.
37 RK, pp. 164ff., 180ff.
38 FCS, pp. 98–100.
39 OSS, pp. 82–3, 92–3.
40 FCS, p. 88.
41 OSS, p. 90.
42 Runciman (1972, 34–5).
43 OSS, pp. 87–91.
44 OSS, pp. 91–3.
45 OSS, p. 92.
46 OSS, pp. 93–4.
47 FCS, pp. 109–12.
48 OSS, pp. 92–100, 106–10.
49 OSS, pp. 106–7.
50 OSS, pp. 100–3.
51 Runciman (1972, 33–48).
52 OSS, p. 111.
53 OSS, p. 111.
54 OSS, pp. 104–6.
55 OSS, p. 112.
56 FCS, p. 88.
57 FCS, p. 88.
58 FCS, p. 92.
59 MEN, pp. 37–48; FCS, pp. 90–3, 109–12.
60 MEN, p. 43.
61 LCS, pp. 169–78.

62 FCS, pp. 96–8.
63 FCS, pp. 114–15.
64 FCS, p. 112.
65 FCS, pp. 113–14.
66 FCS, pp. 115–88.
67 FCS, p. 115.
68 FCS, p. 115.
69 FCS, pp. 116–18.
70 FCS, pp. 118–19.
71 FCS, pp. 118–19.
72 FCS, pp. 119–20.
73 The English translation by Talcott Parsons (Weber 1992, henceforth PE) is based on a later version.
74 PE, pp. 90–2.
75 PE, pp. 27–31.
76 PE, p. 71.
77 PE, p. 17.
78 PE, pp. 17–19.
79 PE, pp. 19–27.
80 PE, pp. 35–78.
81 PE, pp. 35ff.
82 PE, p. 37.
83 PE, pp. 56ff.
84 PE, pp. 98–128.
85 PE, pp. 110–15.
86 PE, pp. 120ff.
87 Durkheim (1982a, pp. 85–97; 1984, pp. 219–309).
88 MEN, pp. 18ff., 27ff.
89 OSS, pp. 51–2; MEN, pp. 18ff.
90 See also Runciman (1972, 25).
91 Coleman (1990).
92 Ringer (1997, 163–7).

Chapter 3 Karl Popper's Falsificationism

1 Note that, while distancing himself from naturalism, Popper used the term differently. He associated naturalism with a misguided inductivist view of science (see Popper 1976, 90–1).
2 See, for instance, Hayek (1944), Gombrich (1960), Gellner (1985, ch. 1).
3 Popper (1991a), henceforth CR.
4 Popper (1991b, 1971a, 1971b), henceforth PH, OS1, OS2.
5 In this context, see, for instance, Hayek (1944) and Popper's 'Utopia and Violence' (CR, pp. 355–63) and 'The History of our Time: An Optimist's View' (CR, pp. 364–76).
6 Popper (1934). See also PH, 137–8.
7 Popper (1992, 31–44), henceforth UQ.

8 CR, pp. 33–9.
9 See, for instance, CR, pp. 337ff.
10 With regard to the relationship between Hayek and Popper, see Simkin (1993, pp. 191–7).
11 PH, pp. 14–16, 155–6; OS2, pp. 212–23.
12 Durkheim (1971), Durkheim and Mauss (1963).
13 Scheler (1980, 67–186).
14 UQ, p. 89.
15 Popper (1959, 15–23), henceforth LSD.
16 LSD, pp. 93–110.
17 LSD, pp. 27–30.
18 CR, pp. 42–59; Popper (1979, 1–31), henceforth OK.
19 LSD, pp. 34–9.
20 LSD, pp. 32–4, 59–62.
21 CR, pp. 39–41.
22 LSD, p. 41.
23 LSD, pp. 78–92.
24 LSD, pp. 112–35.
25 LSD, pp. 136–45.
26 LSD, pp. 286–7.
27 CR, pp. 240–8.
28 OK, p. 15.
29 OK, pp. 319–40.
30 CR, 231–7.
31 Kuhn (1970a).
32 Kuhn (1970a, viii).
33 Kuhn (1970a, 35–42).
34 Kuhn (1970a, 52–76).
35 Kuhn (1970a, 92–159).
36 Kuhn (1970b).
37 Popper (1970, 53–5), henceforth NSD.
38 NSD, p. 55.
39 NSD, pp. 51–4.
40 Kuhn (1970a, 163–4).
41 Kuhn (1970a, 111–35).
42 Kuhn (1970a, 160–73, 205–7).
43 NSD, p. 56.
44 NSD, pp. 56–8.
45 PH, pp. 93–7.
46 PH, pp. 136–43.
47 E.g. Frydman (1982), Heiner (1983).
48 PH, pp. 143–7; OS2, pp. 263–5.
49 OS2, pp. 259–69.
50 PH, pp. 147–52; OS2, pp. 265–9.
51 PH, p. 3.
52 PH, pp. 147–52; OS2, pp. 259–61.
53 CR, pp. 33–7.

54 OS2, pp. 100–10.
55 CR, pp. 336–9; OS2, pp. 85–7.
56 OS2, pp. 269–80.
57 CR, pp. 336–47.
58 CR, pp. 333–4.
59 PH, pp. 120–30.
60 CR, pp. 339–40.
61 PH, pp. 55–8.
62 PH, pp. 58–63.
63 CR, pp. 343–5.
64 PH, pp. 64–70.
65 PH, pp. 83–93; pp. 355–63.
66 CR, pp. 341–2; OS2, pp. 208–11.
67 OS2, pp. 94–6.
68 CR, pp. 341–2.
69 PH, pp. 140–2.
70 Popper (1983, 362–3), henceforth RP.
71 RP, pp. 360–5.
72 CR, pp. 342–3; PH, pp. 60–3.
73 PH, pp. 62–3.
74 See, for instance, Coleman (1990). For a critique, see Baert (1998a) and Green and Shapiro (1994).
75 OS1; OS2; Habermas (1989, 1991a, 1991b, 1991c).
76 Kuhn (1970a, 1–51).
77 NSD.
78 Kuhn (1970a, 160–73).
79 Feyerabend (1975).
80 Occasionally Popper acknowledged that other criteria also matter (for example, simplicity), but his philosophy of science failed to assign a significant role to them.
81 Popper (1950a, 1950b, 1982).
82 PH, p. 62.
83 PH, p. 62.
84 Lakatos (1970).

Chapter 4 Critical Realism

1 Feyerabend (1975); Rorty (1980).
2 Bhaskar (1998) and Giddens (1984). For a comparison, see New (1994) and Archer (1995).
3 Harré (1960); Hesse (1961, 1963).
4 Harré (2002a, 2002b); Harré and Varela (1996).
5 Bhaskar (1978, 1998).
6 Keat and Urry (1982).
7 Archer (1995); Benton (1984); Layder (1990); Lawson (1997, 2003); Manicas (1980, 1987); Outhwaite (1987); Sayer (1992, 2000).

8   Harré and Secord (1972); Will (1980, 1984).
9   Concerning the relationship between critical realism and Marxism, see Bhaskar (1986, 1993) and Collier (1989). For the link with feminism, see, for instance, New (1998). For a more analytical account of critical realist arguments about the emancipatory nature of the social sciences, see Sayer (1997) and Lacey (1997).
10 Harré (1993); Jensen and Harré (1981).
11 See, for instance, Hodgson (1993); Reed and Harvey (1992); Harvey and Reed (1996); and Harvey (2002). For the relationship between realism and evolutionary theory, see Northover (1999).
12 Bhaskar (1993, 1994, 2000).
13 For a balanced review, see Hartwig (2001).
14 In this context, Lawson (2003, 22–7) argues that the anti-realist aspects of mainstream economics inhibit the development of economics into a mature science.
15 For an overview of this issue, see Sayer (1997) and Lacey (1997).
16 With regard to structuralism and realism, see Nellhaus (1998). Will (1980, 1984) defends psychoanalysis from a realist perspective.
17 There are exceptions. For instance, Kaul (2002) argues for a fruitful dialogue between critical realism and postmodernism, and Mäki (1988a, 1988b) and Peter (2001) attempt to reconcile a realist theory of science with McClosley's notion of rhetoric. See also O'Neill (1998) and Lewis (1996).
18 See, for example, Viskovatoff (2002).
19 Bhaskar (1978, 36ff.); Collier (1994, 76–85); Lawson (1997, 33–4).
20 For a cogent summary of the transcendental argumentation in critical realist writings, see Harvey (2002, 164–6).
21 Bhaskar (1978, 21ff.; 1998, 9–13); Collier (1994, 50ff.).
22 Lawson (1997, 25).
23 See, for instance, Lawson (1997, 33–4).
24 Dow (2001, 2002a, 2002b).
25 For a summary of the Humean view, see Harré and Madden (1975, 27–43).
26 Harré and Madden (1975, 27ff.).
27 Lawson (1997, 27–30).
28 See Harré and Madden (1975, 44–53, 118–38).
29 Bhaskar (1978, 50–1); Lawson (1997, 23).
30 Collier (1994, 31–69).
31 Bhaskar (1978, 12ff.).
32 Bhaskar (1978, 43); Isaac (1990, 2–6).
33 Bhaskar (1978, 118–26); Collier (1994, 31–69).
34 Bhaskar (1978, 125–6, 136–7).
35 Lawson (1997, 27–9).
36 Lawson (1994; 1997, 30–2, 282–9).
37 Collier (1994, 160–7); Lawson (1997, 212ff.; 2003, 145ff.).
38 A minority of critical realists are more sceptical of the usefulness of retroduction. See, for instance, Lee (2002).
39 See, for instance, Bhaskar (1998, 19); Lawson (1997, 213); and Runde (1998). See Peacock (2000) for a critique of Bhaskar and Lawson's notion of explanatory power.

40 Peacock (2000, 326–32).
41 Regarding demi-regularities, see, for instance, Downward et al. (2002); Lawson (2003, 105–6); Pinkstone (2002); and Finch and McMaster (2002).
42 Bhaskar (1998, 38ff.).
43 Bhaskar (1998, 34–5).
44 Bhaskar (1998, 39–40); Lewis (2000, 257–8).
45 For instance, Gary Potter (2000a) dismisses Jeffrey Alexander's critique of Bourdieu for failing to realize Bourdieu's implicit commitment to the critical realist account of structure and agency, while Joseph (2000) argues that Gramsci's theory of hegemony is compatible with the transformational model of social action and Mark Peacock (1993) defends a similar realist reading of Friedrich Hayek.
46 See, for instance, Giddens (1984). For a comparison between Bhaskar and Giddens, see New (1994) and Archer (1995).
47 Lawson (1997, 178ff.). For a critical review of the critical realist use of the notion of tacit knowledge, see Faulkner (2002).
48 Lewis (2000, 257–65).
49 Giddens (1984).
50 Jensen and Harré (1981); Harré (1981); and Bhaskar (1981).
51 Hodgson (1993).
52 Lawson (2003, 110–40).
53 Carter (2000).
54 Carter and New (2004).
55 Fleetwood and Ackroyd (2004).
56 Marsh et al. (1999).
57 Marsh et al. (1999, 2–5).
58 Marsh et al. (1999, 6–19).
59 Marsh et al. (1999, 168–88).
60 Marsh et al. (1999, 189–208).
61 See also Baert (1996; 1998a, 189–97).
62 For a discussion of the agency–structure distinction, see Holmwood and Stewart (1991).
63 Dewey (1930, 233ff.).
64 See also Dewey (1908, 53ff.).

Chapter 5 Critical Theory

1 Horkheimer (1972c).
2 Adorno et al. (1950).
3 Adorno (1976b, 118–20), henceforth LSS.
4 Adorno (1992), henceforth CI; Adorno and Horkheimer (1992, 120–67), henceforth DE.
5 DE, pp. 3–80; Adorno (1976a), henceforth SER; Horkheimer (1972a, 138–40), henceforth LAM.
6 See, for instance, LSS, pp. 120–2.
7 DE, pp. 3–80.

8   DE, pp. 3–42.
9   LAM, p. 138.
10 SER, pp. 68–9, 79–83.
11 SER, pp. 71–3, 83–4.
12 Blauner (1964).
13 SER, p. 85.
14 LSS, pp. 116–20.
15 Horkheimer (1972b, 196–7), henceforth TCT.
16 SER, pp. 69–70.
17 SER, p. 76.
18 LSS, pp. 112–18. See also TCT, pp. 206–7.
19 TCT, pp. 204ff.
20 SER, 77ff.
21 SER, pp. 72–3.
22 LSS, pp. 108ff.
23 SER, pp. 73–5.
24 TCT, pp. 231–2.
25 SER, pp. 74–7.
26 SER, p. 78.
27 TCT, p. 232.
28 TCT, pp. 188–91.
29 SER, pp. 77–8; LSS, pp. 105–8.
30 LSS, pp. 110–12; TCT, pp. 197ff.
31 TCT, pp. 208–9.
32 Habermas (1989).
33 Habermas (1987), henceforth KHI.
34 Habermas (1991a, 1991b), henceforth CA1, CA2.
35 KHI, pp. 3–5, 71–90.
36 KHI, pp. 91–186.
37 KHI, pp. 306–8.
38 KHI, pp. 308ff.
39 Durkheim (1989).
40 KHI, pp. 308–9.
41 KHI, p. 309.
42 KHI, pp. 309–10.
43 KHI, pp. 310–11.
44 KHI, pp. 214–300.
45 Habermas (1970a, 1970b, CA1, CA2, 1991c [henceforth CES]).
46 CA1, pp. 286–328; CES, pp. 1–59.
47 Habermas (1970a, 1970b).
48 See also Calhoun (1995).

Chapter 6 Richard Rorty and Pragmatism

1   Rorty (1999, xxii), henceforth PSH.
2   E.g. Rorty (1989); PSH, pp. 131–47.

3 For instance, Williams (1990, 26).
4 Joas (1985, 1993, 1996).
5 Peirce (1934, 276–90).
6 Lovejoy (1963, 1–29).
7 Schiller (1907, 1–21).
8 E.g. Lewis and Smith (1980, 3–150).
9 Rorty (1991, 63–77), henceforth PP1.
10 Dewey (1930, 233ff.).
11 Dewey (1908, 53ff.); PSH, pp. xxiiff., 47–71.
12 See, for example, Mead (1938, 16–18, 64–5, 88–96).
13 See also Dewey (1930); PSH, pp. xvi–xxxii.
14 See, for instance, Rorty (1982, xiii–xlvii), henceforth CP; Rorty (1980), henceforth PMN; Bernstein (1991, 326ff.).
15 James (1907, 46).
16 CP, pp. 162ff.
17 See, for instance, CP, pp. 162ff.; PSH, pp. 23–46; Rorty (1998a, 1–97), henceforth PP3.
18 James (1907, 48).
19 PMN, pp. 315–22.
20 PP1, pp. 64–6.
21 PP1, pp. 66–8.
22 PP1, p. 68.
23 PSH, pp. 175–8.
24 PMN, pp. 322–33.
25 PMN, pp. 324–6.
26 PSH, pp. 178–80.
27 PSH, pp. 178–81.
28 PMN, pp. 322–3.
29 PP1, pp. 67–9; PMN, pp. 322–4.
30 PSH, pp. 180–2.
31 CP, pp. 195–6.
32 CP, pp. 196–7.
33 CP, pp. 197–8. See also PP1, pp. 78–92.
34 CP, pp. 198–200.
35 CP, pp. 200–3.
36 PP3, pp. 228–46; PSH, pp. 201–9.
37 PP3, pp. 228–43.
38 PSH, pp. 201–7.
39 PP3, pp. 239–43; PSH, pp. 208–9.
40 Rorty (1998b, 1–72), henceforth AC.
41 PP1, pp. 76–7.
42 AC, pp. 65–8.
43 AC, pp. 75–107.
44 PP1, pp. 14–16; PSH, pp. 75–107.
45 PSH, pp. 131–47.
46 PSH, p. 145.
47 AC, p. 8.

48 PP3, p. 229.
49 PP3, pp. 234–5.
50 PSH, pp. 210–11.
51 Popper's *Poverty of Historicism* (1991b) was originally published as a set of articles in 1944. *The Open Society and its Enemies* (1971a, 1971b) was originally published in 1945.
52 PP1, p. 48.
53 PP1, pp. 67–9; PSH, pp. 175–89.
54 James (1907, 45).
55 Rorty (1995, 1–6), henceforth PP2.
56 Giddens (1976, 1984).
57 CP, pp. 191–210.
58 CP, pp. 198ff.
59 Taylor (1977).
60 See also PMN, pp. 359ff., for a discussion of Gadamer's *wirkungsgeschichtliches Bewusstsein*.
61 The notion of *Bildung* is here used as self-formation. See also PMN, pp. 315–94.
62 AC, p. 91.
63 PMN, pp. 357–94.
64 See also Baert (1998a, 114–33; 1998b).
65 PP2, p. 173.
66 PP1, p. 2.

Chapter 7 A Pragmatist Philosophy of the Social Sciences

1 See, for instance, Dewey (1916, 1974) and Mead (1934, 1982). For an overview of the intellectual legacy of pragmatism in the social sciences, see, for instance, Denzin (1992, 1–20), Lewis (1976), Petras (1968), Rock (1979, 24–101) and a number of articles in Plummer (1991). For an outline of the various forms of symbolic interactionism, see, in particular, Blumer (1969), Denzin (1992), Charon (1979), Hewitt (1984), Plummer (1991), Rock (1979) and Wood (1982).
2 Regarding the relationship between pragmatism and the Chicago School, see, for instance, Bulmer (1984, 1–44), Fischer and Strauss (1979a, 1979b), Smith (1988, 59–65) and Mills (1966).
3 Joas (1993) has already explored the interplay between pragmatism and European social science. See also Baert and Turner (2004).
4 Habermas (1987) is one of the few exceptions, employing insights of Peirce for his philosophy of the social sciences. Bhaskar (1990) is an example of some of the hostile receptions of pragmatism.
5 Such as Edmundson (1995), Kilian (1998) and Mitchell (1985).
6 See, for instance, Taylor (1985, 1–184). For the convergences between recent developments in hermeneutics and pragmatism, see, for instance, Rorty (1980, 315–56). Gadamer's hermeneutics also occupies a central role in Bernstein's pragmatism. See, for instance, Bernstein (1991, 9ff., 24–5, 48ff.).
7 See, for instance, various articles in the fifth volume of Peirce's *Collected Papers* (1934).

8 Neurath, Carnap and Morris (1955).
9 Compare Popper (1991b, 130–43) with Bhaskar (1998, 1–24); see also Bernstein (1991, 326–7) and Rorty (1980, 315–22).
10 See, for instance, Dupré (1993) and Rosenberg (1994).
11 Dupré (1993, 2).
12 Rosenberg (1994).
13 Examples of the strong programme are Collins (1985, 1990), Collins and Kusch (1998), Barnes et al. (1996), Knorr-Cetina (1996), Latour (1987) and Latour and Woolgar (1979). A similar research programme underlies the work of Shapin (1994) and Pickering (1995).
14 Mannheim (1997).
15 Latour (1987, 63–100).
16 Feyerabend (1988, 129–38).
17 Feyerabend (1988, 67–109).
18 Kuhn (1970a), Feyerabend (1988).
19 See also Rorty (1999, 175–82).
20 Keller (1983), Galison (1987), Geison (1981, 1993).
21 Habermas (1987).
22 Kuhn (1977, 320–39).
23 Danziger (1990), Kusch (1995, 1999).
24 Bhaskar (1978, 118–26, 136–7); Collier (1994, 31–69).
25 Giddens (1984, 334–47). For an in-depth discussion of the philosophical position underlying Giddens's structuration theory, see Doyal and Harris (1986).
26 Dewey (1930, 233ff.).
27 Rule (1997, 174–9).
28 Giddens (1984, xxff.).
29 Layder (1993).
30 Giddens (1984, xxxv).
31 Compare with Bernstein (1991, 326–8).
32 Seidman and Alexander (2001b).
33 See, for example, Bernstein (1991).
34 Bernstein (1991, 336–7).
35 Bernstein (1991, 337–9).
36 James (1907, 45).
37 For a fuller account of the pragmatist position on this issue, see, for instance, Rorty (1982, 195–203; 1991, 78–92).
38 Rorty (1982, 191–210).
39 Gadamer (1975). For other attempts to merge American pragmatism with Gadamer's hermeneutics, see, for instance, Bernstein (1986, 94–114) and Rorty (1980).
40 MacIntyre (1985, 1988).
41 See also Kögler (1996, 159–214).
42 Rabinow (1977).
43 Marcus and Fischer (1999a, x).
44 Jackson (1987).
45 Clifford (1986, 1–3).

46   Marcus and Fischer (1999a, 1–6).
47   Marcus and Fischer (1999a, 7–16).
48   Clifford (1986, 7).
49   Rapport (1997, 179).
50   Rapport (1997, 177–80).
51   Clifford (1986, 8–13).
52   Marcus and Fischer (1999a, 17–44).
53   Marcus and Fischer (1999a, 45–57); Bowman (1997).
54   Marcus and Fischer (1999a, 137–64).
55   Rapport (1997, 190–1).
56   Marcus and Fischer (1999b).
57   Marcus and Fischer (1999b, xviii–xx). See also Hendry (1997).
58   Okely and Callaway (1992).
59   For a history of new archaeology, see, for instance, Wylie (2002, 25–41).
60   Hodder (1991, 3).
61   Shanks and Hodder (1998, 75).
62   Tilley (1998, 320–2).
63   Potter and Leone (1987).
64   Tilley (1998, 324–6).
65   Lowenthal (1996).
66   Tilley (1998, 322–4).
67   Hodder (1991, 167–72).
68   Hodder (1991, 180–1).
69   Meskell (2001).
70   Gosden (2001).
71   Tilley (1998, 315). The italics are mine.
72   Tilley (1998, 318–19).
73   Tilley (1998, 316).
74   Tilley (1998, 319).
75   Nietzsche (1967, 1968, 1969); Foucault (1997a, 1980, 1981, 1987, 1990).
76   E.g. Burchell et al. (1991); Rose (1985, 1990, 1996, 1999); Procacci (1993).
77   Foucault (1977b, 153–4).
78   Foucault (1977b, 154).
79   Nietzsche (1995).
80   Foucault (1977b, 142).
81   Foucault (1977b, 139–45).
82   Geuss (1994, 274–7).
83   Foucault (1977b, 152–7).
84   Foucault (1977a, 3–69).
85   Foucault (1997a, 57–69).
86   Foucault (1997a, 135–69).
87   Foucault (1997a, 135–84).
88   See, for instance, Riley (1988), Barrett and Phillips (1992), Butler and Scott (1992) and Segal (1994, 1997).
89   Said (1980); Bhabha (1994).
90   Danto (1973).
91   Nietzsche (1968, 511) (paragraph 974). Italics are Nietzsche's.

92 Bernstein (1991, 328).
93 For a related argument, see Fraser (1981).
94 Foucault (1977a, 207–8).
95 See, for instance, Joas (1985, 121–44, 199–214).

References and Bibliography

Adorno, T. W. (1976a) 'Sociology and Empirical Research', in *The Positivist Dispute in German Sociology*, ed. T. W. Adorno et al. London: Heinemann, pp. 68–86 [originally in German, 1969; referred to in notes as SER].

Adorno, T. W. (1976b) 'On the Logic of the Social Sciences', in *The Positivist Dispute in German Sociology*, ed. T. W. Adorno et al. London: Heinemann, pp. 105–22 [originally in German, 1969; referred to in notes as LSS].

Adorno, T. W. (1992) *The Culture Industry: Selected Essays on Mass Culture*. London: Routledge [originally in German; referred to in notes as CI].

Adorno, T. W., and Horkheimer, M. (1992) *Dialectic of Enlightenment*. London: Verso [originally in German, 1944; referred to in notes as DE].

Adorno, T. W., et al. (1950) *The Authoritarian Personality*. New York: Harper.

Adorno, T. W., et al. (1976) *The Positivist Dispute in German Sociology*. London: Heinemann [originally in German, 1969].

Alexander, J. (1982a) *Theoretical Logic in Sociology*, vol. 1: *Positivism, Presuppositions, and Current Controversies*. London: Routledge & Kegan Paul.

Alexander, J. (1982b) *Theoretical Logic in Sociology*, vol. 2: *The Antinomies of Classical Thought: Marx and Durkheim*. London: Routledge & Kegan Paul.

Alexander, J. (1982c) *Theoretical Logic in Sociology*, vol. 3: *The Classical Attempt at Theoretical Synthesis: Max Weber*. London: Routledge & Kegan Paul.

Archer, M. (1995) *Realist Social Theory: The Morphogenetic Approach*. Cambridge: Cambridge University Press.

Baert, P. (1996) 'Realism as a Philosophy of Social Sciences and Economics: A Critical Evaluation', *Cambridge Journal of Economics*, 20, pp. 513–22.

Baert, P. (1998a) *Social Theory in the Twentieth Century*. Cambridge: Polity.

Baert, P. (1998b) 'Foucault's History of the Present as Self-Referential Knowledge Acquisition', *Philosophy and Social Criticism*, 24, pp. 111–26.

Baert, P., and Turner, B. S. (2004) 'New Pragmatism and Old Europe: The Relationship between Pragmatist Philosophy and European Social and Political Theory', *European Journal for Social Theory*, 7, pp. 267–74.

Barnes, B., Bloor, D., and Henry, J. (1996) *Scientific Knowledge: A Sociological Analysis*. London: Athlone.

Barrett, M., and Phillips, A. (eds) (1992) *Destabilizing Theory: Contemporary Feminist Debates*. Cambridge: Polity.

Benton, T. (1984) *The Rise and Fall of Structural Marxism: Althusser and his Influence*. London: Macmillan.

Bentz, V. M., and Shapiro, J. J. (1998) *Mindful Inquiry in Social Research*. London: Sage.

Bernstein, R. J. (1986) *Philosophical Profiles: Essays in a Pragmatic Mode*. Philadelphia: University of Pennsylvania Press.

Bernstein, R. J. (1991) *The New Constellation: The Ethical-Political Horizons of Modernity/Postmodernity*. Cambridge: Polity.

Berthelot, J.-M. (1995) *1895 Durkheim: l'avènement de la sociologie scientifique*. Toulouse: Presses Universitaires du Mirail.

Bhabha, H. (1994) *The Location of Culture*. New York: Routledge.

Bhaskar, R. (1978) *A Realist Theory of Science*. 2nd edn, Brighton: Harvester [1st edn 1975].

Bhaskar, R. (1981) 'The Consequences of Socio-Evolutionary Concepts for Naturalism in Sociology: Commentaries on Harré and Toulmin', in *The Philosophy of Evolution*, ed. U. J. Jensen and R. Harré. Brighton: Harvester, pp. 196–209.

Bhaskar, R. (1986) *Scientific Realism and Human Emancipation*. London: Verso.

Bhaskar, R. (1990) 'Rorty, Realism and the Idea of Freedom', in *Reading Rorty: Critical Responses to 'Philosophy and the Mirror of Nature' (and Beyond)*, ed. A. Malachowski. Oxford: Blackwell, pp. 198–232.

Bhaskar, R. (1993) *Dialectic*. London: Verso.

Bhaskar, R. (1994) *Plato Etc: The Problems of Philosophy and their Resolution*. London: Verso.

Bhaskar, R. (1998) *The Possibility of Naturalism: A Philosophical Critique of the Contemporary Human Sciences*. 3rd edn, London: Routledge [1st edn 1979].

Bhaskar, R. (2000) *From East to West: Odyssey of a Soul*. London: Routledge.

Blauner, B. (1964) *Alienation and Freedom: The Factory Worker and his Industry*. Chicago: University of Chicago Press.

Blumer, H. (1969) *Symbolic Interactionism*. New York: Prentice-Hall.

Bohmann, J. (1991) *New Philosophy of Social Sciences: Problems of Indeterminacy*. Cambridge: Polity.

Bowman, G. (1997) 'Identifying versus Identifying with the "Other": Reflections on the Siting of the Subject in Anthropological Discourse', in *After Writing Culture*, ed. A. James, J. Hockey and A. Dawson. London: Routledge, pp. 34–50.

Brandom, Robert B. (ed.) (2000) *Rorty and his Critics*. Oxford: Blackwell.

Bulmer, M. (1984) *The Chicago School of Sociology: Institutionalization, Diversity and the Rise of Sociological Research*. Chicago: University of Chicago Press.

Bunge, M. (1998) *Social Science under Debate: A Philosophical Perspective*. Toronto: University of Toronto Press.

Burchell, G., Gordon, D., and Miller, P. (eds) (1991) *The Foucault Effect: Studies in Governmentality*. Hemel Hempstead: Harvester Wheatsheaf.

Butler, J., and Scott, J. (eds) (1992) *Feminists Theorise the Political*. London: Routledge.

Calhoun, C. (1995) *Critical Social Theory: Culture, History, and the Challenge of Difference*. Oxford: Blackwell.

Carter, B. (2000) *Realism and Racism: Concepts of Race in Sociological Research*. London: Routledge.

Carter, B., and New, C. (eds) (2004) *Making Realism Work: Realist Social Theory and Empirical Research.* London: Routledge.

Cartwright, N. (1983) *How the Laws of Physics Lie.* Oxford: Clarendon Press.

Charon, J. M. (1979) *Symbolic Interactionism: An Introduction, an Interpretation, an Integration.* Englewood Cliffs, NJ: Prentice-Hall.

Chazel, F. (1975) *Durkheim: les règles de la méthode sociologique.* Paris: Hatier.

Clifford, J. (1986) 'Introduction: Partial Truths', in *Writing Culture: The Poetics and Politics of Ethnography,* ed. J. Clifford and G. E. Marcus. Berkeley: University of California Press, pp. 1–26.

Clifford, J., and Marcus, G. E. (eds) (1986) *Writing Culture: The Poetics and Politics of Ethnography.* Berkeley: University of California Press.

Coleman, J. (1990) *Foundations of Social Theory.* Cambridge, MA: Harvard University Press.

Collier, A. (1989) *Scientific Realism and Socialist Thought.* Hemel Hempstead: Harvester Wheatsheaf.

Collier, A. (1994) *Critical Realism: An Introduction to Roy Bhaskar's Philosophy.* London: Verso.

Collier, A. (1996) *Socialist Reasoning: An Inquiry in the Political Philosophy of Scientific Socialism.* London: Pluto Press.

Collins, H. (1985) *Changing Order: Replication and Induction in Scientific Practice.* London: Sage.

Collins, H. (1990) *Artificial Experts: Social Knowledge and Intelligent Machines.* Cambridge, MA: MIT Press.

Collins, H., and Kusch, M. (1998) *The Shape of Actions: What Humans and Machines Can Do.* Cambridge, MA: MIT Press.

Collins, R. (1986) *Weberian Sociological Theory.* Cambridge: Cambridge University Press.

Cooke, M. (1994) *Language and Reason: A Study of Habermas' Pragmatics.* Cambridge, MA: MIT Press.

Cornforth, M. (1977) *The Open Philosophy and the Open Society: A Reply to Sir Karl Popper's Refutations of Marxism.* 2nd edn, London: Lawrence & Wishart [1st edn 1968].

Crotty, M. (1998) *The Foundations of Social Research.* London: Sage.

Cuin, C.-H. (ed.) (1997) *Durkheim d'un siècle à l'autre: lectures actuelles des 'Règles de la méthode sociologique'.* Paris: Presses Universitaires de France.

Currie, G., and Musgrave, A. (eds) (1985) *Popper and the Human Sciences.* Dordrecht: Martinus Nijhoff.

Danto, A. (1973) 'Nietzsche's Perspectivism', in *Nietzsche: A Collection of Critical Essays,* ed. R. C. Solomon. Notre Dame, IN: University of Notre Dame Press, pp. 29–57.

Danziger, K. (1990) *Constructing the Subject: Historical Origins of Psychological Research.* Cambridge: Cambridge University Press.

de Marchie, N. (ed.) (1988) *The Popperian Legacy in Economics.* Cambridge: Cambridge University Press.

Delanty, G., and Strydom, P. (eds) (2003) *Philosophies of Social Sciences: The Classic and Contemporary Readings.* Maidenhead: Open University Press.

Denzin, N. (1992) *Symbolic Interactionism and Cultural Studies: The Politics of Interpretation*. Oxford: Blackwell.

Dewey, J. (1908) 'Does Reality Possess Practical Character?', in *Essays, Philosophical and Psychological, in Honor of William James, Professor in Harvard University, by his Colleagues at Columbia University*. New York: Longmans, Green, pp. 51–80.

Dewey, J. (1916) *Democracy and Education: An Introduction to the Philosophy of Education*. New York: Free Press.

Dewey, J. (1930) *The Quest for Certainty: A Study of the Relationship between Knowledge and Action*. London: Allen & Unwin.

Dewey, J. (1974) *John Dewey on Education: Selected Writings*. Chicago: University of Chicago Press.

Dow, S. C. (2001) 'Hume: A Reassessment', in *Knowledge, Division of Labour and Social Institutions*, ed. R. Scazzieri, P. L. Porta and A. S. Skinner. Aldershot: Elgar.

Dow, S. C. (2002a) 'Historical Reference: Hume and Critical Realism', *Cambridge Journal of Economics*, 26, pp. 683–95.

Dow, S. C. (2002b) 'Interpretation: The Case of David Hume', *History of Political Economy*, 34, pp. 339–420.

Downward, P., Finch, J. H., and Ramsay, J. (2002) 'Critical Realism, Empirical Methods and Inference: A Critical Discussion', *Cambridge Journal of Economics*, 26, pp. 481–500.

Doyal, L., and Harris, R. (1986) *Empiricism, Explanation and Rationality: An Introduction to the Philosophy of the Social Sciences*. London: Routledge & Kegan Paul.

Dupré, J. (1993) *The Disorder of Things: Metaphysical Foundations of the Disunity of Science*. Cambridge, MA: Harvard University Press.

Durkheim, E. (1953) 'The Determination of Moral Facts', in *Sociology and Philosophy*. London: Cohen & West [originally in French, 1906; referred to in notes as DMF].

Durkheim, E. (1963) *Primitive Classification*. London: Cohen & West [originally in French, 1903].

Durkheim, E. (1965a) *Montesquieu and Rousseau: Forerunners of Sociology*. Ann Arbor: University of Michigan Press [originally in French, 1953].

Durkheim, E. (1965b) 'Montesquieu's Contribution to the Rise of Social Science', in *Montesquieu and Rousseau: Forerunners of Sociology*. Ann Arbor: University of Michigan Press, pp. 1–64 [originally in French, 1892; referred to in notes as MSS].

Durkheim, E. (1965c) 'Rousseau's *Social Contract*', in *Montesquieu and Rousseau: Forerunners of Sociology*. Ann Arbor: University of Michigan Press, pp. 65–143.

Durkheim, E. (1971) *The Elementary Forms of Religious Life*. London: Allen & Unwin [originally in French, 1912].

Durkheim, E. (1978a) 'Course in Sociology: Opening Lecture', in *Emile Durkheim on Institutional Analysis*, ed. M. Traugott. Chicago: University of Chicago Press, pp. 43–70 [originally in French, 1888; referred to in notes as CS].

Durkheim, E. (1978b) 'Divorce by Mutual Consent', in *Emile Durkheim on Institutional Analysis*, ed. M. Traugott. Chicago: University of Chicago Press, pp. 240–52 [originally in French, 1906].

Durkheim, E. (1982a) *The Rules of Sociological Method*, in *The Rules of Sociological Method: and Selected Texts on Sociology and its Method*. London: Macmillan, pp. 31–163 [originally in French, 1895; referred to in notes as RSM].

Durkheim, E. (1982b) 'Marxism and Sociology: The Materialist Conception of History', in *The Rules of Sociological Method: and Selected Texts on Sociology and its Method*. London: Macmillan, pp. 167–74 [originally in French, 1897; referred to in notes as MCH].

Durkheim, E. (1982c) 'Sociology and the Social Sciences', in *The Rules of Sociological Method: and Selected Texts on Sociology and its Method*. London: Macmillan, pp. 175–208 [originally in French, 1903; referred to in notes as SSS].

Durkheim, E. (1982d) 'Debate on Explanation in History and Sociology', in *The Rules of Sociological Method: and Selected Texts on Sociology and its Method*. London: Macmillan, pp. 211–28 [originally in French, 1908].

Durkheim, E. (1982e) 'The Method of Sociology', *The Rules of Sociological Method: and Selected Texts on Sociology and its Method*. London: Macmillan, pp. 245–7 [originally in French, 1908].

Durkheim, E. (1983) *Pragmatism and Sociology*. Cambridge: Cambridge University Press [originally in French, 1955; referred to in notes as PS].

Durkheim, E. (1984) *The Division of Labour in Society*. London: Macmillan [originally in French, 1893; referred to in notes as DL].

Durkheim, E. (1989) *Suicide: A Study in Sociology*. London: Routledge [originally in French, 1897; referred to in notes as S].

Durkheim, E., and Mauss, M. (1963) *Primitive Classification*. Chicago: University of Chicago Press [originally in French, 1903].

Edmundson, M. (1995) *Literature Against Philosophy, Plato to Derrida: A Defence of Poetry*. Cambridge: Cambridge University Press.

Elster, J. (1989) *Nuts and Bolts for the Social Sciences*. Cambridge: Cambridge University Press.

Faulkner, P. (2002) 'Some Problems with the Conception of the Human Subject in Critical Realism', *Cambridge Journal of Economics*, 26, pp. 739–51.

Fay, B. (1987) *Critical Social Science: Liberation and its Limits*. Ithaca, NY: Cornell University Press.

Fay, B. (1996) *Contemporary Philosophy of Social Science: A Multicultural Approach*. Oxford: Blackwell.

Festenstein, M., and Thompson, S. (eds) (2001) *Richard Rorty: Critical Dialogues*. Cambridge: Polity.

Feyerabend, P. (1975) *Against Method: Outline of an Anarchistic Theory of Knowledge*. London: Humanities Press.

Feyerabend, P. (1988) *Against Method*. Rev. edn, London: Verso.

Filloux, J.-C. (1977) *Durkheim et le socialisme*. Paris: Droz.

Finch, J. H., and McMaster, R. (2002) 'On Categorical Variables and Non-Parametric Statistical Inference in the Pursuit of Causal Explanations', *Cambridge Journal of Economics*, 26, pp. 753–72.

Fischer, B. M., and Strauss, A. L. (1979a) 'George Herbert Mead and the Chicago Tradition of Sociology (Part 1)', *Symbolic Interaction*, 2, 1, pp. 9–25.

Fischer, B. M., and Strauss, A. L. (1979b) 'George Herbert Mead and the Chicago Tradition of Sociology (Part 2)', *Symbolic Interaction*, 2, 2, pp. 9–20.

Fleetwood, S., and Ackroyd, S. (eds) (2004) *Critical Realist Applications in Organisation and Management Studies*. London: Routledge.

Flew, A. (1991) *Thinking about Social Thinking*. 2nd edn, London: Harper Collins.

Flyvbjerg, B. (2001) *Making Social Science Matter: Why Social Inquiry Fails and How it Can Succeed Again*. Cambridge: Cambridge University Press.

Foucault, M (1977a) *Discipline and Punish: The Birth of the Prison*. London: Allen Lane.

Foucault, M. (1977b) 'Nietzsche, Genealogy, History', in *Language, Counter-Memory, Practice*. Ithaca, NY: Cornell University Press, pp. 139–64.

Foucault, M. (1980) *Power/Knowledge*. Hemel Hempstead: Harvester Press.

Foucault, M. (1981) *History of Sexuality*, vol. 1: *An Introduction*. London: Penguin.

Foucault, M. (1987) *History of Sexuality*, vol. 2: *The Use of Pleasure*. London: Penguin.

Foucault, M. (1990) *History of Sexuality*, vol. 3: *Care of the Self*. London: Penguin.

Fraser, N. (1981) 'Foucault on Modern Power: Empirical Insights and Normative Confusions', *Praxis International*, 1, pp. 272–87.

Frydman, R. (1982) 'Towards an Understanding of Market Processes: Individual Expectations, Learning and Convergence to Rational Expectations Equilibrium', *American Economic Review*, 72, pp. 652–68.

Gadamer, H.-G. (1975) *Truth and Method*. London: Sheed & Ward.

Galison, P. (1987) *How Experiments End*. Chicago: University of Chicago Press.

Gane, M. (1997) 'Durkheim contre Comte dans Les Règles', in *Durkheim d'un siècle à l'autre: lectures actuelles des 'Règles de la méthode sociologique'*, ed. C.-H. Cuin. France: Presses Universitaires de France.

Geison, G. L. (1981) 'Scientific Change, Emerging Specialities, and Research Schools', *History of Science*, 19, pp. 20–40.

Geison, G. L., and Holmes, F. L. (eds) (1993) *Research Schools: Historical Reappraisals, Osiris*, 2nd ser., 8 [special issue].

Gellner, E. (1985) *Relativism and the Social Sciences*. Cambridge: Cambridge University Press.

Geuss, R. (1981) *The Idea of a Critical Theory*. Cambridge: Cambridge University Press.

Geuss, R. (1994) 'Nietzsche and Genealogy', *European Journal of Philosophy*, 2, pp. 274–92.

Giddens, A. (1976) *New Rules of Sociological Method*. London: Hutchinson.

Giddens, A. (1984) *The Constitution of Society: Outline of the Theory of Structuration*. Cambridge: Polity.

Gombrich, E. H. (1960) *Art and Illusion: A Study in the Psychology of Pictorial Representation*. London: Phaidon.

Gordon, S. (1991) *The History and Philosophy of Social Science*. London: Routledge.

Gosden, C. (2001) 'Postcolonial Archaeology: Issues of Culture, Identity, and Knowledge', in *Archaeological Theory Today*, ed. I. Hodder. Cambridge: Polity, pp. 241–61.

Green, D. P., and Shapiro, I. (1994) *Pathologies of Rational Choice Theory: A Critique of Applications in Political Science*. New Haven, CT: Yale University Press.

Habermas, J. (1970a) 'On Systematically Distorted Communication', *Inquiry*, 13, pp. 205–18.

Habermas, J. (1970b) 'Towards a Theory of Communicative Competence', *Inquiry*, 13, pp. 360–75.

Habermas, J. (1987) *Knowledge and Human Interests*. 2nd edn, Cambridge: Polity [originally in German, 1968; 1st English edn, 1972; referred to in notes as KHI].

Habermas, J. (1989) *Structural Transformation of the Public Sphere: An Inquiry into a Category of Bourgeois Society*. Cambridge: Polity [originally in German, 1962].

Habermas, J. (1991a) *The Theory of Communicative Action*, vol. 1: *Reason and the Rationalization of Society*. Cambridge: Polity [originally in German, 1981; referred to in notes as CA1].

Habermas, J. (1991b) *The Theory of Communicative Action*, vol. 2: *Lifeworld and System: A Critique of Functionalist Reason*. Cambridge: Polity [originally in German, 1981; referred to in notes as CA2].

Habermas, J. (1991c) *Communication and the Evolution of Society*. Cambridge: Polity [originally in German, 1976; referred to in notes as CES].

Hacohen, M. H. (2000) *Karl Popper: The Formative Years, 1902–1945: Politics and Philosophy in Interwar Vienna*. Cambridge: Cambridge University Press.

Halfpenny, P. (1982) *Positivism and Sociology: Explaining Social Life*. London: Allan & Unwin.

Harré, R. (1960) *An Introduction to the Logic of the Sciences*. London: Macmillan.

Harré, R. (1981) 'The Evolutionary Analogy in Social Explanation', in *The Philosophy of Evolution*, ed. U. J. Jensen and R. Harré. Brighton: Harvester, pp. 161–75.

Harré, R. (1993) *Social Being*. 2nd edn, Oxford: Blackwell.

Harré, R. (2002a) 'Social Reality and the Myth of Social Structure', *European Journal of Social Theory*, 5, pp. 124–33.

Harré, R. (2002b) 'Tilting at Windmills: Sociological Commonplaces and Miscellaneous Ontological Fallacies', *European Journal of Social Theory*, 5, pp. 143–8.

Harré, R., and Madden, E. H. (1975) *Causal Powers*. Oxford: Blackwell.

Harré, R., and Secord, P. (1972) *The Explanation of Social Behaviour*. Oxford: Blackwell.

Harré, R., and Varela, C. R. (1996) 'Conflicting Varieties of Realism: Causal Powers and the Problems of Social Structure', *Journal for the Theory of Social Behaviour*, 26, pp. 312–25.

Hartwig, M. (2001) 'New Left, New Age, New Paradigm? Roy Bhaskar's *From East to West*', *Journal for the Theory of Social Behaviour*, 31, pp. 139–66.

Harvey, D. L. (2002) 'Agency and Community: A Critical Realist Paradigm', *Journal for the Theory of Social Behaviour*, 32, pp. 163–94.

Harvey, D. L., and Reed, M. (1996) 'Social Science as the Study of Complex Systems', in *Chaos Theory in the Social Sciences: Foundations and Applications*, ed. L. D. Kiel and E. Elliott. Ann Arbor: University of Michigan Press, pp. 295–325.

Hayek, F. (1944) *Road to Serfdom*. London: Routledge & Kegan Paul.

Heiner, R. (1983) 'The Origins of Predictable Behaviour', *American Economic Review*, 73, pp. 560–95.

Held, D. (1980) *Introduction to Critical Theory: Horkheimer to Habermas*. London: Hutchinson; Berkeley: University of California Press.

Hendry, J. (1997) 'Who is Representing Whom? Gardens, Theme Parks and the Anthropologist in Japan', in *After Writing Culture*, ed. A. James, J. Hockey and A. Dawson. London: Routledge, pp. 194–207.

Hesse, M. B. (1961) *Forces and Fields*. London: Nelson.

Hesse, M. B. (1963) *Models and Analogies in Science*. London: Sheed & Ward.

Hewitt, J. P. (1984) *Self and Society: A Symbolic Interactionist Social Psychology*. Boston: Allyn & Bacon.

Hirst, Q. (1975) *Durkheim, Bernard and Epistemology*. London: Routledge & Kegan Paul.

Hodder, I. (1991) *Reading the Past*. 2nd edn, Cambridge: Cambridge University Press [1st edn, 1986].

Hodder, I. (ed.) (2001) *Archaeological Theory Today*. Cambridge: Polity.

Hodgson, G. (1993) *Economics and Evolution: Bringing Life Back into Economics*. Cambridge: Polity.

Hollis, M. (1994) *The Philosophy of Social Science*. Cambridge: Cambridge University Press.

Holmwood, J., and Stewart, A. (1991) *Explanation and Social Theory*. Basingstoke: Macmillan.

Horkheimer, M. (1972a) 'The Latest Attack on Metaphysics', in *Critical Theory: Selected Essays*. New York: Seabury Press, pp. 132–87 [originally in German, 1968; referred to in notes as LAM].

Horkheimer, M. (1972b) 'Traditional and Critical Theory', in *Critical Theory: Selected Essays*. New York: Seabury Press, pp. 188–243 [originally in German, 1968; referred to in notes as TCT].

Horkheimer, M. (1972c) 'Die gegenwärtige Lage der Sozialphilosophie und die Aufgaben eines Instituts für Sozialforschung', in *Sozialphilosophische Studien*. Frankfurt am Main: Athenäum Taschenbuch [originally pubd 1931].

Isaac, J. C. (1990) 'Realism and Reality: Some Realistic Reconsiderations', *Journal for the Theory of Social Behaviour*, 20, pp. 1–32.

Jackson, A. (ed.) (1987) *Anthropology at Home*. London: Tavistock.

James, A., Hockey, J., and Dawson, A. (eds) (1997) *After Writing Culture*. London: Routledge.

James, W. (1907) *Pragmatism: A New Name for Some Old Ways of Thinking*. New York: Longmans, Green.

Jarvie, I. C. (1986) *Thinking about Society: Theory and Practice*. Dordrecht: Reidel.

Jay, M. (1996) *The Dialectical Imagination: A History of the Frankfurt School and the Institute of Social Research, 1923–1950*. Berkeley and London: University of California Press.

Jensen, U. J., and Harré, R. (eds.) (1981) *The Philosophy of Evolution*. Brighton: Harvester.

Joas, H. (1985) *G. H. Mead: A Contemporary Re-examination of his Thought*. Cambridge: Polity.

Joas, H. (1993) *Pragmatism and Social Theory*. Chicago: University of Chicago Press.

Joas, H. (1996) *The Creativity of Action*. Chicago: University of Chicago Press.

Joseph, J. (2000) 'A Realist Theory of Hegemony', *Journal for the Theory of Social Behaviour*, 30, pp. 179–202.

Kaufmann, F. (1978) *Methodology of the Social Sciences*. Atlantic Highlands, NJ: Humanities Press.

Kaul, N. (2002) 'A Critical "Post" to Critical Realism', *Cambridge Journal of Economics*, 26, pp. 709–26.

Keat, R., and Urry, J. (1982) *Social Theory as Science*. 2nd edn, London: Routledge. [1st edn, 1975].

Keller, E. F. (1983) *A Feeling for the Organism: The Life and Work of Barbara McClintock*. San Francisco: W. H. Freeman.

Kilian, M. (1998) *Modern and Postmodern Strategies: Gaming and the Question of Morality: Adorno, Rorty, Lyotard and Enzberger*. New York: Peter Lang.

Kincaid, H. (1996) *Philosophical Foundations of the Social Sciences*. Cambridge: Cambridge University Press.

Knorr-Cetina, K. D. (1996) *The Manufacture of Knowledge: An Essay on the Constructivist and Contextual Nature of Science*. Oxford: Pergamon.

Kögler, H. H. (1996) *The Power of Dialogue: Critical Hermeneutics after Gadamer and Foucault*. Cambridge, MA: MIT Press.

Kuhn, T. (1970a) *The Structure of Scientific Revolutions*. 2nd edn, Chicago: University of Chicago Press [1st edn, 1962].

Kuhn, T. (1970b) 'Logic of Discovery or Psychology of Research', in *Criticism and the Growth of Knowledge*, ed. I. Lakatos and A. Musgrave. Cambridge: Cambridge University Press, pp. 1–23.

Kuhn, T. (1977) *The Essential Tension: Selected Studies in Scientific Tradition and Change*. Chicago: University of Chicago Press.

Kusch, M. (1995) *Psychologism: A Case Study in the Sociology of Philosophical Knowledge*. London: Routledge.

Kusch, M. (1999) *Psychological Knowledge: A Social History and Philosophy*. London: Routledge.

Lacey, H. (1997) 'Neutrality in the Social Sciences: On Bhaskar's Argument for an Essential Emancipatory Impulse in Social Sciences', *Journal for the Theory of Social Behaviour*, 27, pp. 213–42.

Lakatos, I. (1970) 'Falsification and the Methodology of Scientific Research Programmes', in *Criticism and the Growth of Knowledge*, ed. I. Lakatos and A. Musgrave. Cambridge: Cambridge University Press, pp. 91–196.

Lakatos, I., and Musgrave, A. (eds) (1970) *Criticism and the Growth of Knowledge.* Cambridge: Cambridge University Press.

Latour, B. (1987) *Science in Action.* Milton Keynes: Open University Press.

Latour, B., and Woolgar, D. (1979) *Laboratory Life: The Social Construction of Scientific Facts.* London: Sage.

Lawson, T. (1994) 'A Realist Theory for Economics', in *New Directions in Economic Methodology,* ed. R. E. Backhouse. London: Routledge, pp. 257–85.

Lawson, T. (1997) *Economics and Reality.* London: Routledge.

Lawson, T. (2003) *Reorienting Economics.* London: Routledge.

Layder, D. (1990) *The Realist Image in Social Science.* London: Macmillan.

Layder, D. (1993) *New Strategies in Social Research.* Cambridge: Polity.

Lee, F. S. (2002) 'Theory Creation and the Methodological Foundation of Post Keynesian Economics', *Cambridge Journal of Economics,* 26, pp. 789–804.

Lewis, J. (1976) 'The Classical American Pragmatists as Forerunners to Symbolic Interactionism', *Sociological Quarterly,* 17, pp. 347–59.

Lewis, J., and Smith, R. (1980) *American Sociology and Pragmatism: Mead, Chicago Sociology and Symbolic Interactionism.* Chicago: University of Chicago Press.

Lewis, P. (1996) 'Metaphor and Critical Realism', *Review of Social Economy,* 54, pp. 487–506.

Lewis, P. (2000) 'The Problem of Social Structure', *Journal for the Theory of Social Behaviour,* 30, pp. 249–68.

Lovejoy, A. (1963) *The Thirteen Pragmatisms.* Baltimore: Johns Hopkins University Press.

Lowenthal, D. (1996) *Possessed by the Past: The Heritage Crusade and the Spoils of History.* New York: Free Press.

Lukes, S. (1973) *Emile Durkheim, his Life and Work: A Historical and Critical Study.* London: Allen Lane.

Lynch, M. (1993) *Scientific Practice and Ordinary Action.* Cambridge: Cambridge University Press.

MacIntyre, A. (1985) *After Virtue: A Study in Moral Social Theory.* London: Duckworth.

MacIntyre, A. (1988) *Whose Justice? Which Rationality?* Notre Dame, IN: Notre Dame University Press.

McIntyre, L. C. (1996) *Laws and Explanation in the Social Sciences: Defending a Science of Human Behavior.* Boulder, CO: Westview Press.

Mäki, U. (1988a) 'How to Combine Realism in the Methodology of Economics', *Economics and Philosophy,* 4, 1, pp. 89–109.

Mäki, U. (1988b) 'Realism, Economics, and Rhetoric: A Rejoinder to McClosley', *Economics and Philosophy,* 4, 1, pp. 167–9.

Malachowski, A. (ed.) (1990) *Reading Rorty.* Oxford: Blackwell.

Manicas, P. (1980) 'On the Concept of Social Structure', *Journal for the Theory of Social Behaviour,* 10, pp. 65–83.

Manicas, P. T. (1987) *A History and Philosophy of the Social Sciences.* Oxford: Blackwell.

Mannheim, K. (1997) *Ideology and Utopia.* London: Routledge.

Marcus, G. E., and Fischer, M. J. (1999a) *Anthropology as Cultural Critique*. 2nd edn, Chicago: University of Chicago Press [1st edn, 1986].

Marcus, G. E. and Fischer, M. J. (1999b) 'Introduction to the Second Edition', in *Anthropology as Cultural Critique*. Chicago: University of Chicago Press, pp. xv–xxxiv.

Marsh, D., et al. (1999) *Postwar British Politics in Perspective*. Cambridge: Polity.

Martin, M., and McIntyre, L. C. (eds) (1994) *Readings in the Philosophy of Social Science*. Cambridge, MA: MIT Press.

May, T., and Williams, M. (eds) (1998) *Knowing the Social World*. Buckingham: Open University Press.

Mead, G. H. (1934) *Mind, Self and Society: From the Standpoint of a Social Behaviorist*. Chicago: University of Chicago Press.

Mead, G. H. (1938) *Philosophy of the Act*. Chicago: University of Chicago Press.

Mead, G. H. (1982) *The Individual and the Social Self*. Chicago: University of Chicago Press.

Meskell, L. (2001) 'Archaeologies of Identity', in *Archaeological Theory Today*, ed. I. Hodder. Cambridge: Polity, pp. 187–213.

Mills, C. W. (1966) *Sociology and Pragmatism: The Higher Learning in America*. New York: Oxford University Press.

Mitchell, W. J. (1985) *Against Theory: Literary Studies and the New Pragmatism*. Chicago: University of Chicago Press.

Nagel, T. (1986) *The View from Nowhere*. Oxford: Oxford University Press.

Nellhaus, T. (1998) 'Signs, Social Ontology, and Critical Realism', *Journal for the Theory of Social Behaviour*, 28, pp. 1–24.

Neurath, O., Carnap, R., and Morris, C. (eds) (1955) *International Encyclopedia of Unified Science*. Chicago: University of Chicago Press.

New, C. (1994) 'Structure, Agency and Social Transformation', *Journal for the Theory of Social Behaviour*, 24, pp. 187–206.

New, C. (1998) 'Realism, Deconstruction and the Feminist Standpoint', *Journal for the Theory of Social Behaviour*, 28, pp. 349–72.

Nietzsche, F. (1967) *Beyond Good and Evil: Prelude to a Philosophy of the Future*. London: Allen & Unwin [orginally in German, 1886].

Nietzsche, F. (1968) *The Will to Power*. London: Weidenfeld & Nicolson [originally in German, notes written 1883–8, pubd 1901].

Nietzsche, F. (1969) *On the Genealogy of Morals*. New York: Vintage Books [originally in German, 1887].

Nietzsche, F. (1995) 'On the Utility and Liability of History for Life', in *The Complete Works of Friedrich Nietzsche*, ed. E. Behler. Stanford, CA: Stanford University Press, pp. 83–167 [originally in German, 1884].

Northover, P. (1999) 'Evolutionary Growth Theory and Forms of Realism', *Cambridge Journal of Economics*, 22, pp. 33–63.

O'Hear, A. (1992) *Karl Popper*. London: Routledge.

O'Neill, J. (1998) 'Rhetoric, Science and Philosophy', *Philosophy of the Social Sciences*, 28, pp. 205–25.

Oakes, G. (1975) 'Introductory Essay', in M. Weber, *Roscher and Knies: The Logical Problems of Historical Economics*. New York: Free Press, pp. 1–49.

Okely, J., and Callaway, H. (1992) *Anthropology and Autobiography*. London: Routledge.

Outhwaite, W. (1987) *New Philosophies of Social Science: Realism, Hermeneutics and Critical Theory*. Basingstoke: Macmillan.

Outhwaite, W. (1994) *Habermas: A Critical Introduction*. Cambridge: Polity.

Papineau, D. (1978) *For Science in the Social Sciences*. London: Macmillan.

Parsons, T. (1964) 'Introduction', in M. Weber, *The Theory of Social and Economic Organization*. New York: Free Press, pp. 1–86.

Peacock, M. (1993) 'Hayek, Realism and Spontaneous Order', *Journal for the Theory of Social Behaviour*, 23, pp. 249–64.

Peacock, M. (2000) 'Explaining Theory Choice', *Journal for the Theory of Social Behaviour*, 30, pp. 319–39.

Peirce, C. S. (1934) *Collected Papers*, vol. 5: *Pragmatism and Pragmaticism*, ed. C. Hartshorne and P. Weiss. Cambridge, MA: Harvard University Press.

Peter, F. (2001) 'Rhetoric versus Realism in Economic Methodology: A Critical Assessment of Recent Contributions', *Cambridge Journal of Economics*, 25, pp. 571–89.

Petras, J. W. (1968) 'John Dewey and the Rise of Interactionism in American Social Theory', *Journal of the History of the Behavioral Sciences*, 2, pp. 132–42.

Pettegrew, J. (ed.) (2000) *A Pragmatist's Progress? Richard Rorty and American Intellectual History*. New York: Rowman & Littlefield.

Phillips, D. C. (2000) *The Expanded Social Scientist's Bestiary: A Guide to Fabled Threats to, and Defenses of, Naturalistic Social Science*. London: Rowman & Littlefield.

Pickering, A. (1995) *The Mangle of Practice: Time, Agency and Science*. Chicago: University of Chicago Press.

Pinkstone, B. (2002) 'Persistent Demi-regs and Robust Tendencies: Critical Realism and the Singer–Prebisch Thesis', *Cambridge Journal of Economics*, 26, pp. 561–83.

Plummer, K. (ed.) (1991) *Symbolic Interactionism*. Aldershot: Elgar.

Popper, K. (1934) *Logik der Forschung*. Vienna: Julius Springer.

Popper, K. (1950a) 'Indeterminism in Quantum Physics and in Classical Physics, Part 1', *British Journal for the Philosophy of Science*, 1, pp. 117–33.

Popper, K. (1950b) 'Indeterminism in Quantum Physics and in Classical Physics, Part 2', *British Journal for the Philosophy of Science*, 1, pp. 173–95.

Popper, K. (1959) *The Logic of Scientific Discovery*. London: Hutchinson [originally in German, 1934; referred to in notes as LSD].

Popper, K. (1970) 'Normal Science and its Dangers', in *Criticism and the Growth of Knowledge*, ed. I. Lakatos and A. Musgrave. Cambridge: Cambridge University Press, pp. 51–8 [referred to in notes as NSD].

Popper, K. (1971a) *The Open Society and its Enemies*, vol. 1: *The Spell of Plato*. Princeton, NJ: Princeton University Press [originally pubd 1945; referred to in notes as OS1].

Popper, K. (1971b) *The Open Society and its Enemies*, vol. 2: *The High Tide of Prophecy: Hegel, Marx, and the Aftermath*. Princeton, NJ: Princeton University Press [originally pubd 1945; referred to in notes as OS2].

Popper, K. (1976) 'The Logic of the Social Sciences', in *The Positivist Dispute in German Sociology*, ed. T. W. Adorno et al. London: Heinemann, pp. 87–104.
Popper, K. (1979) *Objective Knowledge: An Evolutionary Approach*. Oxford: Oxford University Press [referred to in notes as OK].
Popper, K. (1982) *Postscript to the Logic of Scientific Discovery*, vol. 2: *The Open Universe: An Argument for Indeterminism*. London: Hutchinson.
Popper, K. (1983) 'The Rationality Principle', in *A Pocket Popper*, ed. D. Miller. London: Fontana, pp. 357–65 [originally in French, 1967; referred to in notes as RP].
Popper, K. (1990) *A World of Propensities*. Bristol: Thoemmes.
Popper, K. (1991a) *Conjectures and Refutations*. London: Routledge [originally pubd 1963; referred to in notes as CR].
Popper, K. (1991b) *The Poverty of Historicism*. London: Routledge [originally pubd 1957; referred to in notes as PH].
Popper, K. (1992) *Unended Quest: An Intellectual Autobiography*. London: Routledge [originally pubd 1974 as *Autobiography of Karl Popper*; referred to in notes as UQ].
Popper, K. (1998) *The Open Universe: An Argument for Indeterminism*. London: Hutchinson.
Potter, G. (2000a) 'For Bourdieu, Against Alexander: Reality and Reduction', *Journal for the Theory of Social Behaviour*, 30, pp. 229–46.
Potter, G. (2000b) *The Philosophy of Social Science: New Perspectives*. New York: Prentice-Hall.
Potter, P. B., and Leone, M. P. (1987) 'Archaeology in Public in Annapolis: The Four Seasons, Six Sites, Seven Tours and 32,000 Visitors', *American Archaeologist*, 6, pp. 51–61.
Pratt, V. (1978) *The Philosophy of the Social Sciences*. London: Methuen.
Procacci, G. (1993) *Gouverner la misère: la question sociale en France 1789–1848*. Paris: Seuil.
Rabinow, P. (1977) *Reflections on Fieldwork in Morocco*. Berkeley: University of California Press.
Rapport, N. (1997) 'Edifying Anthropology: Culture as Conversation: Representation as Conversation', in *After Writing Culture*, ed. A. James, J. Hockey and A. Dawson. London: Routledge, pp. 177–93.
Reed, M., and Harvey, D. L. (1992) 'The New Science and the Old: Complexity and Realism in the Social Sciences', *Journal of the Theory of Social Behaviour*, 22, pp. 353–80.
Riley, D. (1988) *Am I that Name?* Basingstoke: Macmillan.
Ringer, F. (1997) *Max Weber's Methodology: The Unification of the Cultural and Social Sciences*. Cambridge, MA: Harvard University Press.
Rock, P. (1979) *The Making of Symbolic Interactionism*. Aldershot: Elgar.
Rorty, R. (ed.) (1967) *The Linguistic Turn: Recent Essays in Philosophical Method*. Chicago: University of Chicago Press.
Rorty, R. (1980) *Philosophy and the Mirror of Nature*. Oxford: Blackwell [referred to in notes as PMN].
Rorty, R. (1982) *Consequences of Pragmatism*. New York: University of Minnesota Press [referred to in notes as CP].

Rorty, R. (1989) *Contingency, Irony, and Solidarity.* Cambridge: Cambridge University Press.
Rorty, R. (1991) *Philosophical Papers,* vol. 1: *Objectivity, Relativism, and Truth.* Cambridge: Cambridge University Press [referred to in notes as PP1].
Rorty, R. (1995) *Philosophical Papers,* vol. 2: *Essays on Heidegger and Others.* Cambridge: Cambridge University Press [referred to in notes as PP2].
Rorty, R. (1998a) *Philosophical Papers,* vol. 3: *Truth and Progress.* Cambridge: Cambridge University Press [referred to in notes as PP3].
Rorty, R. (1998b) *Achieving our Country.* Cambridge, MA: Harvard University Press [referred to in notes as AC].
Rorty, R. (1999) *Philosophy and Social Hope.* Harmondsworth: Penguin [referred to in notes as PSH].
Rose, N. (1985) *The Psychological Complex: Psychology, Politics and Society in England 1869–1939.* London: Routledge & Kegan Paul.
Rose, N. (1990) *Governing the Soul: The Shaping of the Private Self.* London: Routledge.
Rose, N. (1996) *Inventing our Selves: Psychology, Power and Personhood.* Cambridge: Cambridge University Press.
Rose, N. (1999) *Powers of Freedom: Reframing Political Thought.* Cambridge: Cambridge University Press.
Rosenberg, A. (1994) *Instrumental Biology or the Disunity of Science.* Chicago: University of Chicago Press.
Rosenberg, A. (1995) *Philosophy of Social Science.* Boulder, CO: Westview Press.
Rule, J. (1987) *Theory and Progress in Social Science.* Cambridge: Cambridge University Press.
Runciman, W. G. (1972) *A Critique of Max Weber's Philosophy of Social Science.* Cambridge: Cambridge University Press.
Runde, J. (1998) 'Assessing Causal Explanations', *Oxford Economic Papers,* 50, pp. 151–72.
Ryan, A. (1970) *The Philosophy of Social Sciences.* London: Macmillan.
Said, E. W. (1980) *Orientalism.* London: Routledge & Kegan Paul.
Sayer, A. (1992) *Method in Social Science.* 2nd edn, London: Routledge [1st edn, 1984].
Sayer, A. (1997) 'Critical Realism and the Limits to Critical Social Sciences', *Journal for the Theory of Social Behaviour,* 27, pp. 473–88.
Sayer, A. (2000) *Realism and Social Science.* London: Sage.
Scheler, M. (1980) *Problems of a Sociology of Knowledge.* London: Routledge & Kegan Paul [originally in German, 1926].
Schiller, F. C. S. (1907) *Studies in Humanism.* London: Macmillan.
Segal, L. (1994) *Straight Sex: The Politics of Pleasure.* London: Virago.
Segal, L. (1997) *Slow Motion: Changing Masculinities, Changing Men.* 2nd edn, London: Virago [1st edn, 1990].
Seidman, S., and Alexander, J. C. (2001) 'Introduction', in *The New Social Theory Reader.* London: Routledge, pp. 1–26.

Shanks, M., and Hodder, I. (1998) 'Processual, Postprocessual and Interpretative Archaeologies', in *Reader in Archaeological Theory*, ed. D. S. Whitley. London: Routledge, pp. 69–98.

Shapin, S. (1994) *A Social History of Truth: Civility and Science in Seventeenth-Century England*. Chicago: University of Chicago Press.

Simkin, C. (1993) *Popper's Views on Natural and Social Science*. New York: Brill.

Smith, D. (1988) *The Chicago School: A Liberal Critique of Capitalism*. Basingstoke: Macmillan Education.

Solomon, R. C. (ed.) *Nietzsche: A Collection of Critical Essays*. Notre Dame, IN: University of Notre Dame Press.

Taylor, C. (1977) 'Interpretation and the Sciences of Man', in *Understanding and Social Inquiry*, ed. F. R. Dallmayr and T. A. McCarthy. Notre Dame, IN: University of Notre Dame Press.

Taylor, C. (1985) *Philosophy and the Human Sciences: Philosophical Papers 2*. Cambridge: Cambridge University Press.

Tilley, C. (1998) 'Archaeology as Socio-Political Action in the Present', in *Reader in Archaeological Theory*, ed. D. S. Whitley. London: Routledge, pp. 315–30.

Trigg, R. (1985) *Understanding Social Science: A Philosophical Introduction to the Social Sciences*. Oxford: Blackwell.

Turner, S. (1986) *The Search for a Methodology of Social Science: Durkheim, Weber and the Nineteenth-Century Problem of Cause, Probability and Action*. Dordrecht: Reidel.

Viskovatoff, A. (2002) 'Critical Realism and Kantian Transcendental Arguments', *Cambridge Journal of Economics*, 26, pp. 697–708.

Webb, K. (1995) *An Introduction to Problems in the Philosophy of Social Sciences*. London: Pinter.

Weber, M. (1922) *Gesammelte Aufsätze zur Wissenschaftslehre*. Tübingen: J. C. B. Mohr.

Weber, M. (1948) 'Science as Vocation', in *From Max Weber: Essays in Sociology*, ed. and trans. H. H. Gerth and C. W. Mills. London: Routledge, pp. 129–56 [originally in German, 1919; referred to in notes as SV].

Weber, M. (1949a) 'The Meaning of "Ethical Neutrality" in Sociology and Economics', in *The Methodology of the Social Sciences*. New York: Macmillan, pp. 1–47 [originally in German, 1917; referred to in notes as MEN].

Weber, M. (1949b) 'Objectivity in Social Science and Social Policy', in *The Methodology of the Social Sciences*. New York: Macmillan, pp. 49–112 [originally in German, 1904; referred to in notes as OSS].

Weber, M. (1949c) 'Critical Studies in the Logic of the Cultural Sciences', in *The Methodology of the Social Sciences*. New York: Macmillan, pp. 113–88 [originally in German, 1905; referred to in notes as LCS].

Weber, M. (1964) 'The Fundamental Concepts in Sociology', in *The Theory of Social and Economic Organization*. New York: Free Press, pp. 87–157 [originally in German, 1913; referred to in notes as FCS].

Weber, M. (1975) *Roscher and Knies: The Logical Problems of Historical Economics*. New York: Free Press [originally in German, 1903–6; referred to in notes as RK].

Weber, M. (1978) *Max Weber: Selections in Translation,* ed. W. G. Runciman. Cambridge: Cambridge University Press.

⁓ Weber, M. (1992) *The Protestant Ethic and the Spirit of Capitalism.* London: Routledge [originally in German, 1904–5; referred to in notes as PE].

Whitley, D. S. (ed.) (1998) *Reader in Archaeological Theory.* London: Routledge.

Will, D. (1980) 'Psychoanalysis as a Human Science', *British Journal of Medical Psychology,* 53, pp. 201–11.

Will, D. (1984) 'The Progeny of Positivism: The Maudsley School and Anti-Psychiatry', *British Journal of Psychotherapy,* 1, 1.

Williams, B. (1990) 'Auto-da-Fé: Consequences of Pragmatism', in *Reading Rorty: Critical Responses to 'Philosophy and the Mirror of Nature' (and Beyond),* ed. A. Malachowski. Oxford: Blackwell, pp. 26–37.

Williams, M. (2000) *Science and Social Science.* London: Routledge.

Wood, J. T. (1982) *Human Communication: A Symbolic Interactionist Perspective.* New York: Holt, Rinehart & Winston.

Wylie, A. (2002) *Thinking from Things: Essays in the Philosophy of Archaeology.* Berkeley: University of California Press.

Index

Index

hermeneutics
critical theory and   119, 120, 123
pragmatism and   151, 155–6
Rorty   131, 134–5, 141–2
Weber's method and   41–4, 45
Hesse, M.   88, 105
historical-hermeneutic knowledge   118,
119, 123
historical materialism   38–9, 51–2, 74
historicism, Popper and   63–4, 73–6
history
critical realism and   88, 99–101
Durkheim's naturalism and   15–16,
21
ethics   168–9
falsificationism   63–4, 68–70, 72–6
Foucauldian   164–5, 168–9
genealogical   143–4, 163–5, 166
Kuhn–Popper controversy   68–70
pragmatism   135–6, 143–4, 163–5,
166, 168–9
Weber   37, 38–9, 40, 41–6, 47–8,
51–5, 58
Hodgson, G.   89, 98
holism
critical theory   108
Durkheim   16
Kuhn–Popper controversy   70–1
Popper's criticisms   64
Weber's criticisms   39–40
Honneth, A.   107
Horkheimer, M.   7, 106–7, 108, 110,
115, 116, 125
Hume, D.   66, 90, 91–2, 102

ideal speech situation   122–3
ideal types   46–8, 52
idealism, critical realism and   90–1
imaginative component, knowledge
156
imitation thesis, suicide   30
inductivism   62, 66–7, 81–2
instrumental rationality   50
critical theory and   108, 109–10,
112, 116–17
instrumental value   116
interdisciplinarity   108

interpretative method, Weber   5, 37–59
critical realism and   103
critical theory and   109, 111
Durkheim compared   5, 35–6
evaluation   55–9
ideal types   46–8, 52
Methodenstreit   41–6
Popper compared   58–9
pragmatism and   128, 141–2, 152,
155, 156
the Protestant ethic   51–5, 58, 109
Rorty and   141–2
social action   48–51
intransitive objects of knowledge   91
intuition   45–6, 72
irrationalism   70–1

James, W.   126, 127, 128, 130, 140,
154

Kant, I.   90, 120
Keat, R.   88, 105
knowledge   4, 8–9
critical realism   102, 104
falsificationism   65, 66–7
as form of action   154–5
Habermas's classification   118–20
intransitive objects of   91
Mannheim's sociology of   65, 148
non-representational view   104
pragmatism   147, 148, 150, 151–2,
154–7, 166–9
archaeology   163, 166
cultural anthropology   158–9,
166–7, 168
Rorty   129, 140–1, 142–4
self-referential   4, 8–9, 124, 142–3,
155–7, 163, 164–5, 166–9
spectator theory of   104, 126, 129,
151–2
transitive objects of   91
Weber's interpretative method   41,
44–5, 56–7
Kuhn, T.   68–71, 87, 132–3, 149, 150

Labour Party   100
language   117, 118, 120, 121–2, 123